Decoding THE Rise of Made-In-China

Why the Continuity of Catch-up ladder Ultimately Matters

Series on Innovation and Operations Management for Chinese Enterprises

Print ISSN: 2591-7188
Online ISSN: 2591-7196

Editor: Xiaobo Wu *(School of Management, Zhejiang University, China)*

Published:

Vol. 8: *Decoding the Rise of Made-In-China: Why the Continuity of Catch-up Ladder Ultimately Matters*
by Bin Guo

Vol. 7: *Total Innovation Management: Theory and Practice*
by Qingrui Xu

Vol. 6: *Global Manufacturing and Secondary Innovation in China: Latecomer's Advantages*
by Xiaobo Wu

Vol. 5: *R&D Investment of Multinational Corporations and China's Independent Innovation*
by Wen Xiao, Jiadong Pan and Gaobang Lin

Vol. 4: *The Theory and Policies of Mutual Benefit and Win-Win Strategy: Research on Sustainable Development of China's Open Economy*
by Lixin Yu and Wanling Chen

Vol. 3: *The Internationalization of Technological Innovation for Chinese Enterprises*
by Jin Chen

Vol. 2: *Basic Research and Industrial Innovation in China*
by Xielin Liu, Yubing He and Peng Cheng

Vol. 1: *Independent Innovation in China: Theory and Cases*
by Huibo Zhong and Jiasu Lei

Series on Innovation and Operations Management for Chinese Enterprises – Vol. 8

Decoding THE Rise of Made-In-China

Why the Continuity of Catch-up ladder Ultimately Matters

Bin GUO
Zhejiang University, China

World Scientific

ZHEJIANG UNIVERSITY PRESS
浙江大学出版社

Published by

World Scientific Publishing Co. Pte. Ltd.
5 Toh Tuck Link, Singapore 596224
USA office: 27 Warren Street, Suite 401-402, Hackensack, NJ 07601
UK office: 57 Shelton Street, Covent Garden, London WC2H 9HE

and

Zhejiang University Press
No. 148, Tianmushan Road
Xixi Campus of Zhejiang University
Hangzhou 310028, China

Library of Congress Control Number: 2022054807

British Library Cataloguing-in-Publication Data
A catalogue record for this book is available from the British Library.

This edition is jointly published by World Scientific Publishing Co. Pte. Ltd. and Zhejiang University Press. This edition is distributed worldwide by World Scientific Publishing Co. Pte. Ltd, except China.

《大国制造：中国制造的基因优势与未来变革》
Originally published in Chinese by Zhejiang University Press

Series on Innovation and Operations Management for Chinese Enterprises — Vol. 8
DECODING THE RISE OF MADE-IN-CHINA
Why the Continuity of Catch-up Ladder Ultimately Matters

ISBN 978-981-126-521-1 (hardcover)
ISBN 978-981-126-522-8 (ebook for institutions)
ISBN 978-981-126-523-5 (ebook for individuals)

For any available supplementary material, please visit
https://www.worldscientific.com/worldscibooks/10.1142/13110#t=suppl

Desk Editors: Aanand Jayaraman/Pui Yee Lum

Typeset by Stallion Press
Email: enquiries@stallionpress.com

Preface

Ten years ago, I began ruminating over the question: where does China's advantage in economic development come from after all? No doubt, the question seems quite large, even somewhat ambitious.

Yet, such a question managed to attract my attention, largely because I constantly came across doubts and disbelief from some foreign scholars on the sustainability of China's economic growth during my interactions with them on many academic exchange activities.

In fact, the focus of such disbelief about China's economic growth had been evolving over the past few years, shifting from growth data tampering, to the sustainability into the future, which is occasionally accompanied by the Western world's biased rhetoric about "Collapse of China's Economy".

More importantly, as China's manufacturing sector has played a critical role in driving the rapid economic development of the country for a long period of time, some Western scholars and media have often negatively attributed the source of competitive advantage of Chinese manufacturing industry to the global economic system. A typical view attributes such competitive advantages to two critical factors: namely, the advantages of low labor cost and the advantages of imitating the early developed countries. Such attribution can be further interpreted as accusing China of being a "sweatshop" and being "derelict in IPR protection".

Such attribution is not only made by some Western scholars but also by some Chinese scholars.

Though seemingly plausible at first sight, yet when deeply perused, from my perspective, there appears a huge logic loophole in such viewpoints.

It cannot be denied that the above two factors indeed exist and have to some extent driven the growth of China's manufacturing sector. Nevertheless, it's necessary to make it clear that the advantages of low labor cost and being able to imitate the early developed countries are naturally enjoyed by all late-developing nations and regions. As for the first factor, in the early stage of catching-up, the late-developing countries are often troubled by low production efficiency and underutilization of production factors, which result in relative surplus in labor force and low labor cost. As for the imitation advantage enjoyed by a latecomer, it is the natural advantage for any latecomer country, which allows them to acquire knowledge, technology and managerial experience from developed countries at relatively lower costs through observing, imitating and reverse engineering.[1]

As these two advantages are more or less prevalent in all late-developing countries, they cannot be regarded as the key factors to drive the rapid growth of China's manufacturing industry, or China's economy, over the past years.

Yet, it is necessary to point out that China's economic prosperity ignited since its Reform and Opening Up starting from 1978 may very likely be one with the longest span, fastest speed and biggest scale in human history. It is no exaggeration to describe it as a "miracle". For the Chinese people themselves, back to the days in 1978, a starting point when China began to embrace globalization and transfer itself into a market economy, most of them may find the life they enjoy today to be far beyond their wildest or romantic imaginations. This also explains why the former US Secretary of State, Mr. Henry Alfred Kissinger, commented on the significant transformation of China in the China Development Forum, an event hosted by the Development Research Center of the State Council of China in 2015, saying that, "You can imagine what Beijing looked like back in 1971. You may not expect such huge transformations of this country, which to me is a dream beyond human limits."

---

[1]Reverse engineering refers to analyzing, understanding and mastering the structure, module, principle, design and manufacturing of products through dismantling existing products or technologies.

There is no doubt that we need to provide a more solid explanation for China's economic growth miracle and the rapid rise of China's manufacturing industry. Just as nicely put by Justin Yifu Lin, the former World Bank Chief Economist, "China's past four decades of Reform and Opening-up blazed a new trail and achieved unprecedented economic growth never seen in human economic history. By describing it as miracle, it means unexplainable phenomenon beyond the scope of the existing theories.... No existing theory can explain the development wonder China achieved since its Reform and Opening-up. Yet, every phenomenon carries its underlying logic. That's why China's leaders put forward at the 2016 philosophical and social science working conference that 'It's an era that calls for theories and is bound to yield theories. We shall not let down these great times'".[2]

With my deepening reflection on the underlying logic behind the rise of the Chinese manufacturing industry, I changed my mind from initially planning to merely write one paper to finally compiling a whole book, all in the effort to try to answer the above question. One important reason for this is that this seemingly simple question actually is crystallized with so much of content and details that it is impossible to provide a complete framework, sound logic and convincing evidence in merely one article.

Or perhaps I am trying to respond to an overambitious question. So, over the years, whenever I tried to get on with the writing of the book, I always felt more time was needed for my reflection and conceptualization. Therefore, the writing never really started. Until one day I realized that maybe it is not right to pursue perfection, as nothing is perfect in this world. Hence, this book came into being. Even though it has not yet included everything I have conceived, it has sufficiently outlined the key logic I have been pondering over the years.

Over the past years, when I attended academic seminars at home and abroad, when I taught Ph.D., postgraduate, MBA and EMBA students, and even when I delivered lectures to the international exchange students, I had always been trying to share my ideas, in different forms and with different highlights, on China's economic growth miracle, the rise of Made-in-China and all the underlying logical frameworks. During these various forms of interactions, I was impressed by the universal interest

---

[2]Lin Yifu's Keynote Speech at the Founding Conference of the (new) School of Economics of Renmin University of China and the Academic Seminar on 70 Years of Evolution and Development of Chinese Economics on March 23, 2019.

from people of different cultural backgrounds, which also partially motivated me to complete this book.

In this book, I have proposed a theory to explain the rise of China's manufacturing industry, which I call "the catch-up ladders theory". To me, the manufacturing advancement of any country is in essence a process of catching-up in terms of both market and technology,[3] during the process of which enterprises form a ladder-like holistic structure due to their differences in capabilities, technology and market positioning. For an enterprise of any kind, its journey of learning and competence-enhancement is just embedded into such a catch-up ladder. For such a gigantic emerging economy like China, its catch-up ladder carries some particularities, which enable the embedded enterprises to achieve more efficient catch-up. In light of this, the continuity of the catch-up ladder will greatly determine the catch-up efficiency of an industry and even a country at large.

This is a squarely different explanatory framework from the existing theories. In a sense, it is more applicable to large emerging economies, especially those with a population of over one hundred million and thus a huge potential domestic market demand.

What needs to be pointed out is that the catch-up ladder theory showcased in this book does not deny the influences of institutions, cultures, imitation advantages and others on the development of the manufacturing industry in China over the years. However, according to Occam's Razor Principle, when two hypotheses possess exactly the same explanatory and predictive power, the simpler one will be adopted as the basis for discussion. Therefore, it is my hope that the theoretical framework I have proposed is compact and widely applicable. I have long believed that the value of theory lies in helping people comprehend the seemingly complex reality and perplexing phenomena around us in a concise manner, rather than blundering into padding the seemingly simple or intricately complicated phenomena with even more abstruse fillings. This is the power of being concise. Besides, to me, the consistency and completeness of logic far outweighs the richness of mere details, data and facts.

Yet, due to the complexity of China's national conditions, any attempts at using one standalone theory to explain all facts related to China's economic growth will always be a mission impossible. As such, the focus of this book is to shed light onto the "critical yet often neglected"

[3] Institutional factors (changes and perfection of institutions) are here considered as important factors influencing the efficiency of technology and market catching up.

factors and mechanisms behind the rise of China's manufacturing industry.

In some sense, I owe a big thanks to this era. It is China's economic growth and the rise of the Chinese manufacturing industry, along with the continuously increasing influence of Chinese enterprises in the global arena, that give meaning to all attempts to interpret such a phenomenon.

Bin Guo
November 19, 2019

About the Author

Bin Guo is a professor of innovation management and strategy at the School of Management, Zhejiang University, China. He is currently the head of the department of innovation, entrepreneurship and strategy at the School of Management. He received his Ph.D. in management from Zhejiang University (1998). His research interests are in the areas of strategic management of innovation and product strategy in a digital context.

Acknowledgment

The author would like to express gratitude to the National Natural Science Foundation of China and the Fundamental Research Funds for the Central Universities for supporting the relevant research projects that enabled the basic idea, framework and contents of this book.

Contents

Chapter 1

Miracle of China's Economic Growth

The Birth of a Growth Miracle

In 2015, on the 125th anniversary of the well-known scientific journal *Science*, 125 most challenging scientific questions were released in the special issue of the journal published on July 1. The 116th scientific question among them was as follows: "Why are some countries moving forward while others are stagnating?"

There is no doubt that it is one of the most important topics in the macroeconomic field to explain the divergence in the economic development of various countries. What is more, China's economic growth after its Reform and Opening-up in 1978 made it more difficult to answer this question.

In 1978, China's GDP was merely US$367.87 billion, which surged to US$13.6 trillion in 2018.[1] Despite some fluctuations in China's economy in recent years, the economic growth rate of the country has been remaining in the range between 8 and 12% in most of these 40 years. Even in 2018, when China faced huge pressure on its macro economy and a contraction caused by compounding unfavorable factors, its real GDP growth rate still hit 6.6%, while that of the United States was 2.9% in the same period. Comparing China's economic growth data in 1978 and 2018, we can find that China's economic growth is unprecedented in terms of its scale, rate and duration (see Figures 1.1 and 1.2). Putting the three

[1] Data source: https://data.stats.gov.cn/easyquery.htm?cn=C01.

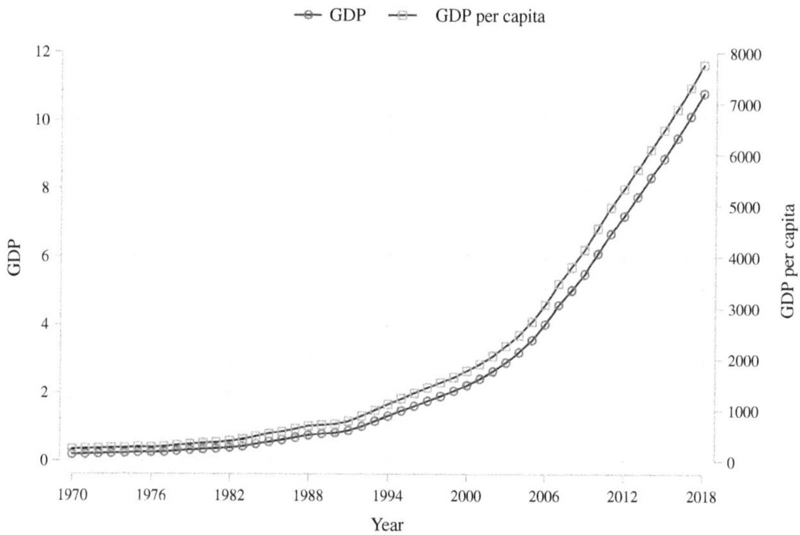

Figure 1.1. China's GDP and Per Capita GDP: 1970–2018

Source: World Bank.

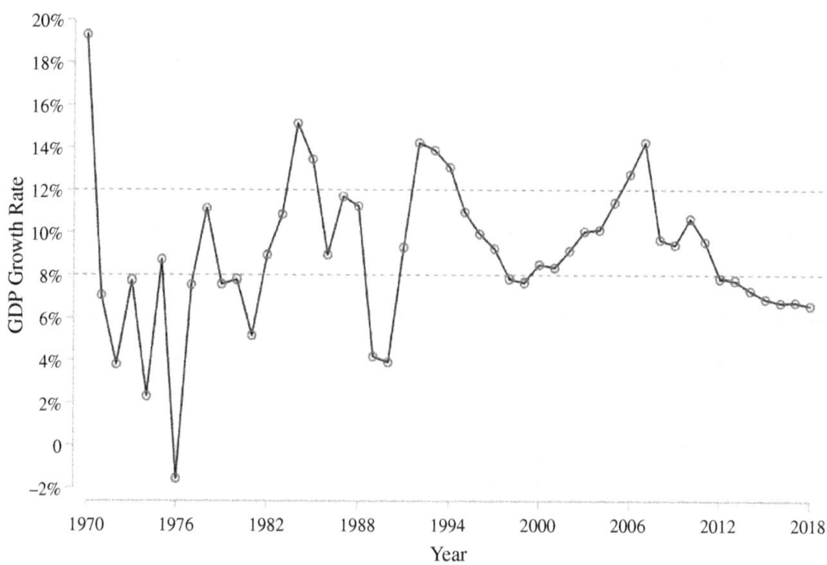

Figure 1.2. China's GDP Growth Rate: 1970–2018

Source: World Bank.

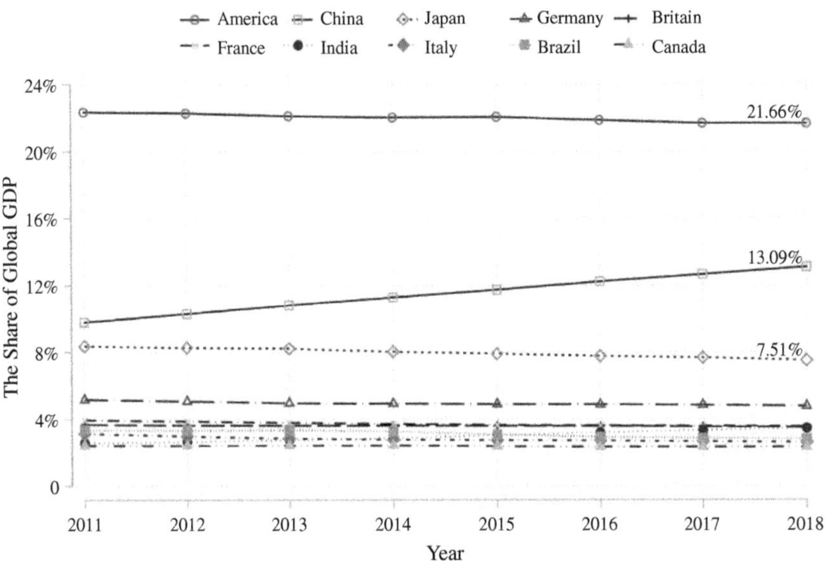

Figure 1.3. Share of Major Economies in Global GDP

Source: World Bank.

indicators together, it is no exaggeration to call this a "miracle of economic growth".

Today, China has become the world's second largest economy which is only second to the United States, with its GDP in 2018 accounting for 16% of the world total (see Figure 1.3). As a very important contributor to the economic development of a country, the growth of enterprises, especially that of the large ones, can be seen as a miniature of the macroeconomic growth of the country. Take the list released by *Fortune* as an example. The magazine releases the world's top 500 companies every year based on the annual income and net profit of the enterprises. In 1995, the magazine included, for the first time, companies from all industries in the list. In that year, only three Chinese enterprises, namely, Bank of China, SINOCHEM and COFCO, were included in the *Fortune* 500 list. By contrast, 151 companies from the United States and 149 from Japan were included. Even in 2002, when China had just joined the World Trade Organization (WTO), only 11 Chinese enterprises were included in the list (see Figure 1.4).

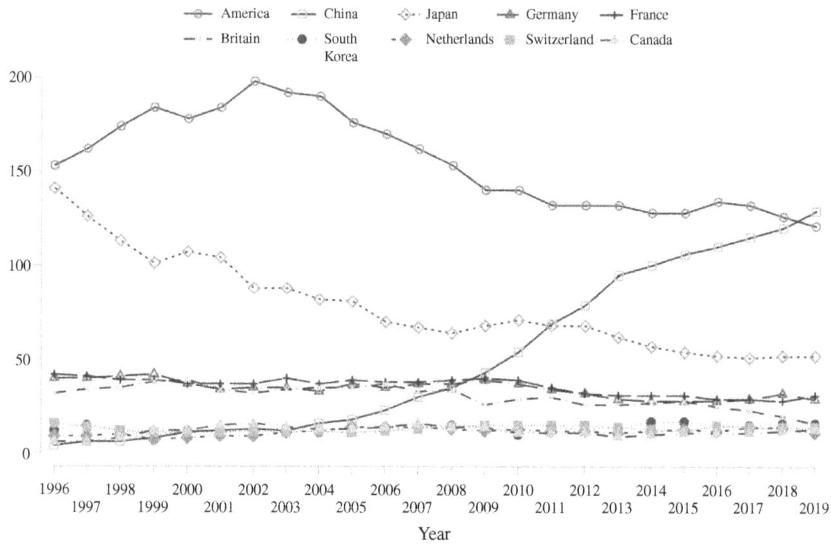

Figure 1.4. Historical Change of Numbers of Enlisted Fortune 500 Enterprises in Different Countries: 1996–2019

Source: http://www.fortunechina.com/fortune500/index.htm.

However, in 2019, when *Fortune* released its global 500 list, it referred to it as "It's China's World" to describe the historic changes of the year. Among the world's 500 largest enterprises listed, 129 were from China (including China Mainland, Hong Kong, Macao and Taiwan). It was the first time that China surpassed the United States with 121 enterprises on the list. In the fields of the Internet, engineering and automobiles, the number of Chinese enterprises on the list exceeded that of the United States. Of the 25 newly included companies, 13 were from China, namely, China Development Bank, CRRC Group, Tsingshan Holding Group, Jinchuan Group, Zhuhai Gree Electric Appliances Co., Ltd., Anhui CONCH Group, Huaxia Insurance, Tongling Nonferrous Metals Group, Shanxi Coking Coal Group, Xiaomi Group, Hailiang Group Co., Ltd., China General Technology (Group) Holding Co., Ltd. and Formosa Plastic Group. Xiaomi, which was included in the list for the first time (ranking the 468th, established in April 2010), became the youngest Fortune 500 company in this year's list.

The Rise of China's Manufacturing Industry: A Historical Perspective

For developing countries, the manufacturing industry has been playing an extremely key role during a very long period of their development, especially in the early stage of their economic catch-up. This is because compared with the traditional agriculture and other primary industries, in these developing countries, the manufacturing industry yields higher productivity and can fully tap into its advantages in low labor costs (see Figure 1.5). As a result of the development in the manufacturing industry, the national revenue of these countries rises rapidly. According to the data from the National Bureau of Statistics, over the past 40 years, the income of Chinese residents has been constantly increasing (see Table 1.1). In 2017,

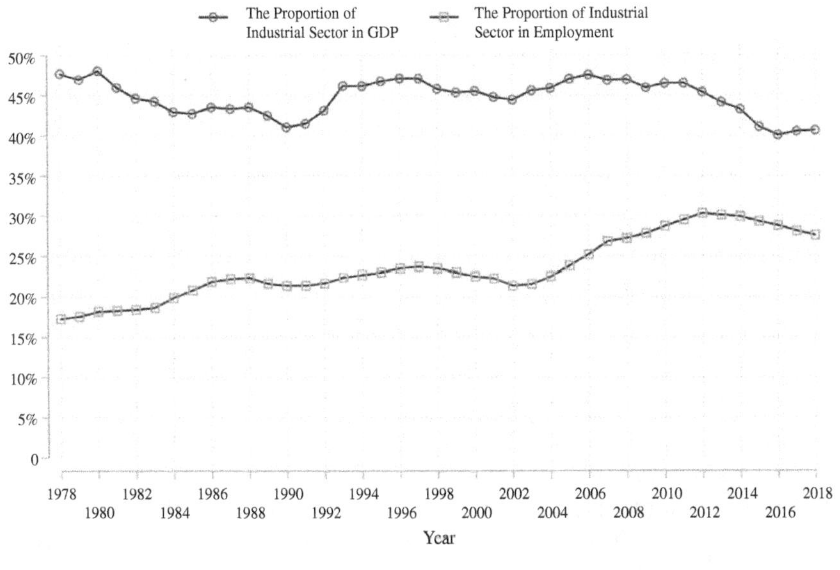

Figure 1.5. Development of China's Secondary Industry: 1978–2018

Note: The national employment data for 1990 and later are calculated according to labor force survey and population census, and the data for 2001 and later are revised according to the data of the 6th Population Census. Data about urban business entities exclude private-owned entities. The data for the year 2012 adopted a new classification standard and shall not be comparable to those from the previous periods.

Source: China National Bureau of Statistics.

Table 1.1. China's Economic and Social Development: 1978–2018

	1978	**1998**	**2018**
GDP Per Capita (US Dollar in 2010)	307.1	1,538.7	7,755.0
Share of Global GDP[a]	1.7%	3.3%	15.9%
Life Expectancy	65.9	70.7	76.5*
Infant Mortality Rate	52.8‰	33.5‰	7.4‰
Urbanization Rate (Proportion of Urban Population to Total Population)	17.9%	33.9%	59.2%
Literacy rate (adult population: 15 years and above)	65.5*	90.9*	96.8

Notes: [a]China's share of world GDP will vary slightly from source to source due to differences in estimation methods (e.g., whether purchasing power parity is taken into account). However, the sustained economic growth after China's reform and opening up is pushing China to gradually realize the dream of the great rejuvenation of the Chinese nation. It is estimated that, by the purchasing power parity, China's share of the world's GDP was once unusual in history, reaching 22.7% and 24.9% in 1000AD and 1500AD, respectively, and even reaching 33% in 1820. However, after this and until 1950, with the rise of the Western world and the rapid increase in productivity, the ratio continued to decline rapidly, plummeting to only 4.6% in 1950.

*Due to the absence of World Bank data, the life expectancy in 2018 is referenced to that in 2017, the literacy rate in 1978 is referenced to that in 1982, and the literacy rate in 1998 is referenced to 2000.

Source: World Bank.

the per capita disposable income of Chinese residents reached RMB 25,974, a 22.8-time increase over that of 1978 after deflating price factors, yielding an average annual real increase of 8.5%. In 2019, the national per capita disposable income of China hit RMB 30,733.

We can see the trend of the rise of China's manufacturing industry through some typical successes achieved in certain related industries.

Take the color TV industry as an example. According to the survey data of Sigmaintell, the global shipment volume of TV sets in 2018 was 239.8 million units. During the five years from 2014 to 2018, the global share of Chinese TV manufacturers increased from 27% to 36%. Among the top 15 companies with the largest global shipment volume (including OEM and private brands), seven were from China.

In the smartphone industry, according to the statistics by Counterpoint, Huawei's global market share was 15% in 2018, ranking third in the world (see Figure 1.6). Moreover, Huawei is in the relatively high-end field of smartphones production. In 2018, Huawei, OPPO and Vivo produced their own best-selling models: Huawei P20 Pro, Huawei Mate 10 Pro, OPPO Find X and VIVO NEX.

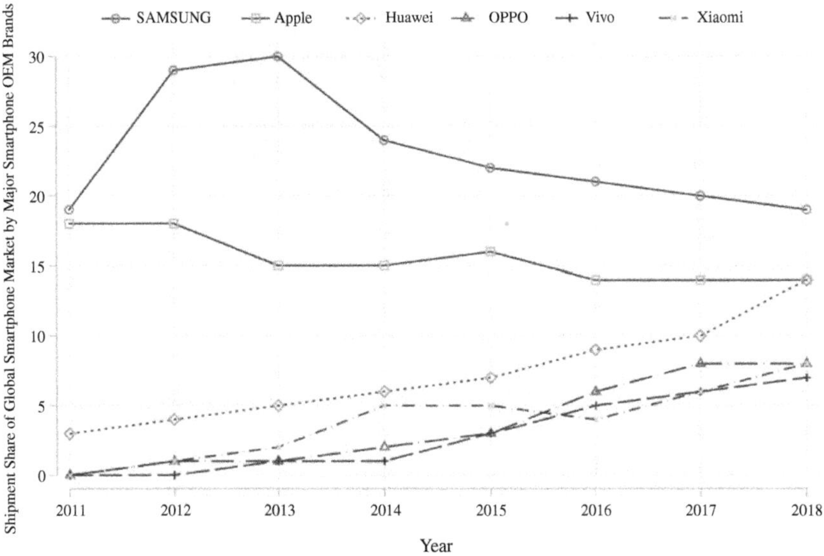

Figure 1.6. Market Performance of Huawei Mobile Phones in Global Competition

Source: Counterpoint, https://www.counterpointresearch.com/global-smartphone-shipments-share-last-eight-years-of-winners-losers/.

In November 2011, Mr. Chengdong Yu, the person in charge of Huawei's mobile phone business, posted two messages in succession on Weibo. The once-called Arabian Nights messages said that "starting from next year (year 2012), we will gradually see great changes in the smartphone industry, and the redefining of product competitiveness specifications ... Next year, we will launch a series of mobile phone products, which, very likely, will indeed realize our goal of gradually surpassing our foreign leading competitors ..."

Today, if you walk along the street in Copenhagen, Denmark, when you approach the brightly colored Nyhavn pedestrian street, you will find a very eye-catching billboard standing on the street with the gigantic Huawei logo on it, so obvious that people passing by will be easily attracted. For Chinese tourists, this is a sign of special affinity, and it also means that the tentacles of Made-in-China are quietly spreading to all corners of the world.

Although China's manufacturing industry is relatively successful in market catch-up, it still has a long way to go in technological catch-up.

Figure 1.7. Changing Images of "Made-in-China" in Western Media

Nevertheless, some new opinions believe China's manufacturing industry has also made impressive progress in technology in some fields.

In fact, the impacts of Made-in-China are not exclusive to Chinese people. Under the tide of globalization, the influence of Made-in-China is also increasingly felt in the everyday life of Western families. As vividly described by US journalist Sara Bongiorni in the book *A Year without "Made in China": One Family's True Life Adventure in the Global Economy*, on the Christmas of 2004, she suddenly realized that 25 of the 39 Christmas gifts along with many daily necessities, such as shoes, socks, toys, lamps and so on, were all "Made-in-China". Therefore, in order to better observe and experience the impact of "Made-in-China" on Western family lives, the author's family started a "life adventure" — starting from January 1, 2005, they began to try not to buy products labeled "Made-in-China" for one year. The experience described in this book is vivid and interesting, which can be seen as a miniature of the global outreach of Chinese manufacturing industry.

Now, it seems that China's manufacturing industry has already obtained a relatively strong viability and competitiveness, showing more confidence in competing on the world arena (see Figure 1.7). However, back in the years before 2001, China was under unprecedentedly huge pressure. When China was determined to fully dock into the globalization system by joining WTO, there was a shared concern among the Chinese government, enterprises and public about the impact China's manufacturing industry might suffer from China's joining WTO. Even some Chinese policymakers felt worried about the hasty opening up to the outside world, for they believed that the Chinese enterprises were not fully prepared for the global competition. Some pessimists even argued that the reduced tariff barriers may cause local Chinese enterprises to quickly lose their market share, hence resulting in the control of many segments of Chinese manufacturing industry by foreign enterprises and leaving local Chinese enterprises gasping with limited survival opportunities in the very low-end markets.

Based on data analysis, Loren Brandt, a professor at the University of Toronto, and Eric Thun, an associate professor at the Oxford University, concluded that those initial worries did not come true.[2] Even though China's joining into the WTO temporarily forfeited some market shares of Chinese enterprises due to the bringing of more competitors, it also forced local enterprises to continuously improve their own capabilities and gradually move upward on the market ladder, ultimately helping local Chinese enterprises to win more market shares in many fields. To a large extent, this is a result of the step-by-step principle followed by the Chinese government in the process of reform and opening up, which is in essence a gradual opening-up approach to promote the transformation of the entire Chinese economy. This is because any change in competition rules, just like the environmental changes catalyzing the biological evolution, will result differently as per the degrees of environmental changes. In order to adapt to this kind of environmental change, the participants either have already acquired certain innate capacity or certain survival ability in the process of environmental changes. In the case of China's economy, in the process of this gradual change, the participants in the system may often lack the motivation to change themselves, and they also lack a clear understanding of the direction of change. The impact of reform and opening up and the competition introduced by the establishment of the market system have greatly promoted the changes in China's economic system. Looking back on the development journey of China's manufacturing industry since 1978, we can find that China's manufacturing industry gradually developed into prosperity as the result of external pressure and competitive environment.

In a sense, the burgeoning "Made-in-China" has even reshaped the world's perception of the value of "manufacturing" in the global competition. This is because in the 1960s, with the large-scale outward transfer of manufacturing from developed countries in Europe and the United States to developing countries, developed countries relatively neglected the importance of manufacturing in the entire industrial value chain, making

---

[2]Brandt, L. and E. Thun (2010). The fight for the middle: Upgrading, competition, and industrial development in China. *World Development* 38(11), 1555–1574.

the manufacturing industry increasingly insignificant in the global competition landscape. Under this context, Zhenrong Shi, the founder of Acer Group, put forward in 1992 the "Smiling Curve" theory which holds that in the whole industrial value chain, the added value is more reflected in the two ends, namely, the research and design on one end, and sales and brand on the other. By contrast, the added value in the manufacturing industry as the intermediate part of the value curve is the lowest and in a subdued position. Therefore, for those latecomer enterprises, their best choice is to gradually move from the trough of the smile curve to its two ends, so as to establish a more meaningful competitive advantage. This view is not only accepted and agreed upon by the industry but also recognized by some researchers from academia.

The view expressed by the smile curve may sound quite reasonable at first sight, especially in the 1990s when China's manufacturing industry was moving upward on the industrial value ladder. However, there are also two potential pitfalls with this view. First is the well-known "Fallacy of Composition", where one infers that something is true of the macro-level from the fact that it is true of some micro-level of the whole. For individual enterprises, there is some rationale behind their following the smile curve to reorient their strategic transformation and positioning. However, from the perspective of the entire Chinese manufacturing industry, it's not always the case. Among the Chinese manufacturing enterprises, although some leading local enterprises have achieved upward migration of their capabilities and market positions in the industrial value chain in recent years, the vast majority of Chinese manufacturing enterprises as a whole are still in the so-called trough of the value curve with the lowest added value: the manufacturing part. Even so, in these years, "Made-in-China" can still make strong influence and demonstrate competitiveness through embracing globalization and deeply embedding itself into the global industrial chain. In the China–US trade conflict, confronted with such strong economic and technological rivals as the US, these forces can even promote China to an evenly matched position with the US. Second, many years ago, a few far-sighted researchers have already foreseen the importance of "manufacturing" to national competitiveness. For example, Teece (1986), an influential scholar in the field of innovation research, wrote the following in a paper published in 1986[3]: "The analysis

[3]Teece, D. J. (December 1986). Profiting from technological innovation: Implications for integration, collaboration, licensing and public policy. *Research Policy* 15(6): 185–219.

provides a theoretical foundation for the proposition that manufacturing often matters, particularly to innovating nations. Innovating firms without the requisite manufacturing and related capacities may die, even though they are the best at innovation". As for the overall situation of China's manufacturing industry, the power of "Made-in-China" does not lie in research, development and branding but relies on a highly efficient and extremely flexible manufacturing chain and a relatively complete local industry chain.

In this regard, China has achieved great success in transforming itself from one of the poorest countries in the world to the world's second largest economy, but the decisive factors behind this success have not yet been well explained or understood.[4] So, how should we interpret the rapid growth of China's manufacturing industry in the past 40 years? What factors or mechanisms are behind the growth? Moreover, there is an interesting question here, that is, why it is China, rather than other economies, that has realized such a growth miracle?

How to Interpret the Source of Advantages of Made-in-China?

It has always been an interesting topic about the real source of the advantages of Chinese manufacturing industry in global competition. It has been interpreted from different angles, most of which can be summarized as follows:

Low labor cost advantage: As a developing country, China has its relative disadvantages in capital and technology and labor supply. Thus, for a long time during the development of its manufacturing industry, the structure and types of the industry have been strikingly different from those of developed countries in Europe and America. The manufacturing industry of China is more based on labor-intensive industries rather than capital-intensive and technology-intensive industries as often seen in developed countries. In this case, low labor cost can become an important source of China's cost advantage.

Imitation advantage as a latecomer: The increment in technology and knowledge is the most important driving force for a country's long-term economic growth. However, there is no doubt that for any country

[4] Yueh, L. (December 9, 2015). China's growth: A brief history. *Harvard Business Review*.

intending to develop technology and accumulate knowledge on its own, besides its capability development, it also needs to make huge investments in talent and capital. Knowledge and technology have a significant "spillover effect", that is, the innovators cannot fully enjoy all benefits from innovation, while the imitators can acquire and absorb such knowledge and further benefit from it at no or relatively lower cost by means of talent flow, imitation, observation and reverse engineering. Therefore, those latecomer countries, as followers or imitators, can obtain latecomer advantages through the spillover effect of technology and knowledge, especially when technology exclusivity and intellectual property protection mechanism is relatively weak. As a latecomer with a strong ability to learn, China has undoubtedly gained considerable benefits from this imitation advantage.

Institutional Advantages: There are some opinions arguing that the Chinese government has designed and implemented effective policies that have enabled China's industrialization process to achieve great success in merely 25 years, whereas in many other economies, the process often takes a century.[5] Back in the earliest years of its Reform and Opening-up, China was still under the influence of the planned economy system, the Chinese government and enterprises were still trying to learn about the market mechanism, and at that time, many institutional designs critical to the economic development of China and the formation of its market economy system were not yet in place. Therefore, on the whole, there were many institutional shackles and institutional deficiencies in the catching-up process of Chinese enterprises. However, with various reforms implemented by the Chinese government in a "local mutation + global asymptotic" manner, and rapid learning and trial and error of the government in view of China's unique institutional environment, corresponding institutional advantages have been gradually accumulated. In particular, because the Chinese government is powerful in resource mobilization and efficient in decision-making and execution, the development of China's manufacturing industry has been effectively driven by the government, obtaining institutionalized development advantages from China's continuously improving market system. This has been fully reflected in the catching-up process of many industries.

---

[5]Ekekwe, N. (September 4, 2019). Why Africa's industrialization won't look like China's. *Harvard Business Review*, 2–5.

The above interpretation seems to be very convincing and consistent with our conventional thinking. However, even if we analyze from our known empirical evidence and the rigor of theoretical logic, we may find these advantages are not sufficient to explain the continuous rise of Made-in-China.[6]

We need to realize that labor cost advantage and latecomer's imitation advantage are not exclusive to China. All late-developing countries, at least in their early stages of catching-up, are sure to possess such advantages. However, in the past 40 years or so, China's sustained and rapid growth is extremely rare. At the same time, in the process of China's economic growth, with the overall increase in the national income and the increasing demand for labor force, the labor cost has actually been presenting an upward trend, especially in the last 10 years. With the more strict enforcement of tax policy and social security system by the Chinese government, the overall labor cost of Chinese enterprises, especially private enterprises, will rise, which will inevitably bring pressure on the operating cost of such enterprises.

Then, a question arises: If labor costs have been rising over the years, leading to the continuous weakening of China's low-cost advantages, then how can the advantages of Made-in-China be sustained for such a long period of time?

Some Western scholars have realized that the low-cost advantage does not always explain the continuous catching-up of some latecomer countries. Jon Sigurdson, a professor at the Stockholm Institute of Economics in Sweden, made some observations on China's textile industry and further pointed out that even in such an industry that is highly dependent on labor costs, the competitive advantages established by Chinese textile

---

[6] J. Stewart Black and Allen J. Morrison summarized the advantages of China's development and thus questioned the sustainability of China's economic growth in the coming years. They believe that the important foundation of China's economic growth in the past — a low starting point of its productivity level (which allows a large possibility and space for improvement), the extremely sufficient supply of rural labor force and the easy acquisition of advanced technology from foreign countries — has been greatly weakened with the passage of time. However, for this view to hold, a strong premise is required, that is, the above three factors are indeed the dominant, and the most important, sources of China's advantages in economic growth. However, in the following discussion, we will find that the continuity of technology ladder and market ladder is instead the core foundation of China's advantages.

enterprises come not only from low labor costs but also from their massive technological upgrades.[7] Take Foxconn as an example. Though now the largest leading enterprise in the global electronic contract manufacturing service industry, it was still a less known electronic contract manufacturing enterprise in Taiwan Province in the 1970s and 1980s. In the early 1990s, Foxconn began to invest and build factories in Chinese Mainland. With the rapid expansion of its scale, from 1990 to 1996, Foxconn's gross profit margin exceeded 20%, while the same figure of its main competitor Compal Electronics Inc[8] was only about 10%. The development of Foxconn at this stage seems to confirm the view about the influence of the advantage of low-cost labor force in Chinese Mainland. However, since 2007, Foxconn has occupied the largest market share in the global electronics contract manufacturing business until now. Then, how can Foxconn's advantages be sustained in the trend of rising labor costs? Obviously, mere labor cost advantage is not enough to explain this.

There is also an interesting paradox regarding the explanations from the institutional perspective. As for some of the same institutional factors, there are often two totally opposite interpretations. Among the institutional factors, the most often cited ones are state ownership (or state-owned enterprises) and government intervention (especially in the form of industrial policies). Western scholars have done substantial research on these two aspects, but their conclusions are quite contradicting. In terms of state ownership, since the 1990s, the mainstream view in academia believes that state-owned enterprises are an inefficient form of industrial organization. Therefore, in China's market-oriented economic reform, this form of organization should be reduced or even eliminated. However, the role played by state-owned enterprises in industrial catching-up and innovation has been neglected. Only in recent years have some researchers begun to notice the positive impact of state ownership on innovation. From the perspective of catching-up, even seen from the historical experience of Japan and R. O. Korea, those large enterprise groups receiving a

[7]Sigurdson, J. (2004). People's Republic of China's Technological Capability. Latin America/Caribbean and Asia/Pacific Economics and Business Association Working paper No. 25.

[8]Compal Electronics Inc. is an enterprise in Taiwan, China. Founded in 1984, it is a global leading company in the notebook computer, liquid crystal video products and intelligent devices manufacturing industry. In July 2018, it ranked 404th in Fortune Global 500 in 2018, and it ranked 390th in Fortune Global 500 in 2019.

large amount of government support have played a key and indisputable role in technological catching-up and market catching-up. As for government intervention materialized in the form of industrial policies, there is also stark disparity between the views espoused by Western liberal economics and the practical experience of the countries in their catching-up. Based on theoretical logic, the believers of market liberalism argue that the government cannot guarantee that it is smarter than the market and that the government's intervention in the market will derail the effective allocation of resources by the market mechanism, thus bringing about negative results.[9] However, in the trade conflict between China and the United States that began in 2018, one of the accusations made by the US government against China was that China's industrial policies had given China's manufacturing industry "unfair" advantages in global competition. This, in turn, seems to prove the effectiveness of China's industrial policy implementation because if the industrial policy implemented by the Chinese government is invalid, it will certainly not be cited as an accusation against China.

This means that we need a different theory to explain the key factors behind the rise of Made-in-China because those universal factors cannot fully explain some unusual phenomena — though we do not deny the influence of the above factors on the rise of Made-in-China. This new interpretation framework is bound to take the particularity of China's national situation into consideration.

With the development of the globalization process, we tend to fall into an illusion that in the era of globalization, the influence of domestic factors seems to exert less influence on the industrial competition and catching-up between countries. This is because, under such

[9]The discussion here does not mean that Western economists hold the same view on the relationship between market economy and the government. Some economists have realized that China can justify its choice in the process of moving towards a market economy. As Stiglitz (2008) put forward, about 30 years ago, China proposed a new road. This road is related to the practical policy of "wading across the river by feeling for stones on the riverbed (trial and error)". The pragmatism behind this practice partly explained China's great success. Now that China has passed the halfway of "this river", it gets a more clear sight of the target riverbank, seeing diversified options to dock with or literately more forms of market economy to choose from. China can now see the influences of its choices, that is, the type of market economy it chooses will affect the type of society it will create.

circumstances, capital, labor, knowledge and other factors of production can flow more freely across national and regional borders. However, as the famous strategic management scholar Michael Porter pointed out in his book,[10] "Competitive advantage is created and sustained through a highly localized process. Differences in national economic structures, values, cultures, institutions and histories contribute profoundly to competitive success. The role of the home nation seems to be as strong or stronger than ever. While globalization of competition might appear to make the nation less important, instead it seems to make it more so".

Some Western scholars have also accepted the idea that China's situation is somehow special, which makes China's development pattern different from those of many other countries. There is no standard answer as to the future of the world but only various possibilities. Every country can and will choose different roads and directions, and most of these choices are influenced by and even decided by their previous choices. James M. Utterback, a professor of MIT, pointed out in the preface to the Chinese edition of his book *Mastering the Dynamics of Innovation* that "Readers must not think that the model they see here can certainly be applied to other countries, such as China. In many ways, our [that of the US] experience in industrialization and innovation is unique ... The direction of innovation in any industry or economy is determined not only by the specific time and place we are in but also by the path we have taken".[11] Joseph E. Stiglitz, a famous economist, wrote in an article on China's economic development model that "Changes in China's circumstances require a different model for the Chinese economic development. Because China's circumstances are different from that of other countries, the model for China inevitably needs to be different from that of elsewhere".[12]

---

[10]Michael, E. P. (1990). *The Competitive Advantage of Nations*. New York: Macmillan Publishers Limited.

[11]James, M. U. (1999). *Mastering The Dynamics of Innovation*. Translated by Gaojian, Li Ming. Beijing: Tsinghua University Press.

[12]Joseph, E. S. (2008). China: Towards a new model of development. *China Economic Journal* 1(1), 33–52.

Catching-up Ladder: A Brand New Way of Interpretation

Understanding the nature of catching-up

We need to rethink about how the competitive advantages of China's manufacturing industry came into being. Before answering this question, we first need to make it clear that the development process of China's manufacturing industry itself is accompanied by the catching-up process of China's economy and its manufacturing industry, including the market catching-up and the technology catching-up (see Figure 1.8). Market catching-up is more reflected in the gradual upward movement of local enterprises in product market positioning and certain global competitiveness of such enterprises in market positioning with higher marginal profits. It is further reflected in the continuous increase of their market share and the improvement of their bargain power (which can also be understood as the acquisition of discourse rights and influences) within the global industrial value chain. Meanwhile, technological catching-up is

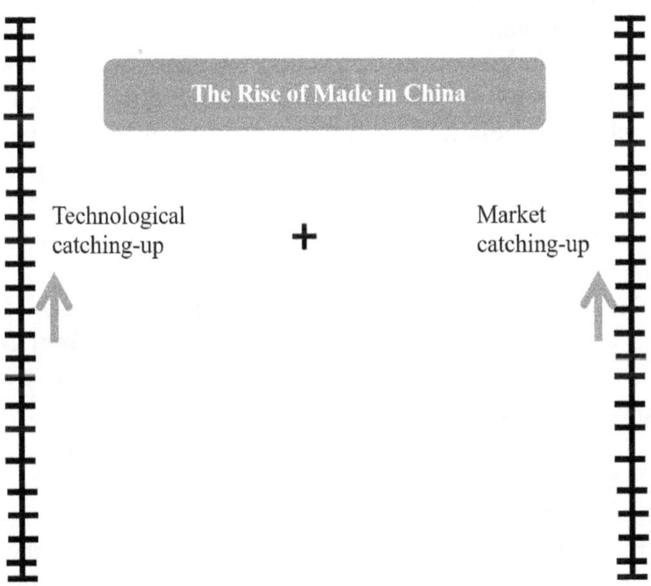

Figure 1.8. The Rise of Made-in-China is Essentially a Process of Technological and Market Catching-up

reflected in the fact that the enterprises gradually acquire research and development capabilities so as to effectively absorb, utilize and develop technologies. For example, they own more patents, narrow the technological gap with leading foreign enterprises, or even develop unique technological expertise in specific segments. In this regard, the process of catching-up can be understood as a learning process in which the latecomers constantly hone their own capabilities. And capability building and development are the core in both technological catch-up and market catch-up.

From the perspective of market catching-up or technological catching-up, any continuous catching-up requires three pre-conditions.

First is huge resource investment. This is because the innate ability of an enterprise can only be acquired through the input of resources. Therefore, in the process of catching-up, besides acquiring external resources as much as possible, it's the priority of an enterprise to obtain the needed resources through market returns and then utilize the resources to sustain more continuous catching-up.

Second is sufficient time. In the process of catching-up, the enterprises need to develop some expertise and abilities, and the gradual acquisition of such expertise and abilities takes time. If we compare the catching-up to a game, then the acquisition of expertise and ability depends on how much time you spend on the game, which is especially true for those complex games. The longer you play, the more likely you are to develop your abilities. The failure of any catching-up is largely due to the fact that the players do not have enough time to develop their ability. If the first-mover's enterprises develop too fast and the environment changes drastically, it will be impossible for the latecomers to realize ability development.

Third is certain absorptive capacity. In the process of catching-up, the latecomer countries often need to obtain technologies from the first-mover countries. According to the classical views of absorptive capacity, the precondition for enterprises to identify and utilize external technologies is that they must have absorptive capacity. Moreover, the stronger the absorptive capacity the latecomer countries have, the more effective their catching-up will be. This seems quite straightforward, but it brings about another question: How to explain the case of "cold start"? In other words, at the beginning, all the late-developing countries lack sufficient absorptive capacity because of the huge gap existing between advanced technology from foreign countries and that of their own. Thus, in some sense, they almost hardly have any absorptive capacity. So, how they use the external advanced technology under the state of "cold start" is an important question to be explained.

Due to the existence of these preconditions, what we try to elaborate here is the particularity in China's catching-up situation and to what extent can it help Chinese manufacturing enterprises meet the necessary preconditions in the catch-up process. Next, we will interpret the first two preconditions from the angle of the particularity of the Chinese market. And then, we will interpret our third question on the "cold start" of absorptive capacity from the perspective of the particularity of China's innovation system.

The home market has always been important

In the process of catching-up, most developing countries will emphasize utilizing foreign capital. For example, they will implement some preferential investment policies to attract foreign capital to their home markets so as to ease the capital shortage commonly faced by them. However, the importance of the home market to the accumulation of resources of domestic enterprises is often overlooked.

For China, the Chinese government has been valuing the role of exports for a long period of time. However, there are still many signs showing that China's home market still means a lot to Chinese enterprises. According to the results of a survey of 11,264 high-tech industrial enterprises conducted by China's National Bureau of Statistics and the Ministry of Science and Technology in 2007, from 2004 to 2006, over 50% of the innovation activities of these enterprises were aimed at their home market. According to China's Industrial Enterprise Innovation Survey 2008, internal funds accounted for 82.8% of the total innovation funds of industrial enterprises above the designated size. This means that Chinese enterprises rely heavily on internal capital accumulation to fund their innovation activities.

Loren Brandt, a professor of economics at the University of Toronto, and Eric Thun, a professor at Oxford University, calculated the data of China's National Industrial Census in 1995 and 2004.[13] According to their

[13] Brandt, L. and E. Thun. (2010). The fight for the middle: Upgrading, competition, and industrial development in China. *World Development* 38(11), 1555–1574.

calculation, in 1995, the total sales revenue (domestic sales plus importation) of Chinese manufacturing enterprises was RMB 5.44 trillion, with the export value 20% higher than the domestic sales. Chinese enterprises roughly supplied 2/3 of the home market demand, while the rest was satisfied by foreign enterprises and imports. The estimated data of 2004 showed that the sales revenue of the manufacturing industry in China's home market in 2004 reached RMB 19.36 trillion, and 72% of all products made in China were sold to the domestic market. Furthermore, US economist Joseph E. Stiglitz pointed out that although exports will continue playing an important role in China's economic development, China is gradually shifting from its export-oriented growth to an economic structure that relies more on domestic consumption and investment and that this trend is actually gaining its momentum. Data from "China and the world: Inside the dynamics of a changing relationship" released by McKinsey Global Institute also support this trend. According to the report, although 110 companies from Mainland of China were included in the Fortune 500 list, their overseas revenues only accounted for less than 20% of their total revenue, while the same figure for S&P 500 companies[14] was 44%.

Before venturing into further discussion about the particularity of the Chinese market, we can have an intuitive guess based on the above data, that is, China's market structure in fact enables Chinese local enterprises to better obtain returns from the home market. This in turn supported them in making more sustained and larger-scale investment in capability development throughout their learning, catching-up and innovation.

A Unique Market

In their development trajectory, many economies, including many Asian countries and regions, such as Japan, R. O. Korea, Singapore and Thailand, have adopted export-oriented policies. Since China is a large

[14] Standard & Poor is a global authoritative financial analysis institution, providing financial services such as credit rating, independent analysis and investment consultation for investors. The Standard & Poor's 500 Index (S&P 500 Index) provided by the agency covers 500 companies with the largest market value publicly traded in the US stock market and is considered to be one of the best indexes reflecting the trend of the US stock market.

emerging economy, its manufacturing industry faces problems similar to that of the above export-oriented economies. However, huge differences existing in some aspects of Chinese manufacturing industry and that of the above-mentioned countries cannot be ignored. For large emerging economies, government policies will not only affect the availability of resources and knowledge on the supply side but also affect the motivation and results of capabilities improving local enterprises. When a country adopts an export-oriented development approach, the government policies only need to provide support from the perspective of resource supply because the demand side is determined by the international market rather than domestic policies.[15] For a large emerging economy like China, its demand side includes not only the international market but also the large-scaled potential home market. Both markets influence the development strategy of local enterprises from the demand side.

So, what are the noteworthy features of the Chinese market?

It is obvious that China's large population base bequeaths the country a huge potential home market demand. We often think that the external manifestation of economies of the scale of the manufacturing industry lies in reduced production cost brought about by its massive scale. Yet, it is actually due to the underlying effective division of labor and the learning effect. In other words, without sufficient effective market size, it is difficult for the manufacturing industry to develop. However, the large size of the home market is not enough to guarantee the survival and development opportunities of the local manufacturing enterprises. Therefore, the feature of a large population base also needs to be associated with another feature of the Chinese market, namely, the highly segmented market structure.

China has a highly segmented market structure featured by the coexistence of the best technology and the poorest technology, the latest products and the most outdated ones, and the most complex product requirements and the entry-level product requirements. All of them constitute various segments in the same market, with each segment having a considerable scale. Walking in any city in China, you can see luxury cars of foreign brands and entry-level cars of local brands harmoniously traveling on the streets at the same time. People come and go on the bustling streets, carrying mobile phones of different brands. In almost any field of

[15]Brandt, L. and E. Thun. (2016). Constructing a ladder for growth: Policy, markets, and industrial upgrading in China. *World Development* 80, 78–95.

life, we can see a highly diversified choice of goods — whether in terms of price, quality, performance, or the country of origin of the brand. Such diversity will be even more obvious when considering China's huge rural population and the income gap between urban and rural areas. Sometimes, it is even difficult for us to use a single word to describe the overall market characteristics of China because of the huge disparity in terms of payment ability and product demands of consumers.

The huge potential domestic market can bring some significant advantages to Chinese manufacturing industry.

First of all, the huge market potential gives local enterprises a stronger motivation to capture those potential market opportunities and also gives entrepreneurs a stronger entrepreneurial motivation. In order to grasp the growth opportunities in these markets as much as possible, the enterprises and entrepreneurs are enthusiastic about developing new technologies and products to continuously enhance the enterprise's capacity. In order to realize the development of products, technologies and capabilities under limited resources, they will try every means to find possible solutions, hence demonstrating a strong risk-taking propensity and a very creative way of thinking.

Second, in such a market, it is easier for local enterprises to find suitable survival space and accumulate financial resources so as to support their long-term catching-up. This is because only when a market has a big-enough home market and a highly segmented structure can it meet the following two requirements. First, the market is sufficiently segmented to allow the local enterprises to avoid head-to-head competition with strong competitors, including international companies. Second, the market size is large enough to sustain economies of scale under a segmented structure. Especially in terms of the development of technological capability, enterprises need to accumulate knowledge and experience through repeated trial and error. For example, they need to proactively invest in knowledge search, high-level talents and the improvement of existing employees' abilities. However, such future-oriented investment highly depends on the chances of success of these enterprises in the home market. A study on Latin American machine tool industry showed that the lack of sufficient domestic market will make local manufacturers in this industry encounter greater obstacles in technological upgrading and capacity-building.[16]

[16] Alcorta, L. (2000). New economic policies and the diffusion of machine tools in Latin America. *World Development* 28(9), 1657–1672.

Moreover, latecomer countries often adopt the strategy of "market for technology" in the process of their catching-up.[17] It means opening up the market (including giving them some attractive preferential policies) to foreign enterprises that can bring in advanced technology and management experience. A huge potential market scale is of great appeal to multinational companies. And it can greatly increase the negotiation chip of the local enterprises in acquiring technology during their joint venture negotiation with these companies. In the early stage of the opening up to the outside world of China's manufacturing industry, when the capabilities of the local enterprises were far from being full-fledged, the appeal of the home market and the relatively low labor costs were almost the only chips for bargain.

It should be pointed out that, with the continuous process of China's urbanization, new incremental demands are continuously generated and released in the domestic market. When rural population floods into cities and towns, the basic needs in daily lives will rise and so will the diversity of their needs. However, these continuously unleashed incremental demands generally lie at the bottom of the market pyramid. Such market demands are often neglected by multinational companies entering the Chinese market, who often focus on high-quality and high-priced markets for a long time after entering China because it makes it easier for them to give full play to their advantages in capability, technology, quality and brand and thus obtain lucrative profits. This will no doubt give more leeway to Chinese enterprises to avoid head-to-head competing against foreign enterprises and to find a market space to survive at their infancy stage. At the same time, with a highly segmented market structure, the consumer needs are often diversified and carry distinctive localized features, which are usually difficult to be addressed by the conventional market strategies of multinational companies. This also brings the local enterprises with survival spaces. This is also why Chinese local enterprises often assimilate localized innovations on the basis of imitation.

[17]For example, the Chinese government has initiated the "market for technology" industrial policy since 1994. Although this policy has been regarded to have played a positive role in some industries, it has been deemed not so effective as expected in some other industries. For the historical changes in the policy after the year 1986, please refer to https://zhidao.baidu.com/question/2141656107932008348.html.

"Cold Start" in Early Catching-Up

Latecomer countries need to overcome not only the "resource constraints" problem[18] but also the "cold start" issue in the early stage of their catching-up.[19] The so-called "cold start" issue can be explained as follows. In the early stage of catching-up, especially technological catching-up, there exists a huge initial gap between the knowledge and capability foundation of domestic enterprises and that of the foreign multinational companies. Thus, it is difficult for domestic enterprises to effectively absorb and utilize advanced technology and management experience of the foreign companies relying on their own innate capabilities.

To comprehend the "cold start" issue in the process of catching-up, we can start with the "absorptive capacity theory", a theory put forward by Wesley M. Cohen,[20] a professor at Duke University, and Daniel A. Levinthal, a professor at Pennsylvania University. According to the **absorptive capacity theory**, even if there is a lot of potentially available external knowledge, it does not mean that an enterprise can absorb and utilize such knowledge because in order to recognize the value of and absorb such knowledge, an enterprise must first have a certain knowledge base or absorptive capacity. In this way, a very interesting paradox arises in the catching-up situation, namely, in the early stage of catching-up, due to the large gap in knowledge or technology between latecomers and forerunners, there is a huge barrier between the capacity base of the latecomers and the potentially available external knowledge. Yet, the logic of absorptive capacity requires an enterprise to first possess absorptive capacity in order to absorb and utilize the external knowledge. This is a classic paradox, i.e., **the premise of an act is exactly the result of this very act**.

The existence of this paradox reveals a very important issue to the researchers, that is, as for the research in catching-up of latecomer

---

[18]This is partly caused by the lack of sufficient capital accumulation for latecomer countries at the early stage of catch-up. In addition, when the domestic financial system is not developed, some institutional deficiencies will make it difficult for most enterprises to obtain enough capital for their product and technology development.

[19]Ishtiaq, P. M. and C. Rufin. (April, 2005). Government's dilemma: The role of government in imitation and innovation. *Academy of Management Review* 30(2), 338–360.

[20]Wesley, C. M. and L. A. Daniel. (1990). Absorptive capacity: A new perspective on learning and innovation. *Administrative Science Quarterly* 35(1), 128–152.

enterprises and countries, it is far from enough to only focus on how these research objects rely on their own innate capabilities to realize their technological capacity catching-up. This is because although the innate capabilities already possessed and the external technology utilization strategies adopted by the enterprises can certainly play a positive role, they still cannot solve the cold start paradox or can they provide practical suggestions for enterprises or industries in their early stage of catching-up.

To solve this paradox, we need to include the home market structure in our analysis. If we arrange all the enterprises in a country's home market (including local enterprises and foreign enterprises operating in the country) in order from low to high according to their market positioning (i.e., the differentiated distribution based on quality and technology levels), we can see the market structure formed by these enterprises as a "ladder".

This market ladder has double connotations. On the one hand, every enterprise will occupy a certain position on this market ladder, and the position depends on its current quality level and technology level. Since enterprises will continuously move up the market ladder through continuous learning in the process of their catching-up, this process is very similar to when we climb the ladders in our daily life. On the other hand, the knowledge gap between any enterprise in this market ladder and its neighboring enterprises (located next to such enterprise) is the smallest compared with the knowledge gaps between such enterprise and any other one on the whole ladder. So, these neighboring enterprises are also the targets of such enterprises to easily infuse knowledge, to learn, and to imitate from. Furthermore, when every enterprise learns and imitates from their corresponding neighboring enterprises above them, the advanced knowledge (whether technical knowledge or management experience) brought by the enterprise at the top of the market ladder can be absorbed step by step like a waterfall and converted into knowledge that can be understood and absorbed by the second-level enterprises, thus enabling all enterprises in the whole market ladder to benefit from it.[21]

---

[21] We will discuss the market ladder in detail in the next chapter. Here, we mainly expound the most basic viewpoints. In addition, there will be horizontal knowledge exchange and knowledge spillovers among enterprises on the same position of a market ladder (that is, they adopt the same market positioning), but we are more concerned about the vertical knowledge spillovers along the market ladder here. It is because horizontal knowledge

Of course, whether all enterprises on the market ladder can obtain the maximum benefits depends, to a great extent, on the continuity of the market ladder under given internal capabilities, knowledge acquisition strategies and resource conditions. We can acquire an intuitive understanding of this from our daily life. It is like when we climb up a mountain. Climbing upstairs step by step, we will eventually reach the top of the mountain and appreciate the artistic conception as described in the verse "Reaching the top, then you can hold all mountains in a single glance". However, let's assume that there exist two climbing ladders as shown in Figure 1.9, where the ladder on the left is more continuous with lower steps so that we can easily mount, whereas the one on the right is less continuous with many higher steps. Then, which one might be more friendly to a mountain climber?

The answer is self-evident: it is the more continuous one on the left side. Then, with the continuity of the market ladder and the technological ladder as the core, we can answer the following question: Which type of

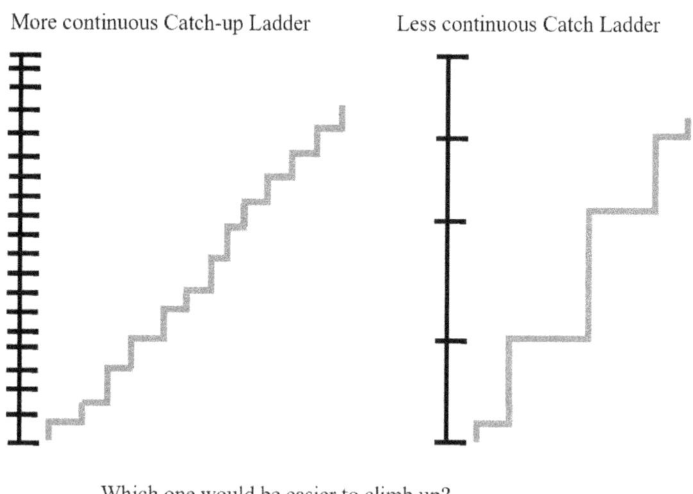

Figure 1.9. Continuity of Catching-up Ladders

exchange often involves complementary technical knowledge, whereas since there is a technological gap between enterprises conducting vertical knowledge spillovers along the market ladder, it will be more difficult for enterprises with relatively low technological potential to overcome this technological gap.

industry is more suitable for Chinese manufacturing enterprises to complete their catching-up? In our observation, we can often find that the answer is those industries with a large number of unsatisfied market demands, modularized products and technologies, relatively complete domestic industrial value chain, and stable yet clear-trended technological development.

Are Chinese Enterprises Facing Globalization or Localization?

Since China implemented the reform and opening-up policy in 1978 and joined the WTO in 2001, China's manufacturing industry has benefited a lot from globalization. It can even be said that China's manufacturing industry has been the biggest beneficiary of China's docking into globalization over the past 40 years.

In the past, when discussing the globalization of enterprises, we often consider whether the enterprises would export their products overseas or deploy their business activities overseas through establishing overseas branch offices, acquiring overseas assets, or founding joint ventures. We might as well call this "active" globalization. However, more and more Chinese enterprises find that even if their products, investments or operations do not really enter the overseas market, all their business activities still mainly take place in the home market of China, and their products are entirely sold in the home market, as local enterprises, they are already involved in intense direct competition with many foreign multinational companies and international brands in the Chinese market. This is what we call "passive" globalization. As more and more foreign enterprises and brands regard the Chinese market as an important link or component in their globalization deployment, "passive" globalization is becoming more and more common. In other words, the overall survival and competing environment of China's manufacturing enterprises are bound to be set against the context of globalization. Just in 2013, Jack Ma, the founder of Alibaba, explained his understanding of globalization back then in an interview, "government officials also said, when talking about globalization, it seems a company is ashamed to claim to be a big one if it has no overseas factory or office. However, a truly globalized enterprise is not defined by the number of its overseas branches or overseas customers but instead, mainly by its global insight, thinking, strategy and organizational culture. Enterprises with global business may not be globalized ones, and globalized enterprises may not necessarily conduct business globally ... In my opinion, the Chinese market is already an international one. Ten years later, the Chinese market will be the hottest marketplace with the most competition. It's already the ideal place you want to conduct business in. Why would we trudge all the way to other markets? I will only flee to other markets if I lose the Chinese market".[22]

For those Chinese enterprises seeking active globalization, they do not necessarily have to abandon their home market in the process of their global expansion. Likewise, even though some Chinese enterprises have been extending their footprint in overseas operations, the home market is still an indispensable part of their globalization road map, which even constitutes the foundation that supports their overseas expansion. When Chinese enterprises operate in both home and overseas markets, this dual-market strategy will bring them some potential advantages and increase their chances of getting returns from the market. For example, they can dynamically adjust their allocation of manufacturing resources according to the asynchronous development of the home and overseas markets so as to better meet the needs of the overseas market, and vice versa. In the same vein, this can alleviate the resource shortage of these enterprises caused by shrinking market conditions that may further affect their capacity-building.

At the same time, the enterprises can also gain synergy advantage from the parallel operations of the home market and the overseas market. For example, they can integrate overseas product R&D and designing capabilities with locally owned manufacturing resources and sales channels and introduce the product design of overseas R&D centers into the Chinese market after localization. It is exactly due to this reason that some Western scholars specially coined a new word: glocal, by combining the two English words global and local. This means that, on one hand, when providing products and services, those globally operating enterprises should consider not only the scale advantages brought about by standardized global operations but also the differentiated local needs. On the other hand, as for the operation management, they need to consider both the efficiency advantage of centralized management in the process of

[22]An Interview with Jack Ma on globalization, http://tech.sina.com.cn/i/2013-07-14/10008537575.shtml.

globalization and the flexibility advantage of decentralized management in localized operations.

In addition, even from the perspective of helping Chinese enterprises overcome resource constraints, the dual-market strategy is also of great benefit. In the era of globalization, Chinese enterprises need a large amount of initial resources and capital for their overseas expansion. This, to a large extent, depends on their cash flow generated in the home market. For example, Lenovo and Huawei all relied on the returns from China's home market to support their expansion to overseas markets and their upward migration in both local and global market ladders. Shaopeng Chen, the senior vice president of Lenovo Group and president of Greater China back then, said in an interview, "We have such a huge base as the Chinese market. At present, in the global PC industry, the largest market is the US market and the second is the Chinese market, but I absolutely believe that one day China will surpass the US to become the largest PC market. For a company to grow sustainably, there must be a sound home market that provides it with sufficient business model and resource accumulation. And Lenovo has such a base. We have grown up in this fastest-growing big market. Therefore, we have become the leader here. At present, we occupy 36% of the market share in China, not calculating our future increase. As long as we can maintain our market share, driven by a rapidly growing market, our development in the global market is bound to be greatly promoted. Such an advantage is beyond any doubt".[23]

[23] Lenova: Three advantages over its competitors, a dialogue between Shaopeng Chen (senior vice president of Lenovo Group and president of Greater China) and Hong Liu (editor-in-chief of China Electronics News), June 6, 2007.

Chapter 2

The Market Ladder

A Market Ladder with Diversity

In any large population, people demonstrate diversified consumption preferences, which are reflected in multiple dimensions, such as differentiated requirements on the function and quality of products. In some cases, such diversified demands cannot be judged as good or bad, but just reveal individual preferences, such as appearance and color preferences. Meanwhile, in a market-oriented system, in order to obtain certain products or services, people need to pay the corresponding cost, especially the monetized cost — the price of the product or service. Then, in a market that is not distorted by human forces, the product price is an external reflection of the product quality (usually indicating the technical level, performance, complexity and other value information of the product). On the demand side, the quality level is parallel with the level that buyers are willing to pay, whereas on the supply side, a higher quality level means better technology and design, better raw materials and parts, and higher level of production process, all of which mean higher costs and higher capacity requirements from the enterprises.

Therefore, taking price as a visible signal, we can arrange the price levels accepted by the demand side in a specific product market in order from low to high, thus getting a market structure description that we described as the "market ladder" in the previous chapter. Externally, different positions on the market ladder reflect the differences in product prices. However, they more deeply reflect the differences in product quality and technical level, as well as a deeper level of enterprise capability.

Such a capability can be simply understood as the ability to provide products of a higher quality level at the same cost level, or to provide products of the same quality level at a lower cost.

Due to China's huge population base, one can easily sense the huge market potential of China. With the long-term growth of China's economy, the purchasing power of Chinese consumers (reflected in the level of disposable personal income) has also continued to rise, which thus enhances the appeal of the Chinese market to Western multinational companies. However, the Chinese market is not only characterized by its "big" size but also by "high segmentation" or diversity. No other country, including the United States or Japan, has so many products and brands like China, where it is often difficult to establish brand loyalty.[1]

As you may well know, when we are too familiar with something, we often tend to take it for granted or even ignore its existence. As the Chinese people are born into such a market system, they may not easily appreciate or perceive its potential in such a strong way. However, in terms of Westerners' perception of the Chinese market, it is a different picture. Before Western companies entered and became familiar with the Chinese market, or before they truly understood the market, they would often subconsciously regard the Chinese market as a relatively homogeneous single entity and were accustomed to describing it with unified labels. As Johnathan Cooley, a part-time professor at George Fox University, said in 2010, "China is often viewed as a single, looming entity of 1.3 billion people, but is actually a diverse country of stark contrasts. One road trip or a business project can bring you to witness its 100 years of technology. When you travel from one province to another, you can experience varying attitudes and unwritten cultural differences. These challenges and other issues are unknown to the Westerners who just begin to deal with China. And those managers with the experience of working and living in China may feel surprised at this. These are our "blind spots".[2]

[1]Tse, E. (2010). Is it too late to enter China? *Harvard Business Review*, April 2010, pp. 96–101.

[2]"China: A Country of Contrasts" by Johnathan Cooley, Managing Partner, Advantage Partners USA & ASIA; CEO/Owner of Advantage Management Software, LLC; Managing Partner of AP Holdings, LLC, Department of Engineering and Technology Management, Technology Management Seminar Series, Graduate Seminars, Portland State University, Spring 2010.

An "Easy Mode" of Catching-Up

How does a highly segmented market structure, or a relatively continuous market ladder, constitute the indispensable condition for the rapid rise of China's manufacturing industry? How does it bring the potential advantages to Chinese manufacturing enterprises?

For Chinese manufacturing enterprises, in the early stage of their catching-up, and even for a long time after that, they are generally faced with the problem of insufficient internal resources, compounded by the so-called "financial constraints" in obtaining external financial resources, which tend to have a negative impact on their innovation and capability development. The main reasons for these problems are the relative shortage of capital, the low efficiency of the banking system and the underdeveloped capital market. Often, such a challenge is felt more by the small and medium-sized enterprises. However, even for the state-owned enterprises that have already developed to a certain scale, they still urgently need to continuously obtain more market returns to support their development strategies. That is to say, whether it is a smaller-sized enterprise or an enterprise with a certain scale, a private enterprise or a state-owned one, when facing the competition from foreign enterprises and the competition from local enterprises, the inevitable questions faced are of how to obtain more survival opportunities in the initial stages and how to accumulate resources quickly through market returns in their following development stages.

In this regard, a highly segmented market structure makes it easier for Chinese enterprises to find an initial market to acquire survival opportunities in their early stages of catching-up. As the capabilities accumulated by multinational enterprises in their past development process are more suitable for those relatively high-quality and high-priced markets, the relatively low-end markets often fall short to meet their financial goals or fit into their existing cost structure. Besides, those market segments are often too small to be noticed by these multinational companies. Therefore, local enterprises can easily find those overlooked low-end markets so as to survive.[3] For example, Huawei started from the peripheral market and gradually enhanced its own capability and knowledge

[3] Spencer, J. W. (2008). The impact of multinational enterprise strategy on indigenous enterprises: Horizontal spillovers and crowding out in developing countries. *Academy of Management Review* 33(2): 341–361.

base and established a complete technical system through its strategy of "encircling the city from the countryside", laying a solid foundation for its future rise.

At the same time, the huge scale and the highly segmented structure of the domestic market also makes it possible for China's manufacturing industry to realize economies of scale and the survival opportunities at the same time. We know that economies of scale are extremely important to the manufacturing industry, and are also a fundamental advantage of the manufacturing enterprises. It is precisely because of the huge size of the Chinese domestic market that even if the market is highly segmented, the size of each segment is still very large, so that the Chinese manufacturing enterprises can still benefit from the effect of scale. To a large extent, such an advantage is exclusive to large emerging economies, a congenital advantage that the small economies cannot enjoy. We can use a simple data calculation to illustrate this point. In 2018, China had a population of 1.395 billion people. Here we assume that 50% of them had valid potential demands, and that 20 market segments are needed to satisfy such demands. Despite our conservative estimation of only 50% potential consumers and as much as 20 market segments (in most cases, the market for a product category is not likely to be so segmented), the size of each segment will still exceed 34 million consumers. You have to know that such a scale even exceeds the total population of most countries. In 2019, there are 233 countries and regions in the world, and only 39 of them had a population equivalent to or larger than 34 million.

Such a market structure also means that the Chinese manufacturing enterprises have a prolonged opportunity for learning. A highly segmented market means that no matter what stage the current capabilities of the local enterprises have developed into, such enterprises can always find market segments that match their ability status best so as to survive. In this regard, the situation of those small economies, including many developed countries, is different from that of China. For example, in the European market, many countries have very small domestic markets. This leads to the problem that if you cannot closely follow the change of trend in the mainstream market, that is, in case the market moves up but your capability cannot keep up with it, you will have less chance to survive in the market because it is difficult for you to find an alternative market in this country. Therefore, the enterprises need to always follow the pace of market change closely. In contrast, things in the Chinese market are quite different. With a highly fragmented domestic market, even if the market segment the enterprise was previously in has moved up and the enterprise's own capabilities may not be able to keep up with this upward shift for the time being, its survival space will be filled by the demand moving up from below. This ensures that no matter whether the enterprise's ability can keep up with the development trend of the target market or not, the local enterprises may have more leeway to survive and thus more chances to catch-up. Especially in the case of catching-up with a time and capital consuming trend, China's market context carries with it incomparable advantages.

The continuous market ladder has also brought China's manufacturing industry opportunities for sustained growth. This is reflected in the gradual upgrading of technology and capabilities of local enterprises along the market ladder, and the further upgrading of product quality and price levels with its upward movement on the market ladder. Moreover, the high-price positioning of foreign-funded enterprises when they enter the Chinese market determines the anchor point for local enterprises to provide products with high cost performance. On this basis, Chinese enterprises can improve their products based on the needs of the local consumers or of consumers from the specific market segment. Take the road sweeper developed by Zoomlion as an example. Because the road conditions in China are quite different from that in Europe, the products produced by European companies cannot work as efficiently as the locally developed ones in China. This has created opportunities for Zoomlion to improve its localized products. With Chinese enterprises making continuous investment into production efficiency and technological development, they will eventually move upward on the market ladder, and even gain certain competitiveness to directly enter the high-end market that was once dominated by the multinational companies.

It is like when game-players start a game, there is often a pop-out reminder to ask them to choose the hard mode or the easy mode. In the hard mode, there is only one chance allowed for each game level, so the player has to make sure he can pass through every level smoothly during the game process. The easy mode is different. Each game level can be archived, so that the players may have many trial and error opportunities until they pass this level. The particular situation of the Chinese market has made it possible for the Chinese enterprises to convert this should-be hard mode of a catch-up game into an easy mode.

How Was the Market Ladder Formed?

China's market ladder was gradually formed in the process of the market-oriented transformation of China's economy. It can be seen as the result jointly produced from China's economic structure before the reform and opening-up, the market mechanism after the reform and opening-up and the incremental adoption of government policies.

More specifically, the reasons for the formation of China's highly segmented market structure, if portrayed by income level or wealth level (as it will largely determine consumers' consumption preference and price acceptance level), can be attributed to the following three aspects: the income disparity between China's urban and rural areas, the imbalance of economic development across regions, and the social stratification gradually formed during the development of China's market economy.

The urban and rural disparity are somehow related to the rural–urban dual policy that China has been implementing since 1949, which resulted in the household registration barriers and the differences in resource allocation of public infrastructure between urban and rural areas. In January 1958, the 91st Session of the Standing Committee of the National People's Congress discussed and passed the "Regulations of the People's Republic of China on Household Registration", marking the formation of China's household migration system with strict restrictions on the flow of rural population to cities as its core. After the Reform, however, the temporary residence permit system served as a continuation of this policy in a sense. At the same time, before the Reform, the distribution of public resources in Chinese society was carried out in the form of administrative redistribution, rather than by market mechanism. As the result, most of the public infrastructure investment went into urban cities rather than rural areas, which led to the gradual formation of a huge gap in disposable income between urban and rural areas. In the past ten years, with the increasing attention of the Chinese government on the issues of agriculture, rural areas and farmers, the per capita disposable income in rural areas has also been rising. However, overall, the gap between urban and rural areas is still relatively significant (see Figure 2.1).

Of course, the development trend of urbanization also affects the urban–rural duality. With more and more of the rural population entering cities and towns, and hence the change of their household registration status, their life demand levels have also changed in quantity, quality and

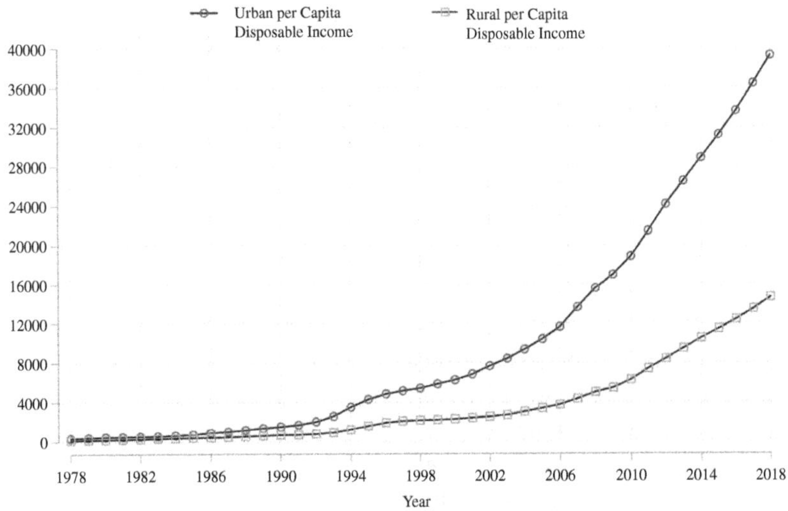

Figure 2.1. Changes in Urban and Rural Disposable Income Level: 1978–2018

Notes: Since 2013, the National Bureau of Statistics of China has carried out successive surveys on income and expenditure and living conditions of households from both urban and rural regions. Related data for 2013 and the years after that were sourced from the aforesaid surveys. Such surveys differed from the previous surveys before 2013 in scope, method and index calibers. Income and expenditure data of urban and rural residents before 2013 were, respectively, sourced from the urban household sample surveys and the rural household sample surveys.

Source: National Bureau of Statistics of China.

structure, which has become one of the reasons for the potential demand in the Chinese market to be continuously released. According to statistics, from 1949 to 2017, China's population increased from 540 million to 1.39 billion, and its urbanization rate soared from 10.64% to 58.52%.[4] Such a huge change in urban population has brought about a huge release of market potential. This newly released demand, at least in the initial stages, comes from the more price-sensitive among the population. In addition, their acceptance of brands and designs still requires a long process of market cultivation. Therefore, foreign-funded enterprises cannot effectively serve such demands. As a result, these demands are met by

[4]https://data.stats.gov.cn/easyquery.htm?cn=C01; http://www.gov.cn/shuju/2018-02/28/content_5269506.htm.

Chinese local enterprises and serve as the potential foundation and opportunities for their further development.

Differences in social and economic development levels across geographical regions are also a typical feature of China. According to the different levels of regional economic development, Chinese Mainland can be divided into eastern, northeastern, and central and western regions. The eastern region is basically a coastal region with a relatively complete market system and the most developed economy. This has led to significant differences in the level of economic development between different regions, which is closely related to the capital flow, market economy transformation and industrial structure change after China's Reform and Opening-up in 1978. China's Reform and Opening-up has been a gradual process, with clear characteristics of learning by trail and error in a way that, first, the market-oriented reforms were conducted in a few pilot regions, then experiences were summed up through continuous trial and error, and then such experiences were promoted in a wider range. As overseas trade in the global market depends heavily on sea transport, coastal regions hold distinctive advantages in attracting foreign capital inflow. Besides, the coastal areas, as traditional trading ports, have inherited the commercial gene and are more prone to accepting the concept of marketization and commercial awareness in the process of China's economic transition to a market economy. As a result, the economic structure of the coastal areas has also realized a rapid transformation to industrialization. As the speed of improvement in productivity in the industrial sector far exceeds that in the traditional agricultural sector, the economic level of these regions was greatly improved, and thus the development of private economy and entrepreneurship in such areas were promoted. The ultimate result is that the per capita income level and wealth accumulation rate of these regions are much higher than that of the other regions of China.

Income disparity across social classes is also an important trend. According to the statistics of *China Statistical Yearbook*, when the total residents in the country are equally divided into five groups by the level of their disposable income, the per capita disposable income of the top 20% residents in 2016 was RMB 59,259.5 yuan. This figure is much higher than that for the remaining 80%, or even that for the mid to high-income group of the second tier (with 31,990.4 RMB yuan per capita disposable income in 2016). However, in 2016, the per capita disposable income of the 20% population with the lowest disposable income was

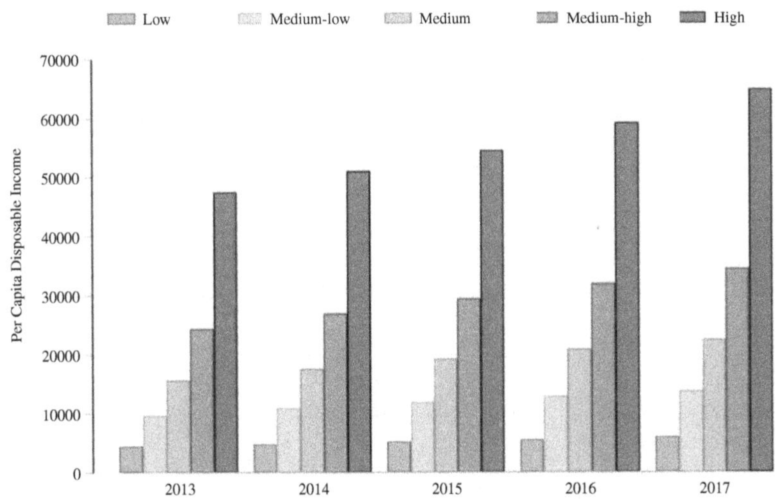

Figure 2.2. Per Capita Disposable Income of Chinese Residents Divided in Five Quintiles

Source: China Statistical Yearbook 2018.

only 5,528.7 RMB yuan, less than 1/10 of that of the high-income population[5] (see Figure 2.2).

Income disparity among different social groups is natural for the market economy. In the market economy system, entrepreneurship and professional ability have more and more value creation opportunities, which leads to higher income levels for business owners, senior managers of enterprises, professionals in finance and other fields. In addition, the increase in wealth accumulation brings about property income, which further widens the gap of wealth possession and income level among different social classes. Thomas Piketty, author of *Capital in the 21st Century*, published a report in April 2017 titled *Capital Accumulation, Private Property and Rising Inequality in China, 1978–2015*. According to his estimation, from 1978 to 2015, the proportion of income of the top 1% population in China rose from 6% in 1978 to 14% in 2015. By contrast, the proportion of income of the bottom 50% of the population dropped from 27% to 15% of the total (see Figure 2.3).[6]

[5]https://baijiahao.baidu.com/s?id=1605603395488126800&wfr=spider&for=pc.

[6]Piketty, T., L. Yang, and G. Zucman (2019). Capital accumulation, private property, and rising inequality in China, 1978–2015. *American Economic Review* 109(7): 2469–2496.

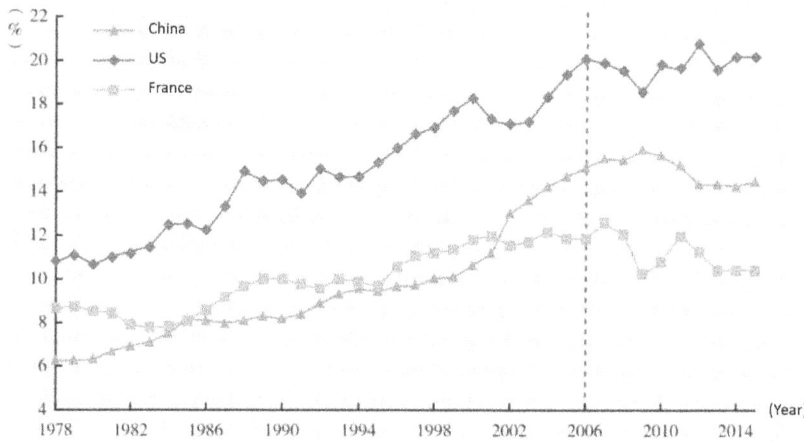

Figure 2.3. Income Proportion of the Top 1% of the Population: A Comparison between China and the Wealthier Countries

Source: Piketty, Thomas, Li Yang, and Gabriel Zucman. "Capital Accumulation, Private Property, and Rising Inequality in China, 1978–2015." *American Economic Review* 109.7 (2019): 2469–96. [Copyright American Economic Association; reproduced with permission of the American Economic Review].

According to the *Global Wealth Report 2011* released by the UBS, in 2011, the number of people with a net worth of USD 1 million in China exceeded 1 million for the first time. More than 5,000 people in China have their personal wealth exceeding USD 50 million, which is referred to as the Ultra High Net Worth (UHNW). And the number of Chinese with UHNW is second only to that of those in the US. China Construction Bank (CCB) cooperated with the Boston Consulting Corporation (BCG) in conducting a comprehensive survey of 3,399 of CCB's private bank customers. On the basis of this survey and extensive data analysis, it was estimated that in 2018 there were a total of 1.67 million high net worth individuals with over RMB 6 million personal investable financial assets. On June 5, 2019, China Merchants Bank and the Bain & Company, an international management consulting company, jointly released 2019 *China Private Wealth Report* with the theme of "Return to the Origin". The report showed that in 2018 there were 1.97 million high net worth individuals in China with an investable asset of over RMB 10 million, whose investable asset added up to RMB 61 trillion yuan and average personal investable assets amounted to RMB 30.8 million. According to the same report, in 2018 there were 170,000 super-rich people with an investable asset exceeding RMB 100 million in China.

Huge purchasing power has been generated precisely due to the expanding middle class population of China. Their demand for brands and quality also keeps rising with time. In fact, China's market ladder not only covers the traditional range of low-end to middle market but also the more high-end luxury market. All China's consumer demands have been covered by the market ladder. Even before and after the global financial crisis in 2008, China's luxury brand market still showed explosive growth. As of December 2009, China's total luxury consumption reached USD 9.4 billion, accounting for 27.5% of the world total, surpassing the US to became the world's second largest luxury goods consuming country.[7] Besides, according to the statistics of Bain & Company, China has become the world's largest luxury goods consumer in 2018, with the spending on luxury goods by the Chinese consumers accounting for about 33% of the world total. From 2012 to 2018, more than half of the growth in the global luxury market came from China. Data from McKinsey showed that in 2018 Chinese consumers spent RMB 770 billion on purchasing luxury goods inside and outside China (about 115 billion US dollars). If this is averaged to every household, the average yearly expenditure of Chinese consumers on luxury goods reached RMB 80,000 per year. In addition, McKinsey predicts that by 2025 the total consumption of luxury goods by Chinese consumers both inside and outside the country will almost double, reaching RMB 1.2 trillion, accounting for 40% of the world's total luxury goods consumption by then.

The Dynamics of the Market Ladder

China's market ladder not only has the typical features discussed above, such as huge domestic market in size, highly segmented structure and high continuity in distribution, but it also has such a typical feature as high dynamics (see Figure 2.4). The so-called dynamics is reflected as follows. On the one hand, the market ladder of China presents an upward migration trend on the whole (which can be understood as the foreseeable dynamics to some extent). On the other hand, due to the fierce competition and uncertainty in this market, it is difficult for enterprises in this market environment to predict the future direction and changing trend,

[7]Top 10 Chinese cities most loved by international luxury brands, by Ivy Wang, March 4, 2011. http://www.china.org.cn/top10/2011-03/04/content_22055707_8.htm.

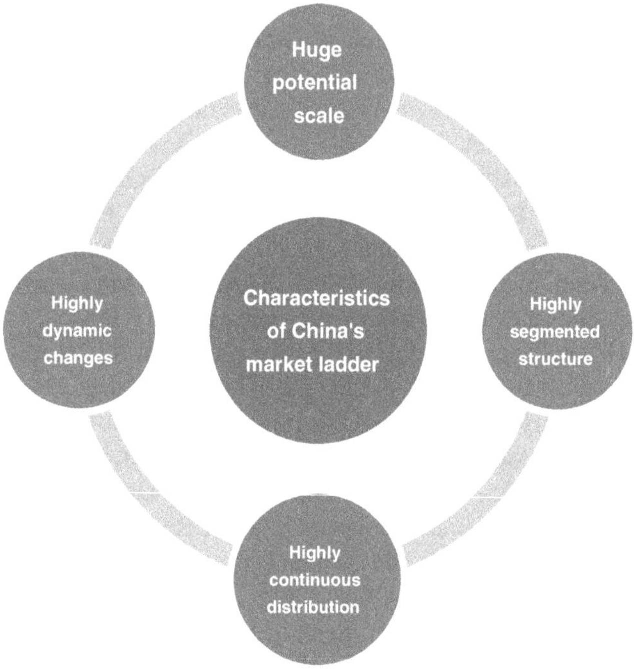

Figure 2.4. Typical Characteristics of the Chinese Market

and they need to endure a highly volatile competitive environment (which can be understood as the non-foreseeable dynamics).

The dynamic change trend of China's market ladder is to a large extent related to the lasting growth on demand side brought by the sustained economic growth and urbanization process of China over the past decades. We can divide the changes in the Chinese market into two types, namely, market upgrading and market expansion. Market upgrading means the market demand continuously moves upward from the bottom of the market ladder. In this process, in order to meet the market's requirements for higher quality and technological complexity, enterprises need to continuously improve their own innate capabilities. Market expansion means in order to accommodate a wider range of market demand with high diversity, the market ladder will evolve into a more complex and further segmented market structure (see Figure 2.5).

In recent years, we have witnessed the continuous consumption upgrading in many product areas. It's evidenced in the fact that people pay

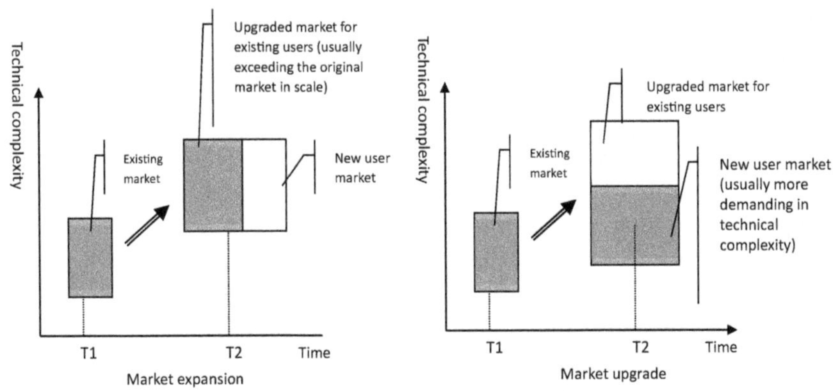

Figure 2.5. Dynamic Changes in China's Market Ladder: Market Expansion and Market Upgrade

more attention to product design, quality and brand. Therefore, their willingness to pay premium for product design, quality and brand is not limited to international luxury brands and foreign branded products, but also extends to many products produced by Chinese local manufacturers. Take smartphones as an example. According to the *ASP 2018* released by Counterpoint, a market data research agency, the average price of Huawei phones increased by 14% in 2017 and 27% in 2018, ranking first among mainstream mobile phone manufacturers. The average price of Apple's mobile phones rose by 11%, ranking the third among mainstream mobile phone manufacturers. At the same time, due to the rising prices of Huawei and Apple mobile phones, the average selling price of smartphones worldwide has seen the biggest increase of the recent years, increasing by 11% in 2018, which is far higher than the 4% in 2017. Yet, the price increase didn't produce any negative impact on the sales volume of mobile phones. In 2018, Huawei's global mobile phone sales surged from 153 million units in 2017 to 206 million units in 2018, witnessing an increase in both price and sales. In June 2019, Bain & Company and Kantar Worldpanel jointly released the *China Shopper Report*. The report also showed that even though the penetration rate and shopping frequency of some categories in fast-moving consumption goods may have reached the peak, there still seems to be sufficient room for the average selling price to rise, which is especially true for the personal care product category. In 2018, the sales of skin care products increased rapidly by 13.7%, with the average selling price up by 7.7%. In 2018, the sales of hair conditioner products dropped by 0.8%, but their sales revenues still increased by 7.3%, mainly because the average selling price was up by 8.1%. This trend also means that enterprises participating in the competition in the Chinese market need to gradually switch the focus of their attention from the quantity-based growth to the quality-based growth, to adapt to the general trend of consumption upgrading in the Chinese market.

As Chinese consumers increasingly shift from being the price-sensitive (paying more attention to the price of products) to the value-sensitive (paying more attention to the high cost-effectiveness of products) type, the core area of market competition has changed. The good-enough market[8] has gradually become a place of strategic importance in the Chinese market. Due to the increased strategic importance and the growth potential of the good-enough market, it even becomes a place where foreign multinational companies and Chinese local enterprises compete on a large scale. In a sense, this is unprecedented because, for a long time, the market positioning strategies of Chinese local enterprises and foreign multinational companies have been perfectly staggered, and there has been almost no overlapping between them in the past. This means the multinational companies usually only needed to maintain their dominant position and competitive advantage in high-quality and high-price markets, so as to completely realize their strategic objectives. And for Chinese local enterprises, they could avoid direct competition with foreign multinational companies through relatively low-end market positioning. However, the gradual overlap of market positioning and the continuous expansion of the potential scale of such overlap make large-scale competitions inevitable between foreign multinational companies and Chinese local enterprises. That's why Gadiesh *et al.* wrote that "Multinationals and local firms for the first time are squaring off in China's rapidly growing

[8]"Good-enough market" is similar in meaning to a market with cheap products with attractive value. In some cases, we may call it "middle level market" or "middle market", in spite of the subtle differences between these terms. Such a market targets value-sensitive consumers, who care more for the balance between quality and price, or the high-cost performance, instead of pure low price. In other words, their value demand is jointly defined by "appropriate quality level" and "attractive price level". For the convenience of our discussion, in this book, we would call it "a cost-effective market".

middle market — a critical staging ground for global expansion and the segment from which world-beating companies will emerge".[9]

Huawei has similar perceptions about the market ladder strategy in the Chinese market. On November 14, 2014, Huawei's President Zhengfei Ren stated in his speech at an "Internal Strategy Brainstorming Meeting", "We must not lose the low-end market while striving to win in the high-end market. We are now implementing the 'needle tip' strategy, drilling forward with all strengths. Yet I feel quite worried that when we manage to win at the 'needle tip', we may lose the 'needle bottom'. If we abandon the low-end products and leave it to others, this might result in incubating our potential competitors who might encroach on the high-end market sooner or later in the future. Huawei entered the high-end by gathering momentum from the low-end market. Why couldn't other competitors of ours replicate our growth path?"

How to effectively cover the market ladder existing in China's local market is a problem that those leading enterprises need to treat with caution. Some overlooked segments in the market ladder can indicate potential opportunities for the leading enterprises, or it may also indicate the foothold for those latecomers to challenge them. In addition, Zhengfei Ren further elaborated on the specific strategy road map that should be adopted when an enterprise is located in a cost-effective market at the low-end of the ladder. He said, "Low-end products should be standardized, simplified, and provide free maintenance services within their life cycle. We will not go down the path of low price with low quality, as that will destroy our power of launching strategic attacks. In terms of technology and service mode, we need to make it impossible for others to compete with us, that is, to streamline the process on a larger scale. If customers want more features, they can buy our high-end products". This means that even if an enterprise is located in the cost-effective market located at the relatively low end of the market ladder, it needs to not only consider the low prices but also the value demands of users. And on this basis, it needs to strike a reasonable balance between the enterprise's own value capture and the value satisfaction of its customers.

In the Chinese market, enterprises also need to manage and adapt to unforeseeable market dynamics. We can demonstrate such dynamics with a seemingly irrelevant simple example. In Western enterprises, we can see

---

[9]Gadiesh, O., P. Leung, and T. Vestring (2007). The battle for China's good-enough market. *Harvard Business Review* 85(9): 80.

that people (especially the managers) will put appointments into their work schedules and handle various management tasks according to the work schedules in most cases. However, in Chinese enterprises, even those already quite large-scale enterprises, managers' work schedules are constantly changing, and some scheduled items will often need to give way to the newly added items with higher priorities. It's often described as "changes run faster than plans" in Chinese. In such a context, a person's plan will present a "ripple effect" due to their interwoven relations in managerial activities. This makes it necessary for everyone to maintain a high degree of flexibility to cope with the high degree of external uncertainty. Although this example is at the individual level, it is also true at the organizational level. Perhaps it is exactly because such volatility of the environment has become a normal that individuals and enterprises within the environment are more likely to acquire the ability to quickly respond to changes. As multinational companies place great emphasis on establishing rigid organizational structures and processes in their organizational design to manage the uncertainty and dynamics of the external environment, they have certain bottlenecks in their organizational flexibility and their responsiveness to a rapidly changing environment. This can become an asymmetric capability advantage that local enterprises can take advantage of when competing with multinational companies in the Chinese market.

Another cause of dynamics is that extremely fierce industrial competition (often in the form of price wars) is very common in the Chinese market. Since the mid-1990s, we have seen a large number of price wars in many industries and business fields. The occurrence of these price wars indicates a similar behavior pattern, that is, although there are already a large number of competitors in some business fields and the market seems to be already saturated, some latecomers would still follow to enter into the market, igniting fierce competition until fierce price wars are triggered.

There was a very interesting anecdote about the product development strategies of Kingsoft Software and Shida Mingtai around the year 2000. Kingsoft Software was considered quite weak according to market analysis back then, so it adopted a product development strategy of developing whatever products were hot in the market. And the product development strategy of Shida Mingtai was even simpler, that is, whatever Kingsoft Software produces, Shida Mingtai would do so, too. Apparently, this anecdote pointed out that the product strategies of Kingsoft Software and

Shida Mingtai indicated they were blindly following market hot spots and were thus clearly irrational.

At first, I also shared the same thought. However, I once heard an entrepreneur talking about why his enterprise adopted the strategy of following the hot spots in the market. I suddenly realized that although this strategy does have irrational characteristics at the industrial level, it is fully rational for individuals at the micro level. At that time, the entrepreneur explained his viewpoint like this, "Let me tell you an example first. What does it mean to you when you walk in the street, seeing a group of people circling around a certain place? This shows that something must have happened there, or otherwise people would not have gathered there. This is just like if many enterprises choose to enter a product category or business area, it must be because this product or business area presents attractive opportunities. I am not always smarter than the market, but there are always many smart people in the market. Since so many smart people have chosen to enter the market, I believe their choice is definitely better than what I made. So I will definitely choose to go in. However, before formally entering the market, I will certainly ask myself two questions. First, if I adopt a similar approach to conducting this business, can I achieve higher efficiency or lower cost compared with others? Second, is it possible for me to find a completely different way to do this business so as to be more efficient or to avoid competition with the existing enterprises? If the answers to both questions are no, then I will finally choose to give up. But if the answer to either of these two questions is yes, I will definitely make a decision to enter the market. For me, I don't care whether it will cause a price war or not, or whether it will aggravate the price war".

His explanation brought me to reconsider this issue, although before this I already knew that the macro level and the micro level are different, and there is always the problem of summation fallacy. Moreover, as the classic prisoner's dilemma tells us, the most rational and right choice each individual makes from his own perspective often adds up to actually the worst choice viewed from the macro perspective.

Behind this problem lie more abundant implications. Hongyi Zhou, the founder of Qihoo 360 Technology Co. Ltd. also made an interesting remark, "Is there really any blue ocean? There is no blue ocean in China, because there are too many smart people, and they have already entered any fields you can think of. You think you finally found a blue ocean and you enter it today. But you will only find you are joined by a big company the next day. Therefore, it's red ocean everywhere. I often say to our product managers that 1,000 people must have thought about the brilliant idea that had enlightened you. Maybe 100 people have already started to roll their sleeves unpacking it, and 10 people may have almost done it. If you search on the Internet, maybe 3 people have already launched the related products".[10] Although there are still some different views on whether there is any blue ocean in the Chinese market, this quote did prove a common phenomenon — there are a lot of trial and error opportunities in the Chinese market. As there are so many enterprises in the Chinese market, these trial and error opportunities and learning will eventually point to the same direction even though they have different starting points. This is also why many entrepreneurs suggest that in the Chinese market it is often impossible to wait until the full maturity of an idea to put it into action. Many times one needs to complete their optimization-oriented thinking while staging rapid action, otherwise he or she will miss many great opportunities that could have been captured from this market.

Still, in the Chinese market, why is such a behavior pattern of seemingly "blindly imitating or following" so common? Judging from the existing observations, there are two important prerequisites for this kind of behavior pattern. First, in terms of the structure, such an industry or business field often lacks enterprises with industrial dominance. Different from the monopolized industries where only a few companies dominate the vast majority of market share, the top few companies in those industries do not have enough market share, leaving the substantial market demand distributing at the end of the long tail. Besides, under such an industrial structure, there are a large number of low-efficiency manufacturers. In other words, there are sufficient opportunities for value disruptions.

These two preconditions are prone to exist in the Chinese context, because the Chinese market carries distinctive features of a huge potential market scale and a highly segmented market structure, which leads to the prevailing long-tail distribution of demand. Moreover, due to these two characteristics, in the initial stages, those manufacturers who are disadvantaged in terms of resources or capabilities can easily find a niche market to survive in at least for the time being. Therefore, though on the surface, the repeatedly occurring "blindly following into the market and

[10] Sina Tech, July 22, 2013. http://tech.sina.com.cn/i/2013-07-22/17448562944.shtml.

imitating behavior" seems to be obviously irrational, from a microscopic perspective we can see the rationality of such irrational behaviors.

Continuity: The Key to the Catch-Up Ladder

Previously, we discussed the features of huge potential scale and highly segmented market structure of the Chinese market, as well as the potential catching-up advantages these features bequeathed to Chinese enterprises. Mindful readers may come up with a question: based on this logic, all large emerging economies, especially the so-called "BRICS" (Brazil, Russia, India, China and South Africa[11]), should all be potentially carrying this kind of advantage. But why, at least until now, are there no other emerging economies which are able to unleash such a manufacturing advantage as that of China? Why did their manufacturing industries generally not develop into highly competitive links in the global industrial value chain and generate important impacts on the global economy?

To successfully capitalize this advantage of the catch-up ladder, a critical precondition is that the existing market ladder in the economy must have sufficient continuity. In other words, the market ladder cannot leave a large gap between the high-end and the low-end enterprises. Otherwise, the local enterprises that gradually migrate upward along the market ladder from the low-end will find it difficult to find a market area matching their ability in the local market to help them further survive and develop. Take India as an example. India has a population of 1.35 billion, 85% of which are under 54 years of age and 65% are under 35. This seems to mean that India, like China, has a huge potential market base. However, in 2018, *The Economist* published an article titled "India's Missing Middle". The article described the current situation of India's large gap between the rich and the poor and the extremely compressed middle class, and expressed such a concern as when the world is looking for the next fast-growing economy after China, India seems to be the most likely candidate. However, India's serious lack of middle-class population may

[11]BRICS is the acronym coined to represent Brazil, Russia, India, China and South Africa. The land area of BRICS countries accounts for 26.46% of the total world territory and their population accounts for 42.07% of the total world population (https://www.fmprc.gov.cn/web/gjhdq_676201/gjhdqzz_681964/jzgj_682158/jbqk_682160/).

make all this come to naught.[12] In other words, the continuity of India's local market ladder is much lower than China's, and there are many breakages and gaps between the high-end demand and the bottom-level demand on its market ladder.

There are two reasons to explain why China's market ladder has a high level of continuity, or why there are a large number of enterprises distributed in every market position from the bottom to the top of the Chinese market ladder. In the era of planned economy from 1949 to 1978, compared with that in the forthcoming years, the internal differences in the level of wealth or income among the Chinese were relatively small. This means an even distribution of wealth or income. Since China's Reform and Opening-up in 1978, such market continuity has been gradually formed through competition and evolution under the market mechanism. It is not a sudden change process. It can be said that thanks to the Reform and Opening-up, China has gradually completed the incremental division of the market ladder, a process that has lasted for more than 40 years now. It is the relative homogeneity at the starting point and the long-term evolution under the market mechanism that has gifted China a continuous market ladder that has not been seen yet in other large emerging economies.

As such, the continuity of the market ladder and the income inequality are not exactly the same thing. Although the continuous market ladder is truly accompanied by certain inequality in income distribution, an economy with income inequality does not necessarily yield a continuous market ladder. It only means that a large amount of wealth or income is concentrated among a small segment of the population. Moreover, the interpretation of the significance of market ladder, in the traditional sense, is more conducted from the perspective of social fairness, with less attention paid to the profound impact of a continuous market ladder on economic efficiency. Actually, for the governments of large emerging economies, harnessing the system design and policy tools to promote the formation of a highly continuous domestic market ladder is an important way to achieve fast economic and technological catching-up, as well as sustained economic growth.

---

[12] Among India's 1.35 billion people, only 27 million middle-class people earn more than \$11,000 a year, accounting for about 2% of its total population.

Underlying Competence for Competing in the Chinese Market

When we turn our attention from the macro level to the micro level and focus on how enterprises can effectively utilize the characteristics of China's market ladder, we need to think about what kind of capabilities enterprises should have in order to better survive and gain competitive advantages in the Chinese market with highly uncertain and fierce competition.

As mentioned earlier, China's market ladder has three basic features: **a huge domestic market size**, **a highly segmented market structure** and **a rapidly changing market environment**. The underlying competency of those successful enterprises (low-cost manufacturing, accurate market positioning, reasonable quality level, manufacturing flexibility, market response speed) is logically closely related to these three features (see Figure 2.6).

The huge scale of the domestic market does not only guarantee a low-cost manufacturing capability but also constitutes a necessary

Figure 2.6. The Underlying Competency for Competing in the Chinese Market

prerequisite to fully tap into the market potential. In a sense, low-cost manufacturing capability constitutes the most fundamental capability of the Chinese manufacturing industry. The value of other capabilities will be based on this fundamental capability.

The highly segmented market structure corresponds to another two competence elements, namely, accurate market positioning and reasonable quality level. In the Chinese market, an enterprise needs to have a very in-depth understanding of the targeted market segments, in order to decide the best market positioning and related strategies that are matched with its own capabilities and resource conditions. Due to the diversity and variability of the market, an enterprise needs to go through the trial and error process very quickly to prevent other competitors from snatching its target markets. On the other hand, amid the competition in the Chinese market, the emphasis is no longer merely on the high quality of the products, but most often on the "reasonable quality level", because high quality usually comes with high costs and high prices. Choosing a reasonable quality level means when an enterprise tries to meet the needs of the target customers, it needs to avoid incompatibility in strategic logic with low-cost manufacturing advantages. In this regard, the strategies that the Chinese local enterprise excels in are clearly different from the high-quality and high-price strategies adopted by foreign multinational companies in the high-end markets.

The rapidly changing market characteristics mean that the enterprises need faster market response speed and greater manufacturing flexibility. Rapid market response will bring a series of challenges to the organizational structure and processes, and even affect the enterprise's decision-making mode. As illustrated in the classical management theory, organizational decision-making requires the establishment of some rules, procedures and processes to maintain the order and stability of the decision-making process. However, such rules, procedures and processes often lead to lowered efficiency of an enterprise in a highly dynamic market environment, causing them to miss the transient market opportunities. Some successful local Chinese enterprises even adopt a strategy like "wading across the river by feeling the stones on the riverbed" (trial and error). They believe in "action before thinking" and even use simple rules to bypass the existing organizational decision-making rules and procedures sometimes. Of course, this is also related to the fact that many entrepreneurs have huge decision-making powers and influence within the enterprise under the Chinese context. The high manufacturing flexibility is, on the one hand, brought about by the internal production mode and manufacturing capacity of the enterprise, and, on the other hand, it is enabled by the external supply chain system the enterprise is embedded into.

Chapter 3

The Technology Ladder

Why Does the Technology Ladder Matter?

In the process of economic catching-up, especially at the early stages, China's manufacturing industry, like manufacturing sectors in other late-developing countries, encountered a similar problem in the process of promoting economic development through industrialization, that is, how to overcome resource constraints and cold start issues in technological development and capacity building?

In fact, the problem of resource constraints in technology development and capability building was not only related to the less developed financial systems and lack of capital accumulation that is typical of developing countries. It was also linked with the default nature of innovation itself. Most often, there is a very long time lag between investment in innovations and visible outcomes generated from such innovations. In other words, such a time lag will lead to low visibility of innovation returns, which will weaken the enthusiasm of enterprises to invest in innovation. Besides, due to the existence of time lag, many unexpected events may occur from the initial investment to the final outcome. There are also a lot of external and internal influencing factors in this process. Hence, such a context will make it more difficult to attribute and evaluate the effect of innovation input.

At the same time, as an investment into the future, innovation is bound to be affected by the enterprises' view of the environment. Due to the high volatility of China's market environment, the outcome of technology investment not only depends on the endeavor made by the enterprise itself, but also is influenced to a large extent by both the ability developed by competitors or potential competitors and their competitive strategies. Given the relatively low market positioning of Chinese manufacturing enterprises in their early days of development, it is difficult for them to fully establish competition barriers in their selected market positioning, and therefore, the investment returns they obtain are more susceptible to the behaviors of their competitors, and they may not get the expected returns if their competitors are more efficient in innovation. In this case, the greater the volatility of those factors that affect the performance of the enterprise in the external environment, the more the likelihood of the enterprise weakening in its motivation to invest in technology and capability development. More importantly, in the process of China's rapid economic growth, the average growth rate of China's GDP has remained between 8% and 12% for most of the past decades. Such a rapid growth means that, in a microscopic sense, Chinese enterprises will face many growth options, or the so-called "barbaric growth" opportunities. However, opportunity-led "barbaric growth" and "innovation-driven" growth are totally different in their strategic conceptions. There are even some conflicts between them. The former's strategic focus is more on the rapid imitation and sale of products, which demonstrates a short-term strategic orientation. However, the latter requires long-term investment in technology and capability building, strategic determination and patience, and sometimes, the abandoning of some short-term foreseeable business opportunities. This is also why although some entrepreneurs understand the importance of innovation and capability development, they often choose to focus on short-term business growth in their practice. After all, such short-term strategies have been proved to be very effective in terms of their financial performance for quite a long time.

However, does this mean that those enterprises that choose the path of "barbaric growth" do not need to invest in their innovation and capability development? It's perhaps not the case. As mentioned earlier, Chinese manufacturing enterprises were constrained by their own capabilities at that time, and thus the thresholds of their selected market segments were often not too high. In addition, Chinese local enterprises were very accustomed to adopting competition strategies of fast imitation. Such competition would promote enterprises to constantly shore up their capabilities, hence forcing them to invest in innovation and capability development. Given the characteristics of China's market ladder, Chinese enterprises can have more opportunities to obtain market returns to accumulate resources and make necessary investments in innovation and capability development.

In this regard, **in the process of technological catching-up, especially in the early stages, the cold start issue exerts greater influence on China's manufacturing industry than resource constraints**. This is because the absorptive capacity of China's manufacturing industry has not yet played its role in the early stages of catching up, and there is a large technology gap between Chinese local enterprises and foreign enterprises as a whole. Even today, when some Chinese enterprises are gradually starting to form their own capabilities, there are still substantial gaps in technology and management levels between many Chinese enterprises and their foreign counterparts. When still lacking sufficient resources and capabilities, how did these enterprises benefit from the advanced technology and management experience brought in by foreign multinational companies? There is no doubt that it's related to the catch-up ladder that they were embedded into.

From the perspective of the market ladder, if Chinese enterprises wish to move upward on the ladder, they need to improve their product quality and technical level. The higher their position in the market ladder, the higher their demand for technological capability.[1] Therefore, behind the migration along the market ladder is implied the migration along the technology ladder in essence. **The so-called technological ladder is formed when we arrange the enterprises of a specific industry in the Chinese market (including local enterprises and foreign enterprises) in order from low to high according to their technological capability level, which produces a technological ladder similar to the market ladder.** The most direct reflection of the differences in technological capability is the differences in productivity, because the productivity of a given enterprise is jointly determined by their technological capability, capital equipment level and management proficiency.

In fact, in 1994, Gary H. Jefferson, a professor of economics at the Brandeis University, and Thomas G. Rawski, a professor from the Department of Economics at the University of Pittsburgh, have already noticed that there is a relatively continuous technological ladder in

[1] It should be pointed out that "technology" here is a broader concept, which includes not only the narrow-sensed technology embedded in products, but also a series of factors that affect product quality and production efficiency, such as production technology, quality control and management technology, that can improve productivity.

China's innovation system, which they referred to as the "quality ladder".[2] They mentioned that in China at that time, if the enterprises are divided by their technical levels, from top to bottom, there was a ladder consisting of multinational companies, joint ventures, large state-owned enterprises, small state-owned enterprises, township enterprises and private enterprises.[3] Due to the high continuity of this ladder, each step of the ladder provided external absorptive capacity for its lower step. For example, after absorbing and transforming the advanced technology of multinational companies, joint ventures then transferred the technology to large state-owned enterprises through a technology spillover mechanism. Then the large state-owned enterprises transformed the technology into technology accessible to small state-owned enterprises and private enterprises through industrial linkages and technology spillovers. In other words, participants located at the upper end of the technology ladder play two roles. One is to act as a conduit for knowledge spillovers that increases the opportunities for participants at the lower end to acquire knowledge, i.e., to serve as the intermediary for knowledge transfer. The other role is to disassemble the knowledge with high complexity from the upper end of the technological ladder and convert it into knowledge that the lower end participants can absorb, i.e., to serve as the dimension reducer for knowledge conversion.

This is especially important for the development of private enterprises in the early stages of the Reform and Opening-up. This is because in terms of technical level and R&D capability, state-owned enterprises were the strongest in technical strength among Chinese local enterprises at that time. The private enterprises, earlier called "township & village enterprises", still rely heavily on state-owned enterprises in terms of capital, equipment, product design, technical information, management skills and subcontracting opportunities. For example, at that time, due to the weak market awareness in China, the state-owned enterprises did not fully understand the value of technology control and protection of intellectual property rights, so many township enterprises actually had state-owned

[2] Jefferson, G. H., and T. G. Rawski (1994). Enterprise reform in Chinese industry. *Journal of Economic Perspectives* 8(2): 47–70.

[3] Jefferson, G. H., and T. G. Rawski (1995). How industrial reform worked in China: The role of innovation, competition, and property rights. *Proceedings of the World Bank Annual Conference on Development Economics 1994*. Washington, DC: The International Bank for Reconstruction and Development/The World Bank, pp. 129–156.

enterprises as their technology sources. Those technicians from state-owned enterprises were once called "Sunday engineers", because they often used their weekend time to provide technical guidance to township enterprises, helping them develop products or solve their problems in production process and technology. Sometimes, local governments even encouraged such forms of technology transfer in order to promote local economic development.

From this standpoint, for China's small and medium-sized enterprises and even state-owned enterprises, the way they absorbed advanced technologies brought by foreign countries was not an individual-firm-based learning as we generally believe. **Rather, it is in the form of the highly efficient group-based catching-up relying on China's national innovation system.** However, when discussing the catch-up in Chinese manufacturing industry, we used to focus on how those Chinese manufacturing enterprises, especially those leading Chinese enterprises that have successfully implemented technological catch-up, managed to achieve their own capability building through certain learning mechanisms, and thus successfully shifted from imitation to catch-up. Such a perspective is necessary. Yet, if it is simply limited to the inside of the catching-up enterprises, we may ignore the important role of the catch-up ladder in Chinese enterprises in their process of catching-up. Only by combining these two perspectives can we form a complete view of the rise of China's manufacturing and reveal the real secrets behind it.

How Is the Continuous Technological Ladder Formed?

China's manufacturing industry has a relatively continuous technological ladder, which is both inevitable and accidental. Apart from the factors of continuous distribution of enterprises along the technological ladder and the important role played by state-owned enterprises in the early stages of the formation of this ladder as we discussed above, the formation of the technological ladder in the Chinese market is also closely related to a set of other participants in China's national innovation system.

In the process of catching-up, Chinese universities and scientific research institutions also played an important role. One of the main driving factors was the great changes to the fund-granting system of

Chinese universities and scientific research institutions in the 1990s.[4] Before that, universities and research institutions were highly dependent on the State's fiscal funds, so their research and development activities were generally separated from the market. After that, when the Chinese government slashed direct fiscal grant to universities and research institutions, they were forced to turn to the market to obtain more contracted projects and funds via servicing the enterprises and the industries. One of the most important reasons for the government to make such policy changes is to push universities and research institutions to better serve the economy and to improve their innovation efficiency through market mechanisms. In order to better meet the needs of the industry and thus obtain the needed research funds, the research work of these universities and research institutions gradually moved closer to the market. They even gradually began to participate in the product development process of some enterprises or try to solve the engineering problems in the production process. From this perspective, even if individual local enterprises lacked sufficient absorptive capacity, universities and scientific research institutions played a role in complementing the capability of the Chinese enterprises, so that they could better absorb and utilize external technology.

Although we seem to have an impression that China has been long faced with the problem of "disconnection between industry, university and research" — many universities and scientific research institutions have relatively low commercialization rate of their research outcomes. This kind of situation does exist in China as a whole, but for provinces with a high economic development level and a well-developed market economy system, the degree of cooperation between industry, university and research are much higher than we assumed. It's even the case for small and medium-sized enterprises in such provinces. For example, Zhejiang Bureau of Small and Medium-sized Enterprises conducted a questionnaire survey in 2008. The survey sampled 1,707 enterprises including both small enterprises (enterprises with an annual sales revenue of less than RMB 30 million) and medium-sized enterprises (enterprises with an annual sales revenue of more than RMB 30 million). The results showed that 48.1% of the surveyed enterprises have established cooperative relationships with universities or scientific research institutions, around 16.5% of the surveyed enterprises had established local research

[4]Liu, X.-L., and S. White (2001). Comparing innovation systems: A framework and application to China's transitional context. *Research Policy* 30(7): 1091–1114.

and development centers with universities or scientific research institutions, 6.3% of them have set up research centers in universities or research institutions, 27.2% of them employed professors or experts as their technical advisors, 14.8% of them have contracted their technology development projects to universities or scientific research institutions, and 8.4% of them have purchased technology from universities or scientific research institutions.[5]

Another point that needs to be emphasized is that the advantages of China's manufacturing so far do not lie in R&D and design in the overall sense, but to a large extent come from the advantages of the engineering capability, that is, the enterprises perfectly combine a set of elements including cost, cost performance and manufacturing flexibility in their manufacturing process, thus enabling China's manufacturing industry to obtain a unique competitive advantage in a cost-effective market. For many years, Chinese manufacturing enterprises have been able to invest almost all their resources in their manufacturing and engineering capabilities, but relatively less in R&D and design. On the one hand, this is due to their relatively low positioning in the market ladder in general. On the other hand, it's because Chinese universities and scientific research institutions, as externally available capabilities of the enterprises, have filled the gaps in capabilities of Chinese enterprises. We will continue elaborating on this in the following chapters.

Of course, in this process, **another technological development mechanism adopted by China, namely, large-scale collective technology research led by the State, also played a pivotal role**. Take the development of high-speed rail in China as an example. The government has adopted the approach of "pooling out all resources to address the major problems". Under the guidance of the government, a large number of scientific research institutions and industrial enterprises formed a complete industrial chain. And adopting such a collective method, the improvement and development of some important technical systems were completed. Viewed from this, China has its institutional advantages in its industrial catching-up. This is because the technical systems with high complexity and technical capabilities of high threshold cannot be achieved by a single or a few enterprises through market mechanism, for failure in technical learning can occur as the result of the overwhelming

[5] Jiaxi, W. (2009). *Zhejiang SME Development Report*. Beijing: Social Science Academic Press.

requirements for the technical capabilities of the participating enterprises, and even if some enterprises succeed in the end, their efficiency will be lower than that in the case of group cooperation. Moreover, since the advanced technology from foreign countries has been continuously developing, efficiency is very critical in the catching-up process of the Chinese enterprises. Otherwise, the targeted technology will have evolved to the next generation before any effective learning and catching-up occur, which will further lift up the threshold and difficulty of the catch-up. From a longer-term perspective, the technology catch-up mode based on group cooperation can increase the number of effective participants in the next generation of technology catch-up, which will definitely increase the possibility of technology catching-up. It is like in the survival and competitive evolution of a species, sufficient population size is very critical for the survival and evolution of the species. Otherwise, despite the existence of powerful individuals in a particular species, it is not enough to maintain the sustainable survival of such a species.

Another important factor also contributes to the formation of China's continuous technological ladder which cannot be ignored, i.e., the foreign-funded enterprises that have been continuously increasing their resource investment and bringing in new technologies into the Chinese market. In the early days, foreign-funded enterprises moved their manufacturing plants to China to take advantage of its low-cost labor. Along with the continuous release of its potential demand, the Chinese market became increasingly attractive to multinational companies. At the same time, competitions arose among multinational companies. And increasing competitions gradually arose between the local enterprises and the foreign enterprises (mainly in good-enough market segments). Such competitions further pressured and motivated foreign enterprises to localize their operations and supply chains to reduce costs and improve market responsiveness. As a result, localization of the industrial value chain would increase opportunities for local enterprises to benefit from technology and knowledge spillovers throughout localized supply chains. In this way, not only in the final product link, but also in the entire industrial chain, China's local enterprises have gained more growth opportunities, forming continuous technological ladders both vertically and horizontally.

The founder of AFRI, Dr. Ndubuisi Ekekwe, proposed his view in *Harvard Business Review*, suggesting that Africa can expand its internal consumption by promoting internal trade among African countries, thus facilitating the process of industrialization, rather than harness the comparative advantage of labor cost as in the traditional mode to establish its comparative advantage in global manufacturing. From the perspective of technology ladder, there may be a potential problem with this view. For late-developing countries and regions, international trade (whether in the form of import or export) not only includes the cross-border flow of commodities, but also the flow of technology and knowledge accompanying the flow of commodities, especially those in terms of knowledge spillovers. It is the inflow, decomposition and recombination of knowledge from the top of the technological ladder that promotes the development of local enterprises' capabilities and the formation of their long-term competitive advantages. Therefore, docking into global manufacturing is an unavoidable choice for those enterprises that wish to move up the market and the technology ladder.

Continuity, Continuity, Continuity!

Similar to the continuity of the market ladder, the continuity of the technological ladder plays an extremely important role in technological catch-up for large economies like China. **The continuity of the** technological ladder determines whether the local industrial chain can enhance its efficiency in dismantling and absorbing foreign advanced technologies, and also decides whether the local enterprises embedded in the technological **ladder can effectively overcome the cold start problem at the individual level and benefit from technology spillovers to the maximum extent**.

As a large emerging economy adjacent to China, in the past 10 years India has made great progress in economic growth. However, compared with China, due to the problem of discontinuity in its technological ladder, its potential in technological catching-up and economic growth has not been fully realized. Although India boasts international advantages in its major industries and even has large global corporations, the industrial connection between these large companies and other local enterprises, especially those local SMEs, is not obvious. In other words, although a large number of enterprises in the Indian market share the intention of serving the needs of the local market, they may not be able to establish links with large enterprises in the industrial chain. Instead, most industrial value chains of its large enterprises are distributed all over the world, mainly targeting the overseas markets. Another example is Russia, one of the large emerging economies. Russia's problems in its catching-up ladder came from the discontinuity of its market ladder — the 1989 economic shock therapy of Russia redistributed the national wealth within a short period of time, which was snatched by the financial oligarchs and oil oligarchs within a few years, leading to a break between the high-end market ladder and the low-end market ladder.

Compared with India and Russia, China has a more continuous technological ladder in its manufacturing industry. This is because the formation of the entire industrial value chain of the Chinese manufacturing industry has been a gradual process. For example, some enterprises started with serving as the supporting suppliers for multinational companies or cooperating with them in setting up joint ventures. When they grew to a certain stage, they began to cultivate their own supplier system, and their suppliers would breed more sub-suppliers. Such a natural decomposition gradually occurring along the industrial value chain can make China's technological ladder more continuous in the process of its growth and the industrial connections among enterprises along the industrial technology ladder closer.

Therefore, **although any large emerging economy should presumably possess the same advantages as China, as what we have discussed earlier, it will often face two great challenges if it wants to fully realize such advantages like what China did. The first challenge is how to build a more continuous market ladder. The second challenge is how to build a more continuous technology ladder.** However, the degree of difficulty of these two challenges depends on whether it enables large local enterprises, including some joint ventures, to form a close industrial relationship with small and medium-sized local enterprises, and to further incubate a continuous market ladder and a continuous technological ladder in its development process with the aid of market mechanism.

Another "Invisible" Technological Ladder

In the era of globalization, those countries or companies that occupy a dominant position in the product market will gradually form their own industrial value chains, which, on the one hand, share and cooperate with their counterparts in other countries, and, on the other hand, compete with their counterparts.

The industrial value chain exists in two different forms, namely, the "manufacturing chain" and the "technology chain". The manufacturing chain is more explicit as its ultimate outcome is presented in the form of products and it is mainly embodied in the application layer of technology. All participants in the manufacturing chain form cooperative relations on the basis of division of labor and finally divide the benefits according to their bargaining power in the entire manufacturing chain. In contrast, the technology chain is relatively implicit as it entails a lot of underlying technologies behind the products. Those underlying technologies are closely related to the product architecture, components, design and production (such as the operating system and chip design we saw in the Huawei Scandal). Different from the relatively discrete pattern of participants in the product market, at the bottom of the technology chain, due to the high technical entry barrier, the core technologies and capabilities are often in the hands of quite a few participants.

This trend of separation between the manufacturing chain and the technology chain means that besides the technology ladder based on productivity level as we discussed earlier, there is also an invisible technology ladder based on industrial control power. And these two types of technology ladders are different from each other. The productivity-based technology ladder is formed in the product market. It is formed based on products and is reflected in the continuous distribution of technologies and productivity levels of enterprises providing the same or similar products and services. We can also call it "the technology ladder in the product market".

The industrial dominance-based ladder exists in two different forms. One is the hierarchical distribution of dominance in value capture along the entire industrial value chain. The typical strategy in utilizing this form of ladder is to become **the "system integrator" in the industrial value chain**. A system integrator does not need to produce all parts or subsystems in a product system, and sometimes even does not need to have its own manufacturing capacity. Rather, it integrates the capabilities and resources owned by other enterprises via leveraging their own advantages in brand, technical architecture or management competence. Some leading manufacturing enterprises developed from the China's domestic marketplace are gradually becoming this type of companies. Another form, with technology units as the core, is the continuous distribution of enterprises according to their discourse power, influence and dominance along the industrial value chain centering around specific businesses or products. Such dominance within the technology chain is manifested in whether it is substitutable, the degree of exclusivity the technology holder has over the underlying technologies, the entry threshold of the underlying technologies (which usually requires a very long period of technology and knowledge accumulation). We can also call this technological ladder **"a technological ladder on the technological chain"**. The typical strategy in seeking this form dominance is to become the underlying dominator of the technology chain. It must be pointed out that at present, such underlying dominators are almost leading companies from the Western countries.

Hence, there are differences between the industrial value chain perspective at the national level and that at the enterprise level. Such differences are mainly reflected in the following aspects. At the enterprise level, in the conventional sense, as product providers or system integrators, the enterprises do not need to possess complete capabilities along the entire industrial value chain (no matter the manufacturing chain or the technology chain). This is because for them, it is a more reasonable choice to integrate their internal and external resources and capabilities through division of labor based on specialization, thereby maintaining the best balance between efficiency and flexibility. However, at the national level, for the sake of industrial security, it is not enough to have only the advantages in the manufacturing chain. This is evidenced in the industrial continuity issues China is now facing from the escalating Sino-US trade conflicts. In the long run, the result of the competition and the gaming between countries in terms of industrial value chains depends, to a large extent, on the technology chain rather than the manufacturing chain.

In fact, China has gradually established significant advantages in terms of its manufacturing chain in its development process of the past four decades. This is evidenced in several aspects. In many industries, China has established a relatively complete industrial manufacturing chain with some large-scale system integrators and acquired various discrete advantageous manufacturing capacities throughout the entire manufacturing chain. In other words, the Chinese manufacturing industry already has some comparative advantages in both breadth and depth of their capability distribution in the manufacturing chain. In many industrial fields, the gap in manufacturing chain between China and the United States is continuously narrowing. However, compared with Western developed countries, China's advantages in the technical chain of its manufacturing industry still lag behind in terms of both breadth and depth.

This is reflected in the fundamental core technology of the technology chain, the underlying architecture design, industrial computing software and irreplaceable core equipment. Therefore, although many Chinese companies have become very competitive in the global product market, they often depend on others in the underlying technology chain, and lack sufficient top companies with competitive and dominance power. These challenges cannot be bypassed if China's manufacturing industry is to become a global benchmark for manufacturing competitiveness.

An Indispensable Instrument in Global Industry Gaming

After the international financial crisis in 2008, the global economy has not yet realized full recovery and stable growth. Although the growth rate of the global economy experienced a transient peak in 2010, such a peak has not appeared since then. The global economy has been maintaining a relatively stable moderate and low growth rate. In the ten years from 2008 to 2017, the average global economic growth rate was 3.2%, and that of the developed economies was only 1.1%.[6] Major economies in the world are facing a pattern similar to a zero-sum game, or at least in their mindset, they tend to take the growth of other economies as a pressure factor for their own economic growth. At the same time, China's economic growth is seen not only in its scale. Especially in some key industries and emerging technology fields, China has been trying to establish its own advantages in technology and products. In other words, China is no longer satisfied merely with participating in the global value chain division at the middle and low end of industrial value chain with its advantages in low cost. Rather, it has strong motivation and potential to migrate to the core links of the global value chain. Although China still has a long way to go to achieve this strategic goal, such a development trend will no doubt change the situation where Western economies have dominated and controlled the global industrial value chain over the years, thus causing the United States to worry about its leading position in the global economy.

From a series of US government's accusations against China in recent years and a series of related documents issued on Sino-US trade

[6] See www.gfmag.com/global-data/economic-data/economic-dataworlds-gdp-growth-by-region.

conflicts, four key words have repeatedly appeared: industrial policy, state-owned enterprises, technology and intellectual property rights, and Made-in-China 2025. When making accusations against China, the United States certainly demonstrates its political stance in using these key words, and there are some considerations under the surface. But why are these key words frequently mentioned?

It should be pointed out that, first of all, the important information is often not revealed from the literal exposition of these core issues, but rooted in the repeated mentioning of these key words. Secondly, for these key words, the important meaning arises when they are combined instead of when they are separated. In other words, in the past, when interpreting these topics, we often separated these keywords. However, what we really need to think about is what can we see if we put these key words together?

The true meaning of the word combination arises from the intersection of the four key words. China's rapid development in the past decades carries typical features of technological catching-up, with China constantly striving to improve its technological competences. However, as China benefits from globalization and gradually deeply integrates itself into the global industrial value chain, China's manufacturing industry needs support from the global industrial value chain, thus forming a close cooperative relationship between China and other participants in the global industrial value chain. On the other hand, with the enhancement of China's own capabilities and its upward migration in the core links of the industrial value chain, it will inevitably compete with the global, especially the Western, industrial value chain participants.

The historical industrial catch-up experience of Japan and R. O. Korea shows that in the process of rapid catching-up of late-developing countries, the governments of these countries need to have strong industrial policy instruments to effectively implement their industrial and technological catching-up so as to realize the target of obtaining a favorable position for domestic industries in the global industrial game. Japan's Keiretsu (such as Mitsubishi and other large industrial groups) and R. O. Korea's Chaebol (such as Samsung Group)[7] served as important industrial policy instruments of the government. They were closely

[7]Keiretsu is a common form of industrial organization in Japan, and its member enterprises form a huge industrial group through mutual shares holding and close cooperative partnership. By contrast, as an industrial group, a chaebol in Korea demonstrates distinctive features of family control.

related to the implementation of the government's industrial policy and played a vital role in the technological catch-up of Japan and R. O. Korea.

For an enterprise to serve as a policy instrument for industry catching-up, or a tool for participating in global industry games, two important prerequisites are required. In the capability dimension, sufficient technical and economic strength are required for assuming the role as an industry gaming tool. In the motivation dimension, to serve as an instrument of industry catching-up and gaming, an enterprise needs to pay a price for the development of industrial technology (which means that the benefits brought by such development demonstrate significant spillover effect, that is, other local enterprises will benefit from the development without the need to pay for the direct cost). In fact, in the process of China's development, **only large-scale state-owned enterprises or those large-scale enterprises that have acquired a certain position in the global value chain can meet the above two prerequisites. They are not only important instruments for China's industrial policy implementation, but also important tools for China to participate in the global industrial game.** Other enterprises either lack sufficient strength or lack sufficient motivation.

What truly worries the United States is not the competitive advantages gradually established by Chinese enterprises in certain product markets (especially in those product categories that significantly rely on the comparative advantage of low-cost labor force), but the capability continuously acquired by Chinese enterprises at the underlying layer of the industrial value chain, or the technological chain, which leads the United States to face challenges from China in their industrial dominance that involves their core interests. With the "Made-in-China 2025" as the goal, the Chinese government uses state-owned enterprises as a policy instrument to implement its industrial policies, aiming at building a global competitive advantage in technology and intellectual property in the core technology fields. Such a conception will no doubt be seen by the United States as a great challenge or even a real threat to its core and strategic interests. Nevertheless, China will not limit its competitiveness to those low-end value chains, because this is definitely not in line with China's own strategic interests.

Chapter 4

Decomposition and Recombination in Technological Catch-Up

The Cold Start Paradox in Technological Catching-Up

We know that different positions on technical ladders essentially represent the differences in quality and technical level of the products of enterprises. To be able to shift upward along the technological ladder means that the enterprises need to provide higher product quality, and meet higher technical performance and more complex functional requirements. We can call such requirements behind the technology ladder the "technology" level requirements. This so-called "technology" is a broad term, which not only refers to some constituent technologies the products are designed with, but also includes the capabilities the enterprises need to have to achieve this higher quality and narrow-sense technology requirements. For example, in order to make the manufacturing process more efficient, enterprises may need to have stronger capabilities for equipment improvement, production quality management, manufacturing process optimization and so on.

Therefore, **during the upward migration of Chinese enterprises along the technological ladders, two issues need to be addressed. First, how to develop the required technology in a more effective way?** These technologies can derive from the assimilation, utilization and integration of external technologies and knowledge. They can also come from the process of internal capability development. **Second, how to**

develop their underlying capacities? Moreover, such capacities can help enterprises effectively absorb, utilize and integrate external technologies and knowledge.

Considering that for China's manufacturing sector this upward migration along the technological ladders happens in the context of technological catch-up, it is necessary for us to discuss what restraining factors the late-comers in technology catch-up will encounter. It is these restraining factors that hinder the absorption, utilization and integration of externally accessed technologies and the development of competences of the enterprises.

According to the Absorptive Capacity Theory (ACT), if an enterprise wants to acquire and absorb knowledge from outside effectively, it needs to have a certain level of prior knowledge base. The significance of such a prior knowledge base lies in the fact that only when you have accumulated certain prior knowledge can you identify valuable information from the vast amount of information and knowledge outside, understand it, and then successfully transform it into knowledge that can be understood, transferred and utilized within an organization. From the perspective of absorptive capacity, technology gap has a very important influence on late-comer enterprises in their absorption of the advanced technology introduced from foreign countries. Such an influence is two-fold. On the one hand, technology gap means potential learning opportunities. The wider the technology gap is, the more the potential technical knowledge that can be absorbed and utilized, and the more the possible technology spillover opportunities. On the other hand, technology gap may constitute an obstacle to absorbing and utilizing external technical knowledge in the process of technological catch-up, because at this time, it raises higher the requirements for prior knowledge base from enterprises. In other words, the greater the technological gap, the higher the threshold of absorptive capacity that enterprises need to reach.

In the early stage of technology catch-up by late-comer countries, there is a big gap, in both technical level and technical competence, between domestic enterprises and foreign counterparts from developed countries. This will lead to the so-called cold-start paradox of technological catch-up, namely, the local enterprises need to have a certain degree of absorption capacity before they can identify and absorb advanced technology and management experience from foreign multinational companies, yet the local enterprises happen to lack such absorptive capacity (due to their lack of sufficient prior knowledge base). Therefore, this creates an infinite loop.

In reality, **how to break the paradox of cold start induced by absorptive capacity has become the key issue for Chinese enterprises to start their technology catch-up from the beginning**. From a theoretical point of view, if we can't reasonably explain this cold start paradox, it will be difficult for us to truly understand how Chinese manufacturing industry has successfully realized the technological and market catch-up in many fields in the past decades.

Another problem that Chinese enterprises need to crack in their technological catch-up is the problem of resource constraints. In late-developing countries, due to the relatively insufficient domestic capital and the underdeveloped financial system, enterprises are generally faced with the problem of financial constraints, especially in the early stages of their technological catch-up. However, the capability building in technological catch-up is a learning process which is generally time- and resource-consuming, and the late-comer enterprises need to undergo a lot of trial and error in this process to gradually accumulate technical expertise and learning ability. Therefore, the late-comer enterprises need to effectively overcome both the paradox of cold start and the problem of resource constraints in their learning and capability-building process, for the sake of their technology acquisition and development.

Learning in Technological Catch-Up: Decomposition and Recombination

By observing the catching-up experience of Chinese manufacturing industry, I would like to put forward the following analytical framework to explain how Chinese enterprises effectively solved the cold start paradox and the resource constraints problem. The core of this analytical framework is "learning by decomposition" and "learning by recombination". **Learning by decomposition can effectively solve the cold start paradox in the process of technology catch-up, especially in the early catching-up stages, whereas learning by recombination can help late-comers to better develop their unique capabilities, and hence make up for their resource insufficiency through more efficient gaining of market returns** (see Figure 4.1).

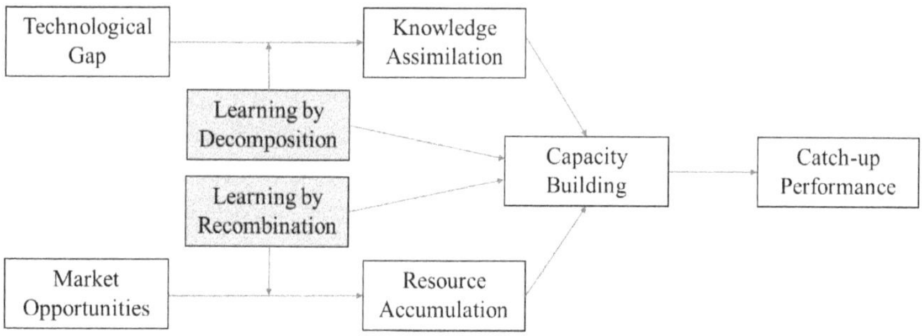

Figure 4.1. Learning by Decomposition and Recombination

Learning by decomposition can be interpreted with such an analogy. When we human beings need to think about how to solve a very complex problem, we tend to deconstruct the complex problem into several sub-problems that can be solved separately, thereby reducing the difficulty of thinking by focusing on specific sub-problems, and thus solving all sub-problems one by one, and finally obtaining the complete answer to the original complex problem. For example, when we see a large-sized image, we tend to sub-divide it into several blocks and zoom into such blocks to observe and then restore these deconstructed images into a holistic one in our brain. In the same vein, when we plan to develop a complete set of technical capabilities for a complex product system (which includes many subsystems or modules), we can start with the sub-systems or modules that require capabilities that are closer to our current ones, and then gradually move on to other subsystems or modules with higher capability requirements when our capability reaches a higher level. This process continues until we have mastered all the basic knowledge modules needed for the whole product system. This is quite similar to a jigsaw puzzle, where all we have to do is constantly search for and generate various graphic fragments until we get all the fragments needed for a complete picture.

Therefore, **learning by decomposition is a learning process in which, based on his or her current absorptive capacity, the learner deconstructs a complete technology that he or she needs to absorb and master, so as to divide the complex technology into various lower-dimension blocks that can be utilized under his or her current absorptive capacity.** In this way, after the decomposition, the threshold for absorptive capacity can be effectively lowered. In the meantime, the time and resources needed for technology absorption are also accordingly reduced. Therefore, the problem of resource constraints will be alleviated to some extent. In this regard, enterprises can adopt different strategies in learning by decomposition to effectively lower the learning costs. Further discussions will be made in Chapter 6 "China's Advantages in the Field of Complex Product Systems".

Decomposition is not only a process of learning, but also an important way for enterprises to build their capabilities. Decomposition itself requires certain capabilities, because deconstructing a complete whole effectively also requires a lot of trial and error and experience-based learning. As described in a story from the ancient Taoism classic *Chuang Tse* titled "A magical and skilled form of craftsmanship", "His cook was cutting up an ox for the ruler Wen Hui. Whenever he applied his hand, leaned forward with his shoulder, planted his foot, and employed the pressure of his knee, in the audible ripping off of the skin, and slicing operation of the knife, the sounds were all in regular cadence... The ruler said, 'Ah! Admirable! That your art should have become so perfect!' (Having finished his operation), the cook laid down his knife, and replied to the remark, 'What your servant loves is the method of the Tao, something in advance of any art. When I first began to cut up an ox, I saw nothing but the (entire) carcass. After three years I ceased to see it as a whole. Now I deal with it in a spirit-like manner, and do not look at it with my eyes. The use of my senses is discarded, and my spirit acts as it wills.... Now my knife has been in use for nineteen years; it has cut up several thousand oxen, and yet its edge is as sharp as if it had newly come from the whetstone.' The reason why "the Cook" can reach such a culminated state of his skill is not only his iterative practice and experiential learning, but also his phased-in development of specific competence to realize an elevation from "skills" to "Tao".

More importantly, the subjects of learning by decomposition are not limited to the enterprises themselves, and the activities of learning by decomposition do not necessarily occur only within the enterprises. The enterprises always have many horizontal or vertical links with the industry chain outside. Therefore, they can collaborate with their external partners to complete the technical decomposition. In this way, they can greatly reduce the time, effort and resources consumed in the learning process through cost and risk sharing, and utilize these externally accessible expertise and capacities from outside to enhance their efficiency of learning.

In fact, this kind of learning by decomposition was discovered many years ago when people studied the phenomenon of industrial clusters. In industrial clusters, there are a large number of enterprises, which either produce similar products or form a complete upstream and downstream industrial chain around a few backbone enterprises. In a sense, the enterprises in a cluster have been embedded into a network or an ecosystem composed by enterprises. On the basis of division of labor, through distributive learning and innovation, these enterprises can complete learning by decomposition within market mechanism in a subconscious way. This is similar to the logic we discussed earlier. Functioning as an ecosystem, an industrial cluster can reduce the learning cost and entry threshold for any enterprises within this ecosystem. This is because every enterprise inside the cluster can concentrate its attention and resources on a few selected areas of their expertise. As a consequence, the seemingly weak individual enterprises in the cluster can demonstrate amazing learning efficiency and adaptability to the dynamic environment when they are integrated as a whole.

If learning by decomposition aims to efficiently internalize external knowledge and thus lay the foundation for the development of absorptive capacity, then learning by recombination is all about integrating and utilizing knowledge from different sources. In this sense, learning by decomposition and learning by recombination thus form a closed-loop process, both for learning and for capability building.

Learning by recombination involves two specific processes. First of all, diversified knowledge and technologies from different periods and sources are integrated and applied into developing new products and technologies, or improving the efficiency of the manufacturing processes. This kind of knowledge integration can involve the recombination of multi-domain technologies and knowledge accumulated in different time periods, or the recombination of imported technologies from different external sources to create new products and technologies, or even the integration of external technologies with internal technologies and expertise. For example, Dahua Technology Co., Ltd. is a company engaged in security monitoring. During its evolution from a mere DVD producer to an overall solution provider in the security monitoring industry, it gradually established its expertise in various fields including front-end information collection, encoding and transmission, high-definition storage, high-definition display and platform control, and expanded the scope of its business to cover infrared intercom, intelligent access control, video intercom, smart locks and other intelligent building products and technologies, so as to acquire its ability to provide one-stop overall security solutions.

Secondly, the enterprises need to find the most matched market opportunities for the technologies or products created through recombination. In doing so, they have to consider specific localized needs before developing the technologies and products, and make appropriate adaptive improvements. This is of critical importance to solving their resource restraints issue during technological catch-up. Most often, even when faced with similar technology and market opportunities, the effectiveness of different enterprises to make use of these opportunities may vary. The enterprises' ability to capture and match market opportunities will determine the efficiency of their transforming of the results of their learning by recombination into resource accumulation in the process of their catching-up.

Finally, from a longer-term perspective, learning by recombination refers to the building of enterprise-specific advantages through creating new technologies and expertises on the basis of recombining knowledge, technology, experience and know-how internally developed and/or externally acquired. This means that, on the one hand, late-comer enterprises need to employ their established absorptive capacity to refine and transform their technical knowledge accumulated from various sources. On the other hand, it also means they need to harness their existing technical knowledge to produce new knowledge combinations or new knowledge and expertise based on their existing knowledge. This will bring them a process of positive feedback — the knowledge and expertise acquired through the learning by recombination can be used in the specific market scenario to build unique competitive advantages, bringing the enterprises more opportunities to continuously obtaining market returns in a longer period of time. As a result, the enterprises are enabled to continuously invest in highly uncertain long-term capacity-building activities such as R&D and innovations. Such continuous investment in capability building will help enhance both the capability and efficiency of technology decomposition and recombination of such enterprises, which will eventually be translated into advantages in market competition and long-term market returns.

Strengthening Decomposition and Recombination Capabilities via Purposive Business Strategies

During their product design and development, some enterprises will attempt to strengthen their capabilities for decomposition and recombination through some carefully designed business strategies. Because, be it learning by decomposition or learning by recombination, as long as the two processes are continuously repeated, the late-comer enterprises will gradually acquire the underlying capabilities for decomposition and recombination.

Take the technology ecosystem of smartphones as an example. Many smartphone manufacturers, such as Meitu, VIVO, OPPO, etc., will all consciously choose many same-type manufacturers as their technical service providers. Meitu's beauty filter and other functions are derived from the software development kit (SDK) of Sensetime, its censorship function is grafted upon the application program interface (API) of Tupu Technology, and its face unlocking technology comes from the technical solution of Megvii Co., Ltd. In the case of VIVO smartphones, its face unlocking feature is supported, respectively, by Sensetime and Megvii Co., Ltd. Depending on different models, the facial recognition technology of VIVO flagship smartphone X20 comes from Sensetime, whereas its face unlocking technology used in its smartphone products sold in the overseas market like India comes from Megvii Co., Ltd. In light of this, Hu Baishan, the executive vice president of VIVO, disclosed to the media that the rationale behind VIVO's adoption of multiple technical service providers not only can help reduce the risk of over-dependence on any single supplier, but also forces these suppliers to spare no effort in technical improvement. If these technology suppliers can't continuously improve their products and technologies, their market opportunities will be gradually taken away by other competitors. Choosing multiple technology service providers will eventually make it possible to integrate various advanced technology elements into a product. Of course, this also means that as the system integrator, smartphone makers need to build stronger integrative learning ability, so as to more efficiently integrate multiple technology units and technical elements into an overall solution that meets the market demand. In this regard, the technical decomposition and recombination for the smartphone industry not only takes place inside the end device makers, but also in the whole industrial value chain via market mechanisms.

Another common strategy is related to the development of low-cost manufacturing capability. As we know, even today, low-cost manufacturing capability is one of the very fundamental competences of Chinese enterprises. By observing various industries, we will find that in the early stages of catching-up, the phenomenon of labor replacing capital often occurs. Specifically, when introducing foreign advanced production technology, even if a complete set of fully automated production equipment and technologies are already in place, Chinese enterprises will not consciously choose to transform some parts of the assembly line into manual mode at the cost of overly compromised production quality, so as to generate a hybrid production system with both automatic and manual modes. Undoubtedly, this can greatly reduce the capital requirements for capital and equipment investment. Meanwhile, it can endow the entire production system with greater flexibility. For example, Mu Qing, a professor at Shanghai University of Finance and Economics, and Keun Lee, a professor of economics at Seoul National University in Korea, cited the example of Shanghai Bell Co., Ltd. (a company established on December 15, 1983) which adopted a hybrid production system in the process of technology introduction.[1] This means, in the process of establishing low-cost manufacturing capabilities, enterprises need to consider deconstructing the production system technology, redesigning some elements, and adding those more cost-effective domestic alternative solutions into the new production system. It will promote Chinese manufacturing enterprises to establish their decomposition and recombination capabilities in manufacturing. Although this capability is not as visible as the technical recombination of products, it can provide the underlying foundation for Chinese enterprises to establish market competitiveness especially at the early stages of their catching-up.

The Role of Universities and Academic Institutions in Deconstructing Technology

Universities and research institutions played a very important role in forming China's continuous technological ladder for catch-up. On the

[1] Mu, Q., and K. Lee (2005). Knowledge diffusion, market segmentation and technological catch-up: The case of the telecommunication industry in China. *Research Policy* 34(6): 759–783.

whole, Chinese universities and independent research institutions have become an indispensable part of China's national innovation system. For many years, people have been paying close attention to the relationship between universities, research institutions and the industry. And the focus of such attention was primarily on the efficiency of industry–university–research cooperation.

Especially in the 1990s, the weak connection among industry, education and research and the inefficient commercial transformation of scientific research outputs were deemed as urgent issues for resolution when China was promoting enterprises to become the main undertakers of innovation. Back then, a large number of research results by universities and research institutions had never been applied, or even if such research results were transferred to the enterprises, they could not be commercialized because they failed to meet the industrialization requirements of the enterprises. This gap between research and industrialization led governmental departments, industry and the public to call for "the universities to venture out of the Ivory Tower". Since the 19th century, the phrase "Ivory Tower" has been used to refer to a scenario where academic pursuit is separated from reality, which thereafter was directly designated to denote academic communities or universities, sadly with a bit of a derogatory tone.

With China gradually transforming from a planned economy to a market economy, the Chinese government has formulated a series of strategic guiding policies to motivate universities and research institutions to serve national economic development with their science and technology.[2] The "Decision on the Reform of Science and Technology System" issued in 1985 unveiled an all-around reform of the science and technology system. Starting with reforming the funding system and opening up the technology market, China's science and technology work was reoriented to "face the main battlefield of economic construction". After that, the "Decision on Accelerating the Progress of Science and Technology" was issued in 1995, which established the strategy of "rejuvenating the country through science and education" and started the pilot work in restructuring scientific research institutions. The year 1999 witnessed the issuance of the "Decision on Strengthening Technological Innovation, Developing High-tech and Realizing Industrialization", which marks the beginning of

[2]Baidu Baike, Reform of scientific and technological system. https://baike.baidu.com/item/科技体制改革/3829882.

systematical adjustment of the deployment structure of research institutions. It's from this period that the policy interest was more focused on strengthening the construction of the national innovation system and accelerating commercialization of science and technology achievements. There is a clear logical vein behind these policies, that is, allowing the market mechanism to play an increasingly important role in technology development and innovation.

Such reform promotes the universities and research institutions to be more proactive to respond to the commercialization demand of the industry. On the one hand, the government has downsized the direct funding earmarked to research institutions, making them feel the pressure of survival and turn to the market to obtain the funds via commercialization of research outputs to sustain their own operations. After the year 2000, funding by the government was cut off for more than 5,000 research institutions. Instead, they could only access research funding through competitive research projects sponsored by various ministries.[3] On the other hand, research institutions could obtain income through more diversified and market-oriented means, i.e., technology licensing and transferring, revenues from providing technical consulting services, or even direct entry into the market through industrialization (such as setting up spin-offs or spin-outs).

Universities underwent similar changes in those years. Though universities still needed to function as knowledge disseminators (mainly in the form of talent development) and places of knowledge generation (mainly in the form of research activities), they seemed to be less pressured in marketization than research institutions (see Figure 4.2).

It could be concluded from the preceding chapters that the technological catch-up of Chinese manufacturing enterprises is not only dependent on their own internal efforts, but highly dependent on the whole technological ladder within the national innovation system to a great extent. Therefore, the role played by universities and research institutions in technology decomposition is closely related to the securing of the continuity of the technology ladder. It is accomplished mainly through the following three ways.

---

[3]Liu, X. L., and S. White (2001). Comparing innovation systems: A framework and application to China's transitional context. *Research Policy* 30(7): 1091–1114.

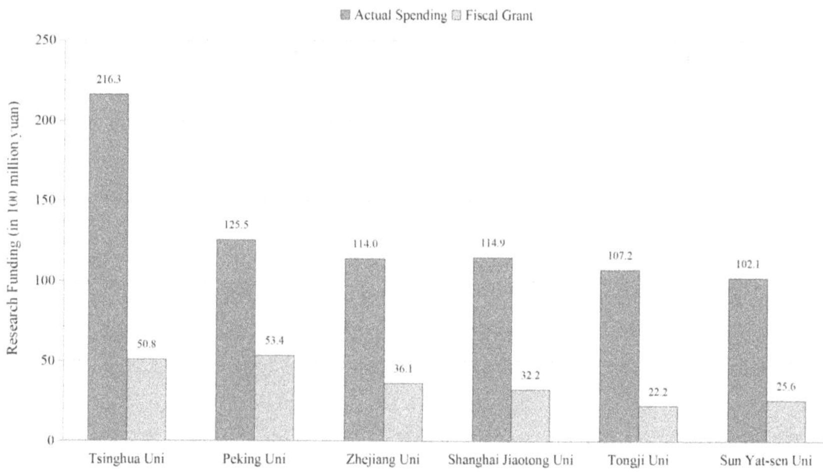

Figure 4.2. Research Funding of Chinese Universities (2018)

Source: https://www.163.com/dy/article/DGEFF6010516MOTB.html, https://www.163.com/dy/article/DGVMOQ150516MOTB.html.

1. The **introduction of foreign capital** is the main storyline of China's economic catch-up. Although the introduction of foreign capital started from addressing the scarcity of capital of a developing country, the introduction of advanced technology and management experience during the introduction has had a far-reaching significance. At the beginning of any catching-up, as the result of the big technology gap between Chinese enterprises and foreign-funded enterprises, universities and research institutions often served as the "technological dimensionality reducers" in introduction, digestion and absorption of technology, using their comparative advantages in technology understanding to complete the absorption of foreign advanced technologies and converting them into technologies and knowledge that the local enterprises can master and use. This is why when looking back at the development history of many industrial technologies in China, we may find many groundbreaking key projects, about importing, digesting and absorbing technology, were often backed by universities and research institutions.
2. **Providing complementary capabilities to Chinese local enterprises** is also one of the important roles played by universities and research institutions. Specifically, local enterprises, particularly those weak in

R&D, would often directly consign universities and research institutions to conduct research projects on their pending technical problems. In this way, universities and research institutions had to act beyond their established positioning in the innovation chain. Instead of focusing on pure "research", they needed to provide local enterprises with products and technical solutions that could be directly applied in the "development" stage. As a result, with the help of imitation, technology spillovers and complementary capabilities infused from the universities and research institutions, many SMEs can continuously launch new products and improve their production efficiency without investing in developing their own internal R&D capabilities. Likewise, universities and research institutions are playing an increasingly important role in promoting the continuous upgrading of the local technology ladder. On the technological ladder, both the technology and knowledge from the top multinational companies and the new technologies created by local enterprises in the relatively high positions of the technological ladder can horizontally permeate among their counterparts and vertically penetrate into the upstream and downstream of the local innovation chain when universities and research institutions are providing solutions to technical problems.

3. With the continuous improvement of the local enterprises' technological competence and the continuous broadening of the technological ladder, the roles of universities and research institutions were also undergoing some **new changes**. For the local enterprises located in a relatively high position on the technological ladder, along with their narrowing down of the technology gap from multinational companies, the uncertainty of technological development also went up. Under such circumstance, these enterprises need universities and research institutions to track and analyze the development trend of technology, providing guidance and decision-making consultancy for them on this basis. Thanks to their research orientation, universities and research institutions are more adept at **tracking the latest progress in research fields**.

Innovation Generated from Imitation

Imitation and innovation have very delicate connections.

Imitation means convergence, that is, when you start imitating, you often end up acting more like the imitation target. On the contrary, innovation means finding and establishing differences with competitors or substitutes. Theoretically, it's pointing to an utterly opposite direction from imitation.

Nevertheless, the answer might look certainly different if we peruse the relationship between imitation and innovation in the context of the real world. In Chinese traditional culture, calligraphy has been granted a vital position. When Chinese people practice calligraphy, they often start with imitating the calligraphy copybook or stone inscriptions. It is not until the calligraphy practitioners can imitate these fonts freely can they really start to practice calligraphy more freely and even form their own style. There are many wide-spreading anecdotes about great calligraphers in history, such as Xizhi Wang and Banqiao Zheng, starting from imitating predecessors' styles to creating their own calligraphy classics.

The Japanese scholar Tatsuhiko Inoue wrote in his book *Good Imitation to Great Innovation*: "Even the distinctively styled novelists often start out from imitating other writers. Through repeatedly imitating and failing in imitation, they formed the style that other writers cannot completely replicate. It can be said that the same is true in the business world. Even if a company owns an idea no other counterparts can replicate, by careful investigation, we would find that the conceptualization of such an idea actually is formed by some big or small imitations. The non-replicable ideas are often rooted back to imitation. This is the so-called 'imitation paradox'".[4]

The technological catch-up of enterprises of late-comer countries shares much similarity with the aforesaid examples. Those enterprises that finally venture in the space of innovation often started as faithful imitators of others. This mode is so common that if we observe the countries that have successfully achieved technological catch-up in the past decades, we may find that almost all of these countries' indigenous enterprises have gone through this process, be it Japanese enterprises, R. O. Korean enterprises[5] or Chinese enterprises.

Evidenced from the experience of Japanese, Korean and Chinese manufacturing enterprises, a lot of learning by decomposition and learning by recombination happened in the process of imitation and innovation. Moreover, these late-comer enterprises generally adopt the following

[4]Tatsuhiko, I. (2014). *Good Imitation to Great Innovation.* Trans. Xingyuan. Beijing: World Book Inc.

[5]Linsu, K. (1998). *Imitation to Innovation: The Dynamics of Korea's Technological Learning*. Trans. Liu Xiaomei, Liu Hongji. Beijing: Xinhua Publishing House.

rules when transforming from imitation to innovation via learning by decomposition and learning by recombination:

1. **Taking imitation as the basis and innovation as the target.** Although all imitation behaviors look similar on the surface, there are still differences between simple imitation and imitation for innovation. Simple imitation is often limited to the imitation of products or services, with its goal as just short-term market results. As for imitation for innovation, the most important outcome is not the product or service itself, but the learning and capability enhancement behind it. Learning by decomposition often plays an important role in this process. Because market demand and imitated products could constantly evolve, imitation strategy requires the imitators to improve their organizational efficiency in all aspects, including the efficiency in imitation behavior itself. Learning by decomposition can help imitators greatly reduce the cost and time of imitation.
2. **Achieving mastery by absorbing an eclectic range of knowledge.** In the transformation process from imitation to innovation, these enterprises will disassemble the technologies or skills embedded in the products, and set different learning targets for each technology or skill. This mode of learning from multiple sources can greatly enhance the absorptive capacity of enterprises, as in this case, the knowledge base of enterprises, with its advantage of diversity, is more efficient in identifying new external technological opportunities. Enterprises carry the need to integrate technologies from multiple sources to create new technologies and products. They also need to incorporate the technologies acquired from outside and developed inside themselves into product design. This will motivate enterprises to conduct more learning by recombination. For example, Geely Automobile has conducted many cross-border M&A since 2006. In 2006, Geely Holding acquired a 19.97% stake of the London Taxi Company (manufacturer of the London classic black taxi that we often see in Western movies). In 2013, Geely Holding spent 11.04 million pounds (about RMB 96.95 million yuan) in acquiring the core assets and business of the London Taxi Company (LTC), which was renamed London Electric Vehicle Company (LEVC) in July 2017. In 2009, Geely Holding acquired the Australian gearbox company DSI with HK$ 257 million, so as to reinforce Geely's R&D capability in gearbox technology. In 2010, Geely Holding acquired 100% equity of Volvo Cars. In 2017, it acquired 49.9% of Proton Automobile (owned by DRB-Hicom) and

51% of Lotus Automobile. These M&A deals surely have multiple goals, such as the consideration of brand, technology, market, etc., whereas a very important strategic consideration is to recombine Geely's internal capabilities — "We integrate global resources at the group level and enhance our capabilities of design, R&D, production and sales, and hence grow into a global enterprise rooted in China yet embracing the world".[6] In the end, this kind of learning by recombination happens many times, and enterprises will build experience and skills in such process, thus providing the necessary capacity foundation for imitation for innovation.

3. **Innovation through recombination.** It has been said that if we carefully observe the so-called new products we find, most of them are actually just the result of recombination of the existing elements. Such combined innovation may fall into two basic types. As for the first type, innovation may not occur to the constituent elements but is realized through innovative recombination of such elements. As for the second type, enterprises develop new elements based on the existing ones, and thus produce better or more differentiated products. Take the Chinese smartphones for example, they have been acquiring new design space through recombination of the existing technologies from other fields (i.e., MP3 players, digital cameras and GPS) along their technological evolution history. In this case, the more the elements that can be combined, the more the new combinations that can be created, which means more opportunities for innovation through recombination. Because the Chinese market is huge and highly segmented, the interplay of innovation through recombination and the segmented and continuous market ladder will provide a lot of survival and growth space for local enterprises, providing rich application scenarios for element recombinations.
4. **Continuous incremental improvement.** During the repeated iterative imitation, enterprises will try some minor improvements at first and learn through trial and error in this process. In a short time, such an improvement might seem trivial and so simple as if it were just another imitation. But as time goes by, it will demonstrate its power. With the accumulation of experience and skills, late-comer enterprises can gradually make some substantive improvements and will eventually yield unique innovations from such continuous incremental improvements.

---

[6] Sohu, Interview with Li Shufu: Geely M&A evolution. *Talent Magazine*, June 4, 2018. http://www.sohu.com/a/234031871_120079.

Never Underestimate the Significance of Manufacturing Ability in the Transformation from Imitation to Innovation

The transformation from imitation to innovation is a goal that all enterprises from late-comer countries wish to achieve in their catching-up. To this end, these enterprises in late-comer countries need to conduct learning by decomposition and learning by recombination effectively. In the aforesaid paragraphs, we discussed the significance of imitation for innovation. At the beginning, enterprises' learning by decomposition and learning by recombination are inseparable from their imitation activities. The result of imitation will inevitably cause more competition, because homogenization makes it harder for enterprises to differentiate themselves from the competitors. Competition will pressurize these enterprises to be more efficient in imitation, so as to conduct faster imitation to get a place in the market, or to get greater user base via low cost. Manufacturing capability has become a feasible option for enterprises to build differentiation advantages in speed or low cost.

For emerging economies like China who gradually transform from imitation to innovation, most of their local enterprises are positioned at the low end of the market ladder in their infant stage. Their imitated products and technologies are relatively low in complexity, making it less likely for them to differentiate themselves by innovation through recombination. This almost leaves no other options for local enterprises than just focusing on low-cost manufacturing.

On the basis of observations of R. O. Korean enterprises' experience from imitation to innovation, Linsu Kim, a Korean Scholar, pointed out that the late-comer countries often reverse the order of research, development and manufacturing in the process of technological catching-up. In other words, developed countries in Europe and America usually develop corresponding technologies in the sequence of research, development, engineering and manufacturing, whereas late-comer countries often solve engineering and manufacturing problems first, then slowly build up product and process development capabilities, and ultimately shore up their research capabilities.[7] In fact, this development sequence not only applies

[7]Linsu, K. (1997). *Imitation to Innovation: The Dynamics of Korea's Technological Learning*. Boston: Harvard Business School Press.

to the manufacturing industry of R. O. Korean, but also to that of China. At the beginning of the development of the Chinese manufacturing industry, a similar sequence pattern can be detected, i.e., from technology introduction to imitation and then to improvement.[8] Gary Jefferson and Thomas Rawski reached a conclusion after analyzing China's manufacturing industry before the mid-1990s: "China's industrial products are rarely comparable to that produced by the world's leading enterprises in quality and features. But for those most capable Chinese companies, they can produce acceptable low-cost alternative products by themselves or through cooperating with foreign companies".[9]

For many years, out of worries about the prospects of Chinese manufacturing industry, many Chinese scholars have been stressing the importance of developing R&D and design capabilities for the Chinese enterprises. In the long run, such an argument surely has its point. However, it also harbors a biased view, namely, it underestimates the importance of the manufacturing capability to China's economic growth. Even in some cases, some opinions often associate manufacturing with low added value, equating it to low-end labor-intensive. Manufacturing was hence considered the toughest, least rewarded and least dominant part in the whole industrial value chain.

Nevertheless, we need to admit that, with the development of capabilities, Chinese local enterprises no longer lack unique technology and capabilities, as in their early stages of development. The majority of the local enterprises will shift their strategic positioning from purely low cost to cost performance, that is, to achieving the ultimate balance among quality, functional performance and low cost as much as possible, which still needs to be grounded on low-cost manufacturing capabilities. Otherwise, it will be very difficult for the enterprises to maintain low product cost and price level while improving quality.

Viewed from a longer-term perspective, the development trajectory of Chinese enterprises' manufacturing capability is likely to be one that gradually evolves from low-cost manufacturing to high-efficiency manufacturing. Although high-efficiency manufacturing has the potential to

---

[8] Interestingly, all these English words, namely, the "importation", "imitation", "improvement" and "innovation" all started with "i" in initials.

[9] Jefferson, G. H., and T. G. Rawski (1995). How industrial reform worked in China: The role of innovation, competition, and property rights. *Proceedings of the World Bank Annual Conference on Development Economics 1994*. Washington, DC: World Bank, pp. 129–156.

reduce manufacturing costs, in general, **what high-efficiency manufacturing emphasizes is an extreme balance between high quality, lowest cost and greatest output efficiency per unit time. This raises higher requirement of manufacturing capability.**

In light of this, the rise of Made-in-Japan and Made-in-China are two very important landmarks in the development history of global manufacturing. In the different historical periods and through different ways, they showcased the significance of manufacturing to a nation's economic take-off and the changing of the industry landscape across the globe. In the process of the rise of Japanese manufacturing, quality and efficiency factors have been elevated to an unprecedented height, and thus bestowed Japan the competitive advantages in the global market. By contrast, the rise of Made-in-China has brought the roles of low cost and high-price performance to their full. Different from its Chinese counterpart, Made-in-Japan, from World War II until 1980s, adopted a high-price–performance competition strategy in its manufacturing industry, so as to move upward along the market ladder. However, when Made-in-Japan developed to a critical threshold in technology and quality, since it strongly depends on export and global market, it gradually abandoned the cost-sensitive low-end market, but instead ventured into the value-sensitive and high-quality high-premium market. In the case of Made-in-China, to date, its dependence on the domestic market is still quite high, exhibiting an extended positioning in the market ladder — covering a wide range from the low-end market, price-sensitive good-enough market to the value-sensitive good-enough market. With the rise of some local leading companies, Chinese manufacturing even has begun to try out in the high-quality premium market. This not only proves the importance of manufacturing capacity for sustainable catch-up in late-comer countries, but also shows that the selection of development strategies in manufacturing industry is closely related to the domestic situation (especially the generic positioning in market ladder, the industrial catch-up policies, the capability development status which is path-dependent, and the scale and structural characteristics of the domestic market).

Never Ignore the Value of Implicit Innovation

The development process of China's manufacturing industry will inevitably shift from imitation to innovation over time. However, when talking about innovations, we could easily focus our attention on the more visible innovations — for example, the technical improvements embodied in products or newly introduced technical attributes, or the technical improvements to those patented critical production processes. These innovations can be referred to as "explicit innovations". The reason why it is called "explicit innovation" is that this kind of innovation usually has two traits. On the one hand, they can be easily seen by consumers or users as outsiders. On the other hand, they can often be protected by exclusivity mechanisms such as patents and trade secrets.

The opposite of "explicit innovation" is the so-called "implicit innovation", whose manifestation and commercial value are often overlooked.

Implicit innovation has at least the following two typical manifestations:

First, it is often reflected in **process improvements**, especially those not completely presented in the form of technology. For example, why can Chinese enterprises combine reasonable quality and low price in their products? The buttress underneath is not directly perceived by our consumers, as the major part of it remains invisible. Without such an invisible buttress, the Chinese enterprises cannot reach such a balance. In addition, as claimed by Nirmalya Kumar, a Canadian social activism and leadership training expert in his TED sharing of "India's Intangible Innovation", this kind of innovation is also not exclusive to China.[10] For example, India provides IT outsourcing, which is one of the best offshore IT services in the world. Actually, if interpreted simply from the conventional perspective, it does not involve much innovation, and nor does it produce any better R&D-based products or introduce any unique IT technologies. However, there are a lot of process innovations behind it, which is reflected in effective coordination of highly complex processes and efficient completion of operations through labor division.

Second, it may also take the form of **distributed product improvement**. In China, due to the massive geographic concentration of enterprises within a certain region (such as the formation of industrial clusters), or the highly subdivided and cooperative industrial value chain formed around specific products and businesses, market players often cooperate and compete at the same time. This is reflected in the improvements of products or technologies. Due to mutual imitation, knowledge spillovers and distributed cooperation, the improvements of those products (even

[10]Kumar, N. (2012). India's invisible entrepreneurs. Ted, April, 2012. https://www.ted.com/talks/nirmalya_kumar_india_s_invisible_innovation.

some important ones) are actually not done by a single enterprise, but by a number of enterprises through their informal collaboration. In some extreme cases, an individual enterprise doesn't even need to know or does not know who completed the preceding improvement. And every enterprise has left some traces on the product improvement in its own way. This is like a co-completed or collaborative work. It is just that the participating individuals never realize or need to know how others participated in the creation process. In this regard, the competitiveness of the Chinese manufacturing enterprises does not come from a single enterprise, but from the collective strength of the entire supply chain the enterprise is embedded in. Therefore, in some sense, the innovations (including product and process improvements) of the Chinese manufacturing enterprises cannot be attributed to the contribution of any individual enterprise, as such innovations are often the result of joint efforts of a cluster of enterprises.

In the past innovation practice, Chinese enterprises would tailor-make some implicit innovations to some specific market segments or specific unmet needs. A typical example is that China's mobile phones are designed with dual SIM card slots, which was not seen in overseas markets early on. This product was first developed for the Chinese market.

It can be seen that more and more Chinese enterprises not only focused on just the Chinese market, but also gradually started to transplant their experience accumulated from the Chinese market, namely, their experiences in designing, business operations, market understanding and business model innovations, to their overseas markets, especially to large emerging economies such as India, South Africa and Brazil. This is actually very interesting. We can see that we are living in a wonderful era, an era when China starts to move from imitation toward innovation. Made-in-China is no longer the synonym of low labor costs or low-end manufacturing capabilities. Chinese enterprises have already arrived at a crossroad. They can not only meet China's local market demands, but also tap into their accumulated experience and expertise in innovation to acquire competitiveness in the global market.

Seize the Time Window of Catching-Up

When researching into the catch-up at the economy level or industry level, researchers have long noticed the existence of the time window for catch-up. That is to say, the probability of catching-up is not always evenly distributed on the time axis. In a specific time period, the success rate of catching-up may be much higher than that in other periods.

The time window of catching-up is a complicated issue due to two factors. On the one hand, the technology involved in catching-up is constantly developing and changing. And the catching-up behavior of competitors in the process of catching-up will also exert a noticeable impact on the environment where catching-up takes place. For this reason, the window time of catching-up is generally limited. As the core of the catching-up process, the efficiency of learning and ability building will determine whether the late-comers can seize the time window, and ultimately determine the results of catching-up. On the other hand, catching-up depends not only on the capability enhancement of late-comers themselves, but also on their relative capability status compared to the leading enterprises. This is like shooting a moving target. A constantly moving target will be more complicated and more challenging to shoot than a stationary target.

Interestingly, there seem to be some different research findings about the influence of technical characteristics over the catching-up window and the success rate. For example, Kyoo-Ho Park, a scholar at R. O. Korean Hanshin University, and Keun Lee, a professor at Seoul National University, Korea, used patent data from USPTO (The United States Patent and Trademark Office) to conduct an empirical analysis on industrial technology catch-up of R. O. Korea and Taiwan of China. They concluded that the shorter the technology life cycle, the higher the probability of technological catch-up. However, China's industry catching-up experience shows that the Chinese enterprises are successful in both industries with long technology life cycles and those with short technology life cycles. What are the causes of such differences in the catch-up experience?[11]

In industries with longer technology life cycles, e.g., in color TV, air conditioners, personal computers industries, etc., the speed of technology development will be relatively moderate, which allows a longer time for the late-comers to catch up. It is especially the case in terms of capacity development, where the relative certainty of future technology development direction will lead the late-comers to make long-term investment. At the same time, we usually think that the accumulated advantages of the

---

[11] Park, K.-H., and K. Lee (2006). Linking the technological regime to the technological catch-pp: Analyzing (R. O.) Korea and Taiwan (China) using the US patent data. *Industrial and Corporate Change* 15(4): 715–753.

leading enterprises (especially those multinational companies) in industries with slow technological development will be very difficult to break. Therefore, it would be very unfavorable for the catch-ups by late-comer companies. However, this problem will be significantly alleviated in China. This is because, as mentioned earlier, the huge and highly segmented Chinese market makes it easier for local enterprises to find enough market space to avoid direct competition with those leading companies. The existence of a continuous technology ladder can help late-comer enterprises greatly reduce the costs of learning by decomposition and learning by recombination.

For industries with short technology life cycle, the technological development is often uncertain in the early stages, and the future development direction of technology often changes frequently and dynamically, so the first-mover advantages of those leading companies are easily to be reduced, or even destroyed. Therefore, we often say that "everyone starts from the same starting line". In this case, the establishment of advantages will depend on two factors. First, who can complete iterative improvement faster and surpass the performance threshold of technology? Second, who can perfectly match technology with market demand with higher efficiency? Fast iteration depends on the high flexibility of the enterprise and its quick response to the market, whereas high-efficiency matching depends on in-depth understanding of the local market and localized innovation capability. In terms of these aspects, there is no obvious capability gap between Chinese enterprises and foreign multinational companies. Even to a certain extent, Chinese enterprises might be more advantageous in flexibility and responsiveness when compared to their foreign competitors.

Another question we need to consider is whether this catch-up happens in a stock market or an incremental market. In a stock market, late-comers need to face direct competition from existing enterprises, whereas in an incremental market, they might get more chances of survival. In the Chinese market, those enterprises from abroad usually take the high-end market as the entry point, as it is more matched with their advantages in quality, technology and brand, and it is easier for them to meet their targets in cost structure and financial returns. As time goes by, this market segment will become a place with gradually stabilized competition pattern and relatively fewer growth opportunities for multinational companies. The "economical market", which is located at a lower position in the market ladder compared with the high-end market, develops much faster than the high-end market. And it has some typical features (which is true no matter in European and American countries or China). Unlike in the high-end markets, clients in the economical market can sacrifice some innovation, quality and service to a certain extent for lower price levels. Although they care much about the price of products, they still have certain requirements for reasonable product quality, performance, safety and services. However, when their basic expectations are met, their willingness to pay for additional value or service usually becomes lower.[12] For example, Philips's large medical equipment in the Chinese market originally targeted the top hospitals in first-tier and second-tier cities. These hospitals hold stronger financial ability to afford those functionally complex and financially expensive products. However, with more enterprises in this market segment purchasing such equipment, the market increment will gradually reduce. Compared with such hospitals, hospitals located outside these cities, including the Grade B or even Grade B secondary hospitals in prefecture-level cities, tend to accept lower price levels. Moreover, as such hospitals are less likely to face intractable disease cases, they usually do not have medical research needs like the Grade A tertiary hospitals in first-tier and second-tier cities, and therefore do not require high-end features from the equipment. This market segment has the potential for rapid growth, and is more in line with the decomposition and recombination capabilities the Chinese local enterprises have acquired. Hence, the local enterprises need to seize this opportunity to establish their differentiated competitive advantages with attractive price, reasonable quality level and quick market response as the core in this market before foreign multinational companies take the initiative to migrate down the market ladder.

[12]Llewellyn, C., D. Podpolny, and C. Zerbi (2015). Capturing the new "value" segment in medical devices, January, 2015. https://www.mckinsey.com/industries/life-sciences/our-insights/capturing-the-new-value-segment-in-medical-devices.

Chapter 5

Competing in a Good-Enough Market

A Good-Enough Market Is Becoming More Important Than Ever Before

A conventional way to depict market structure is to divide the positioning on the market ladder into three typical types, namely, the high-end market (or premium market), the mid-end market and the low-end market mainly based on the price level of products. This division is easy to understand because the price level reflects customers' willingness to pay for quality and branding on the demand side. It also mirrors the quality and technical level of products on the supply side. In such a market structure, we often think that customers in the high-end market have higher purchasing power and higher requirements for product quality and performance than those in other market types. In contrast, the products in the low-end market are of relatively low quality, mainly meeting customers' basic needs, and the buyers are very sensitive to price.

This conception about market structure is in line with the situation of the Chinese market that has existed for many years now. Typically, in many product fields, foreign multinational companies occupy a dominant position in the high-end market after entering the Chinese market, which is characterized by high quality, high price and usually high profit margin. Accordingly, the technology and quality requirements are very high, which are reflected in higher requirements for product components and production technology and equipment, as well as huge R&D and branding investments. Inevitably, the entry threshold becomes relatively high, especially for Chinese local enterprises in the early stages. Products that the nowadays urban families have found very common in their lives, like color TV sets, refrigerators, air conditioners, etc., were beyond the wildest imaginations of many families back in 1980s. Perhaps many people may still remember that when a household bought in a color TV set, all their neighbors would swarm into their living room and watch TV with them with much curiosity. At that time, foreign brands were better in quality and more expensive in price. It probably cost two years' worth of income of a household or even more to buy an imported color TV of ordinary size.[1] This situation remained until 1996. In 1996, China's color TV import tariff was adjusted from 35% to 23%, and international brands such as Philips, Sharp, Toshiba, Panasonic and Sony began to occupy the Chinese market. In March 1996, Sichuan Changhong increased its market share of color TV sets from 22% in 1995 to 35% by initiating a price war in the market and became the No.1 domestic brand of color TV sets in China at that time. Since then, color TV sets have become a standard choice in the shopping list of Chinese households.

For many product categories, due to the limited purchasing power of Chinese consumers from the 1980s to the early 1990s and a market situation of relatively insufficient supply, although the mid-end market existed, it was generally small in size. In most cases, people either chose entry-level local products or high-end products of foreign brands. With the passage of time, Chinese local enterprises have accumulated mature experience in low-cost manufacturing, and also effectively honed their technology and market competence amid fierce market competition. It is an obvious fact that as a result of the low entry barrier of the low-end market, with more local enterprises joining in the competition, the profitability of enterprises will become even lower over time. As a result, inevitably, some local enterprises that have acquired sufficient financial resources and technical capabilities will gradually migrate upward along the market ladder, which will extend the Chinese market structure and expand the scale of the mid-end market.

In the recent twenty years, another silent change has been occurring in the Chinese market, that is, the good-enough market is expanding in China's domestic market and has already become a competition arena that attracts the attention of local and foreign enterprises. Such growth was,

---

[1]Mao, C. (2018). The first wave of color TV buyers in Hunan province: A 14-inch color TV took a year and a half's salary. Sina, June 18, 2018. http://hunan.sina.com.cn/news/s/2018-06-18/detail-iheauxvy8580731.shtml.

first, a result of the change of the Chinese people's consumption patterns. With the upgrading of Chinese people's consumption levels, a considerable number of Chinese consumers have gradually shifted from being price-sensitive to value-sensitive. This has provided a continuously expanding potential market for cost-effective market positioning. During this period, the quality of Chinese local manufactured goods has been gradually improved, which can hence satisfy a considerable number of value-sensitive users. For example, in the field of smartphones, the launch of Xiaomi phones in 2010 triggered the explosive demand of young Chinese consumers for cost-effective mobile phones. And the slogan "born to fever" proposed by Xiaomi also changed people's perception about the locally made mobile phones. With Huawei, OPPO and Vivo devoting to the production of mid-end to high-end mobile phones in recent years, the gap between the product quality and brand image of domestic mobile phones and that of Apple and Samsung has been greatly narrowed. At the same time, previously, those Chinese consumers with strong purchasing power and clear requirements for quality used to have only two options: relatively low-end positioned local products and relatively high-end international brands. However, now, these good-enough products made in China have gradually entered their field of vision and become a reasonable option for them. It is like while in the 1980s the Chinese consumers were very concerned about whether the color TV sets they bought were imported "complete built unit (CBU)" or "complete or semi-knock down", many consumers now do not feel the need to buy CBU TV sets of international brands.

Second, due to the fierce price competition in the Chinese market, domestic enterprises are also continuously pressured to control their costs. Purchasing raw materials or equipment based on cost-effective consideration has become an increasingly common strategy. Even those enterprises with certain natural monopoly advantages will be forced by intensifying competition to make some adaptations. In the past, they may have preferred to buy high-priced international first-line brands, even when the quality or performance of these products exceeded the existing demands. One of the biggest incentives of doing so is that the management can be exempted from accusation of "negligence" — as when problems arise, they can write in their report that "We have purchased the best products in the world. It's not our fault if things go wrong, because there is simply no better choice". If it's decided to buy a local product with lower cost, there will be a happy ending when nothing goes wrong.

However, if there is any problem, the management would probably be blamed: "Why did you buy this product? Why didn't you buy an international brand which is better in technology and quality?"[2]

Finally, looking beyond the Chinese market, we can find the demand for good-enough products made in China gradually goes up in the global market. The Asian financial crisis in 1997 and the global financial crisis in 2008 greatly impacted the regional and global economy, leading to shrinking consumer expenditure worldwide and increased pressure on the enterprises to reduce costs. In this case, because the products made by Chinese enterprises have strong advantages in cost performance, these good-enough products won more favors among the consumers.

The expansion of demand for good-enough products is also subtly changing multinational companies' perceptions about the Chinese market. In the opinion of Gadiesh *et al.*, in the future, the good-enough market will become the core area of competition between multinational enterprises and local enterprises, producing world-class companies. If the enterprises can find ways to gain advantages in a good-enough market, the "strategically vital point" inside the Chinese market, then they will be able to secure their longer-term growth.[3]

Two Types of Good-Enough Markets

Although a good-enough market has often been equated to a mid-end market in previous literature, through careful observation of the Chinese market we can find that the two are not always the same. Or more precisely, there are two different sub-types of good-enough markets located in different positions of China's market ladder (see Figure 5.1).

The first type of good-enough market, which we refer to as the low-end version good-enough market, or price-sensitive good-enough market, is located in the upper half of the low-end market in the traditional sense. In other words, although they generally fall into the category of the low-end market, these products still focus on high price–performance ratio, which has low product price as its core. Although their

---

[2]This is a classical principal–agent problem, since the goals of the management team and that of the enterprise are not always the same.

[3]Gadiesh, O., P. Leung, and T. Vestring (2007). The battle for China's good-enough market. *Harvard Business Review* 85(9): 80.

Figure 5.1. Positioning of a Good-Enough Market

quality is sometimes not so satisfactory, their advantage in price makes them quite attractive to consumers in the low-end market. **The second type of good-enough market is what we refer to as the premium version good-enough market or value-sensitive good-enough market. It covers the mid-end market and the bottom part of high-end market in the traditional sense.** Such price–performance ratio is essentially based on reasonable quality as the core. In other words, its attractiveness to users is not entirely based on the price factor, but a comprehensive advantage in product quality and price.

Examples of the strategy to divide a good-enough market into value-sensitive and price-sensitive types can be seen in first-line local mobile phone manufacturers, such as Huawei's sub-brand, the Honor, which was positioned somewhat close to the price-sensitive good-enough market in the beginning. Of course, because the positioning of Huawei Mate and Huawei P series mobile phones is constantly migrating and expanding upward from the value-sensitive good-enough market, the current market ladder of Honor mobile phones has exceeded the price-sensitive good-enough market.

In the new retail business in China which combines conventional retail business with e-commerce, we can also see some examples of the dividing of price-sensitive and value-sensitive good-enough market types. For example, FreshHema and HemaMini cover different market areas. Many areas that could not be covered by FreshHema will be left to HemaMini, including the suburbs of first and second-tier cities, the entire third- and fourth-tier cities and some counties. Moreover, different market coverage does not only involve geographical areas but also involves adapting the products and services to the localization needs of the target market. Different from the exquisitely packaged vegetables in FreshHema, HemaMini will introduce more vegetables in loose packaging. The iconic multi-category seafood package of FreshHema has been downsized to just selective categories in HemaMini including Dungeness crab and Boston lobster, with some commonly seen fresh-water aquatic products such as carp added to the category. Many ready-to-serve steamed stuffed buns and steamed buns, dumplings, wonton and cold dishes with pot-stewed vegetables have been added to the shelves of HemaMini, so as to accommodate the local everyday diets. To save cost, the overhead order-gantry and the order-split-consolidation system of FreshHema have also been omitted. More importantly, such differentiation is also seen in the organizational design: where HemaMini adopts a new store-manager-partner system, FreshHema still follows its conventional centralized management model. These differences in operational details vividly reflect the significant differences between price-sensitive and value-sensitive market positioning.

It is precisely due to the existence of these two types of good-enough markets that many growing Chinese domestic enterprises adapt their strategic settings when moving up the market ladder. For example, the initial strategic vision set by Geely Automobile was to "build cars that ordinary people can afford", for back then, Geely was still looking for its initial living space in the price-sensitive value-for-money market. However, after 2007, Geely began its strategic transformation, with its strategic vision evolving into "build the safest, most environmentally friendly and most energy-efficient cars, and bring Geely cars to the world". This switch from price-sensitive to value-sensitive good-enough market can be intuitively seen in the design and configuration of new models launched by Geely. It's also exemplified in the expanded price range of Geely's product portfolio.

Therefore, the good-enough market we mentioned earlier is not equal to the mid-end market, because it falls into two types: the price-sensitive market and the value-sensitive market. However, although these two market types have different positions on the market ladder and differentiated focus on product design, they have one thing in common, that is, a straightforward rule they all embrace: when the quality of this product is the same as that of other competitive products in this good-enough market, the price of such a product should be the most competitive, and when such a product is equally priced as that of other competing products in the same market, its quality shall be the best.

How to Survive in a Good-Enough Market

Although a good-enough market seems to be very attractive to those enterprises seeking growth opportunities, it is not easy to capture such business opportunities and survive in this market. This is not only because of the fierce competition but also because there are some special competition rules in this market. Behind these competition rules, there are actually specific capability requirements for market entrants.

The blank-filling market positioning strategy

The continuity of China's market ladder indeed brings Chinese enterprises more opportunities for catching-up, but it is more reflected at the macro level. For individual enterprises, the continuity of market ladder inevitably means that there are usually more competitors in the existing market positioning. In order to avoid direct competition with the existing competitors, enterprises need to develop better insights into the unmet needs in the market and provide corresponding products and services to fill these "blanks on the market ladder".

In the Chinese market, such market blanks are usually defined by two dimensions, namely, category and price. In this regard, enterprises can try to expand or even create some new categories, or redefine the price range on their existing categories.

In the past forty years, many Chinese enterprises have capitalized on the market ladder blanks to achieve rapid growth and even their "counterattack".

Great Wall Motor (GWM), a Chinese car maker founded in 1984, has successfully applied this blank-filling strategy in the production of its pickup trucks and SUVs and gained opportunities for its rapid development. A pickup truck is a light-duty passenger-cargo dual-purpose truck that has an enclosed cabin and an open cargo area with low sides and tailgate.[4] As a private enterprise, GWM started with pickup trucks. From

[4]Baidu Baike, Pick up. https://baike.baidu.com/item/皮卡/35161.

the beginning, GWM chose pickup trucks as its market entry point mainly out of a very important consideration that automobile joint ventures entering the Chinese market care less about this market segment and seldom invested any market resources in it, or even if they made any investment, it was mainly focused on premium ones with relatively higher price, and meanwhile, domestic car producers also undervalued this subcategory and focused more on the passenger vehicle category. In 2006, GWM launched its pickup trucks, and in 2008, it became the No.1 producer of this category in the Chinese market, a position that it has maintained till now.[5] In terms of the category of SUVs, Great Wall Motor had a clear customer profiling since the launch of its first SUV models, namely, the young people who love fashion but are slightly less able to pay, who therefore emphasize on price–performance. In 2002 and 2003, GWM launched the SUV models SAFE and SING, which occupied 25% of the total share of the Chinese SUV market. After that, based on the reverse engineering of the fourth generation Honda CR-V, GWM launched the first generation Haval-6 in August 2011. This model quickly became the first choice of young consumers in third-tier cities and below. The biggest attraction of the model lies in its fashionable appearance, attractive price, and more diversified choices in interior configuration compared with other higher-priced joint venture brands. There is no doubt that it is more in line with the demand in a value-sensitive good-enough market.

However, it should be pointed out that, due to the remarkably dynamic market ladder of China, any efforts to find and define market blanks on the market ladder can only bring enterprises with growth opportunities in the market for a limited period of time, the length of which depends to a great extent on the "moat" established by enterprises to protect their advantages and how they achieve rapid upgrading of their products and technologies. The SUV of GWM managed to become the value benchmark in China's domestic SUV market for a long time. Yet, as GWM failed to adapt to the general trend of consumption upgrading in the Chinese market in recent years, it did not do very well in developing new products or upgrading its existing products. What is worse, with more international brands sinking to this market segment while the domestic brands keep moving upward on the market ladder, the business of GWM has been in decline since 2017.

---

[5]The market share of Great Wall pickup trucks in 2017 and 2018 was 29% and 31%, respectively (https://www.cnpickups.com/news/783893.html).

An ultimate balance between low cost and reasonable quality

In emerging markets, good-enough segments hold great growth potential, especially for those with a large population base. This is mainly because emerging markets with a large population tend to have highly discrete demands, making it impossible for them to meet the customer demands with either low-quality and low-price strategy or high-quality and high-price strategy.

Chinese enterprises are using the good-enough strategy to gain more market opportunities, even sometimes those outside of their home market. Take the mobile phone market as an example: after entering the Indian market in 2014, MI mobile phone has rapidly expanded its share in the Indian market by virtue of its advantages in cost performance. According to data from IDG, in 2018, Xiaomi had the largest market share in India, which was as high as 28.9%, surpassing that of Samsung (22.4%). Moreover, Redmi 5A and Redmi Note 5/Note 5 Pro series became the fastest growing mobile phone models in the Indian market in 2018, with their global shipment exceeding 10 million units. To achieve this, low-cost manufacturing capability has been very critical. In April 2018, at the MI 6X launching conference and also in an internal circulation letter, Lei Jun, the founder, chairman and CEO of MI, unofficially disclosed a resolution approved by MI's board, "From now on, Xiaomi would like to give a solemn promise to our users that the overall annual after-tax net profit of all our hardware businesses (including mobile phones, IoT and consumer products) will not exceed 5%. If it exceeds this figure, we will return in a reasonable manner any surplus above the 5% back to our MI users". Moreover, in an internal circulation letter, he summed up MI's business model as "pricing the well-designed quality products close to their hardware cost, delivering products to users via our own or direct-supply efficient retail channels online and offline, and continuously providing users with diversified services on-line". This also represents MI's consistent practice in market competition. On the basis of maintaining the quality and performance as much as possible (even with improvement in some aspects), the product pricing of MI is greatly reduced to trigger the rapid explosion of demand. For example, as for the 10,000 mAh mobile power bank with market rate often above RMB 200, MI beat down the price to only RMB 69 yuan. And it reduced the price of a mainstream air purifier product which was originally priced above RMB 2,000 yuan to below RMB 1,000 yuan. Even though the capital market still has some doubts about whether such strategies might sustain MI's growth into the future, it for sure has somehow changed the landscape of the related markets in China.

In order to realize low-cost manufacturing and maintain differentiated advantages in quality, many successful manufacturers making cost-effective products often try to self-make or improve some key special equipment and try to continuously optimize and streamline their manufacturing process, so as to maintain or even simultaneously improve the product quality level while up-lifting operational efficiency. For example, Phoenix, a German hidden champion company, is the world market leader in industrial connection technology and automation. It even fabricates screws itself within its factory in Bloomberg, producing 7 million pieces of screws every day. It also develops a lot of special equipment, which is aimed to protect its own advantages and for its own differentiated product competitiveness.

Some Chinese companies even tried to transplant this strategy to their markets in developed countries. Mr. Ren Zhengfei, President of Huawei, once said in a company internal speech in 2018, "We should not think that only (the markets of developing countries like) India require low cost. Actually, developed countries also need substantially large bandwidth but cheap networks. That's why it'll be surely right for us to work hard in this direction". In his view, low cost can even serve as a booster of high quality. As he mentioned: "We emphasize embracing the future information society with extremely low cost, and we must build very low cost, follow Moore's Law to reduce the unit cost per byte, and push ourselves to uplift the quality to extreme and lower our cost to a certain degree. In this way, no one can compete with us".[6] In the past, we've often held the stereotype that those products emphasizing cost advantage are often positioned for the low-end market. However, we have to admit that apart from luxury goods with Veblen effect[7] and the Giffen products[8] rarely seen in the real

[6] Sina Finance (2018). Zhengfei Ren: A concise victory means the future: Inside the simplicity is complexity, August 22, 2018. https://finance.sina.com.cn/chanjing/gsnews/2018-08-22/doc-ihhzsnec2650663.shtml.

[7] Veblen effect refers to the case where the degree of consumer demand for a commodity increases with the increase of price, which is different from the normal case where the demand decreases with the increase of price as in most commodities.

[8] Giffin goods refer to goods whose demand changes in the same direction as their price. This concept originated from the discovery of Robert Giffin, a British economist in the 19th century, who discovered that when a famine occurred in Ireland in 1845, the demand for potatoes increased with the rising price of potatoes.

world, people's pursuit of high quality and attractive price level is a lasting normal. There is huge reservoir of commercial potential behind this.

The support of a complete industrial chain

The influence of a complete industrial chain on the efficiency and competitiveness of China's manufacturing industry is often overlooked. Because most of the time, we only focus on the competitive advantage of every single enterprise. In fact, the reason why many Chinese manufacturing enterprises are able to establish strong low-cost manufacturing advantages is that not only have they internally established strong resources and capability bases, they have also benefited from being embedded in a strong industrial value chain. On the one hand, this complete and efficient industrial value chain can help enterprises embedded in it to concentrate their resources on specific parts within the entire value chain, which not only greatly alleviates the negative impacts of the classical resource constraint issue, but also more effectively helps enterprises build continuously improving ability base in certain value chain links. On the other hand, it can also help these enterprises develop extraordinary flexibility in depending upon the industrial value chain, so as to better survive and capture the rapidly changing opportunities in the highly volatile market environment of China.

In the early development stages of China's manufacturing industry, the industrial value chains the SME manufacturers were first embedded in were often highly condensed in some geographical areas, that is, regional-based value chains were formed. For example, in China's coastal provinces, there are a large number of industrial clusters, and many cluster enterprises can purchase almost all raw materials and parts locally. The resulting extremely low transportation cost greatly reduces the product cost. With the increased scale, product quality and technical level of some Chinese manufacturing enterprises, the industrial chains they are embedded in are continuously upgraded and expanded, gradually bringing them into the global value chain system. This means that enterprises can integrate more competitive manufacturing resources at a global scale, thus creating configuration advantages by coupling the localized manufacturing ecosystem with the global manufacturing chain.

Such industrial value chains that have been gradually generated with the rise of China's manufacturing industry, especially the high-efficiency local industrial value chain, have been formed as the result of a series of factors. As we know, due to the huge potential of China's domestic market demand, it's naturally conducive for multinational companies to form a complete industrial value chain in China. In this process, especially in terms of the developing of manufacturing capability, it requires a lot of repetitive learning and improvement, whereas the resources and time costs incurred from this need to be shared by opportunities that can be replicated and has a certain scale. This includes not only the tangible investments in equipment and other manufacturing facilities, but also entails the intangible investment into training and developing of Chinese manufacturing workers with discipline and skills. The huge market potential will cause large-scale imitations in geographic areas where the early successful enterprises are located. The high-degree aggregation of these imitating enterprises in a few geographical locations will catalyze the formation of a somehow shared production network in these areas and reduce the transportation cost and resource development cost through collective assets developing, resource sharing (such as that of human resources, product technology, regional brands, etc.) and geographical location concentration. Moreover, these enterprises are also direct competitors of each other. And the rapid imitation of the best practices makes it necessary for enterprises to continuously improve and innovate to maintain their competitive edge, which will further stimulate these enterprises to constantly improve their efficiency in business operations and management.

Second, the development of Western multinational companies in China has also greatly promoted the upgrading of China's local manufacturing value chain. After making tentative investment in China, Western multinational companies find the Chinese market increasingly attractive and even gradually consider it as a critical part of their global strategic map. Against such a backdrop, out of the previously mentioned two reasons, Western multinational companies will gradually localize their supply chain. First, the localization of supply chain can greatly improve the speed of responding to Chinese market demand, and reduce the cost of manufacturing and services to a certain extent. On the other hand, with the continuous improvement of its comprehensive capability, China's local manufacturing chain has gradually become a competitive and potentially available manufacturing capability and resource pool within the global value chain. Therefore, those Chinese local enterprises that have been pushed to join the production system of multinational corporations will get the opportunity to enhance their competitiveness directly as the result of the knowledge transfer and learning opportunities provided by these multinational corporations, and further indirectly promote the capability improvement of other local manufacturing enterprises through various mechanisms of knowledge spillovers. Thanks to the more rigorous standards and sound management systems of multinational companies on product quality, production process and factory management, local enterprises are pushed to quickly learn in a relatively short period of time, or be flushed out of the supplier system as the result of the competition mechanism.

Third, the localization policy implemented by the Chinese government in many manufacturing industries has somehow accelerated this process. As domestication is often one of the requirements for joint ventures or one of the additional requirements for technology and equipment importation by the technology-importing enterprises, those joint ventures or technology-importing enterprises (usually enterprises with a certain scale) are often pushed to cultivate a relatively complete industrial value chain in the local market in order to secure domestication progress of some important product categories (such as color TV sets, refrigerators, automobiles, etc.).

Under the interplay of these factors, China has formed a wide-reaching, highly efficient and relatively complete industrial value chain, which has become the launch pad for the Chinese manufacturing industry to obtain a comprehensive advantage of low cost and high flexibility. So we can be sure that, as far as the completeness of industrial value chain is concerned, across the world, no country can boast surpassing China now, especially when products are required to cover all segments on the market ladder ranging from low-end to mid-end and high-end. By now, China has already developed 41 major industrial categories, 207 middle industrial classes and 666 industrial sections, forming a relatively complete modern industrial system, making China the only country in the world with all industrial categories listed in UN ISIC standard classifications. Just as clearly stated by Mr. Chu Shijia, Director General of the General Affairs Department of the Ministry of Commerce of China, in a press conference on "Stabilizing Foreign Trade, Securing Foreign Investment and Promoting Domestic Consumption" held by the Ministry of Commerce on July 2, 2019, the comprehensive advantages of China's industrial chain cannot be substituted by any other country at present. Instead, it can only get better with the emergence and infusion of new industries.[9]

Giving full play to the market ladder: Encircling the cities from the rural area

Using the continuity of the market ladder to realize the upward migration from the bottom market segment is a common market development strategy adopted by many Chinese manufacturing enterprises. This kind of strategy is vividly described by researchers and industrial practitioners as "encircling the cities from the rural area". The reason why this strategy is often used in the early stages of enterprise development is that the caviar part of the market is usually occupied by multinational companies at first. At that time, it's frankly not a smart strategy for local enterprises, which are often short in technical ability, capital and market resources, to directly compete against their powerful rivalries. A more rational choice is to look for those niche market segments that have been ignored by multinational companies, that is, the market segments with relatively low positioning on the market ladder or those remote markets that bring about high service costs. Such so-called "remote markets" or "rural markets" have become the initial solid foothold for local enterprises, as well as the starting point for Chinese enterprises to unveil their great ambitions and journey to the future. In this sense, much greatness may begin with a seemingly "humble" starting point.

Take Huawei as an example. When Ren Zhengfei started his entrepreneurial journey in 1987, the telephone exchange products market in Chinese first-tier cities and provincial capitals was mainly dominated by Siemens, NEC Corporation, Fujitsu, etc. Through its initial positioning of serving the lower-end market, Huawei managed to avoid the head-to-head competition against the multinational giants, and at the same time made its first bucket of technology and funds accumulation to finance its future development. Locally designed and manufactured stored program control (SPC) exchanges were seen in Chinese rural markets ever since 1992. People may be curious why multinational companies or joint ventures

[9]Ni, H. (2019). Huanqiu, Mofcom: The comprehensive advantages of China's industrial chain are irreplaceable in the world, July 2, 2019. http://world.huanqiu.com/exclusive/2019-07/15081119.html?agt=15438.

don't care to penetrate this market. Qing Mu and Keun Lee explained this in a study that "Even if they had wanted to enter the rural market, their products may not match with the local needs ... Considering the low network adoption rate and poor network performance, the systems provided by foreign multinational enterprises basically cannot run on the rural networks. In addition, the systems provided by foreign companies were based on the premise of using as few lines as possible. However, due to the low telephone penetration rate and high-frequency usage of single route telephones in the Chinese rural market, the systems provided by foreign companies were often encountered with bugs and sometimes even crashes in local network environment".[10] This so-called strategy of "encircling the cities from the rural areas" was even adopted in Huawei's overseas market expansion. Since 1997, when Huawei gradually ventured into the overseas markets, it started from Russia and Brazil, which were relatively overlooked or less explored by enterprises from developed countries back then.

The strategy of "encircling the cities from the rural areas" is not only adopted by manufacturing enterprises but also has become a common strategy for Chinese enterprises in other business areas. For example, on November 20, 2017, the Internet giant Alibaba became a shareholder of Sun Art Retail, whose subsidiary retail brands such as Auchan and RT-Mart ranked the largest and fastest-growing hypermarket operators in China back then largely due to the market strategies they adopted. Foreign giants running supermarket chains in the Chinese market such as Wal-Mart, Carrefour, etc. successfully expanded from first-tier cities to second- and third-tier cities. RT-Mart, on the contrary, chose to establish its own market foundation and influence first from second and third-tier cities where there is huge consumption potential but less attention of business giants. For example, the best-performing RT-Mart store in China is located in Kunshan, instead of in first-tier cities like Beijing and Shanghai.[11]

Despite the new trend of retail business brought about by the development of the Internet, the data and facts still show that the market at the

---

[10] Mu, Q., and K. Lee (2005). Knowledge diffusion, market segmentation and technological catch-up: The case of the telecommunication industry in China. *Research Policy* 34(6): 759–783.

[11] Sohu, RT-Mart was acquired by Jack Ma for 22.4 billion yuan, and Mingduan Huang, chairman of RT-Mart, resigned: He won all opponents but lost to the times, February 6, 2018. https://www.sohu.com/a/221341414_733114.

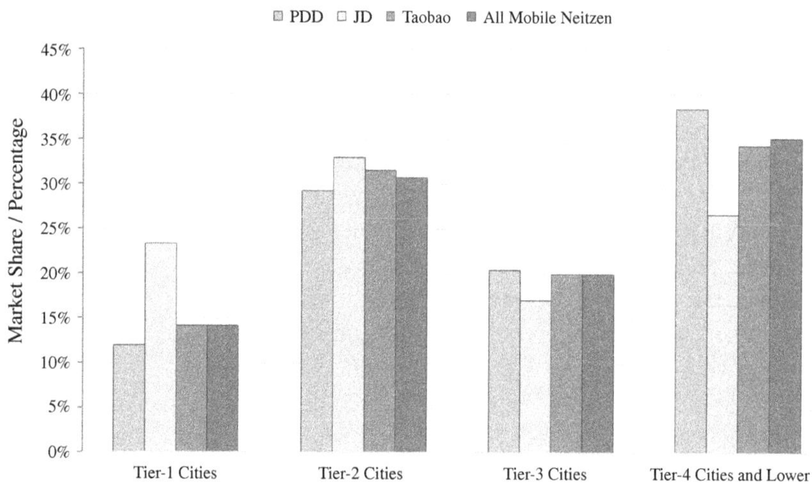

Figure 5.2. City Distribution of E-commerce Platform Users in China in 2018

Source: QuestMobile.

lower end of the market ladder can bring opportunities with growth potential. Take Pinduoduo, an e-commerce platform established in 2015, as an example (see Figure 5.2). For a long time, the majority of the users of Pinduoduo have been from third-tier cities or below, accounting for roughly 2/3 of the total user population. This positioning has helped Pinduoduo find market opportunities that have not been fully attended to by existing e-commerce giants like Alibaba and JD.COM. Therefore, Pinduoduo quickly established its own user base. According to the data disclosed in 2019, in January 2019, the proportion of Gross Merchandise Volume (GMV) users of Pinduoduo from first and second-tier cities was 37%. By June 2019, this figure rapidly surged to 48%.

Product Development Strategy in a Good-Enough Market

As we discussed earlier, China's good-enough market can be divided into two types according to the characteristics of customer demand, namely, the value-sensitive and price-sensitive type. In light of the starkly different demand profiles of these two market types, the enterprises would need to focus on different points in designing, developing and providing products for these two types of markets.

In a price-sensitive good-enough market, the market segments are usually located at the bottom of the whole market ladder, so low price (especially much lower than the regular market price) becomes a very conspicuous label. In order to achieve such a low price, enterprises often simplify the product or lower the quality standard of the product as compared with the regularly designed ones (although the whole quality level must still meet the minimum quality requirements of the low-end market). For enterprises, although the gross profit margin of their products is very low, their low pricing will trigger a lot of potential demand, which can bring attractive profit-making opportunities for them.

The development process of price-sensitive good-enough products is roughly carried out as follows[12]:

Step 1: Determining the target pricing of products. This kind of price setting can be based on the existing benchmark products, but the more common case is to directly set the price range of products, so that it is very convenient for the enterprises to choose a market segment that is not occupied by their existing competitors or competitive products.

Step 2: Selecting the product benchmark. A very easy-to-follow rule is to select the best-seller products in the current market as the benchmark products. The basic logic behind this choice is: those best-seller products have already stood the market tests, so their market risks will be relatively low. Moreover, the reason why this kind of product is welcomed by the market must be that its functionality and design details are very welcomed by users, making it easier to digest and capture market demands through improvement and reinforcements on the basis of its design.

Step 3: Disassembling and analyzing design details of the benchmark product. It is necessary to try every means to keep those product features that are popular in the market and achievable at a relatively low cost, and at the same time eliminate those product features that require higher realization costs in the new product design. This is what we often refer to as "purposive subtraction".

[12]It is worth nothing that the steps of product development process described here may not strictly follow the above sequence. There may be some slight changes in industrial practice. Nevertheless, the basic logic still holds.

Step 4: Selective strengthening of one or a few product functions or product features after purposive subtraction, adding some low-cost minor innovations tailored to the local demands, so as to enhance the attraction to the target market. This is "addition based on subtraction". In this regard, even these cost-effective products aimed at the low-end market are not necessarily "low-end duplicate" as the result of simple imitation or copying. Rather, it involves a lot of micro-innovations in terms of product design and the production process.

Step 5: Launching new products into the market at the fastest pace. Due to the low imitation barriers of these products, speed has become an important weapon for these enterprises to compete in the market. In some special circumstances, the imitator may outperform the imitated in product launch speed. Take the copycat mobile phones as an example, some copycat mobile phone companies occasionally attempted to predict the appearance and functional configuration of Apple's new iPhone series based on some market intelligence. They designed their envisaged versions on this basis, so as to preemptively approach low-end target customers before authentic new iPhone series could enter the market. Such market intelligence might be collected based on the analysis and projection about every new generation of iPhone from some industry experts' analysis or news reports.

The target customers of value-sensitive good-enough products are not satisfied only with relatively low price. To attract their attention, local enterprises need to combine high-performance design with attractive pricing into product design. In other words, such cost-effective customer experience cannot be generated simply from low prices. The customers have certain comprehensive requirements for product quality, performance and brand. This means that manufacturers providing such products need to face two challenges. On the basis of low-cost manufacturing, they need to have the in-house design capabilities or be able to access external design resources. At the same time, they also need to establish a brand and market image with certain reputation in the local market. Although enterprises in a price-sensitive good-enough market can have their own brands, such brands are regarded more as a product symbol that can help distinguish the enterprises from other competitors, and this symbol will not make customers be willing to pay a premium for it. Yet, in contrast, the brands in the value-sensitive good-enough market can bring certain value perceptions to the target customers. And customers are willing to pay a corresponding premium for it.

In the process of product development, there are both similarities and obvious differences between value-sensitive products and price-sensitive products. The development process of value-sensitive products is largely conducted in the following steps:

Step 1: Similar to the development process of price-sensitive products, enterprises need to set a range for market pricing.

Step 2: Setting the product benchmark. Yet, value-sensitive strategies usually do not involve setting benchmark products completely based on market popularity. First, enterprises often identify the benchmark enterprises they want to compete with, which could be leading enterprises from the Chinese home market or multinational companies from abroad. Products with excellent market performance from these benchmark enterprises are then selected to serve as the value benchmarks, based on which new products are designed and developed.

Step 3: Analyzing benchmark products and preserving as much of the product features of such products as possible. Of course, it is necessary to find a low-cost implementation method for incorporating these product features as much as possible. This can be realized with the help of some more cost-effective technologies, or through manufacturing with a lower cost.

Step 4: The "addition" to product designing, that is, introducing some market-attracting designs which take the forms of improving the performance of some specific product attributes (e.g., providing a camera function module with higher pixels in a smartphone), or introducing innovative designs according to the characteristics of localization requirements (e.g., the "dual SIM cards & dual standby" function of mobile phones).

Step 5: Good-enough marketers need to keep up with the pace of new product market launch of benchmark enterprises, so as to adapt to the changes of market trends and maintain their stable growth trajectory.

We can use Table 5.1 to summarize the essential differences between value-sensitive and price-sensitive good-enough products. It is important to point out that, unlike what is normally often believed, the product development strategy in the good-enough market is not based on simple imitation and pure replication, but requires the introduction of a large number of micro and localized innovations on the basis of low-cost manufacturing, which also constitutes a very special competitive advantage foundation of Made-in-China.

Table 5.1. Comparison of Price Sensitivity and Value Sensitivity in a Good-Enough Market

Good-Enough Market Types	Price-Sensitive	Value-Sensitive
Product selling points	Low cost+reasonable quality	High-performance design+attractive pricing
Benchmark	Best-selling products	Leading competitors
Competition focus	Competing on selected product features	Competing on as wide product features as possible
Rhythm of product improvement	As fast as possible	Keeping pace with leading benchmark companies as much as possible

A Good-Enough Market Is Different from the Bottom of a Pyramid Market

"Bottom of the Pyramid" (abbreviated as BoP) was originally proposed by C. K. Prahalad, a professor of business management at Michigan Ross School of Business, and Stuart L. Hart, a professor at Cornell University School of Management, in an article titled *The Fortune at the Bottom of the Pyramid* published in the *Strategy+Business* magazine.[13] Later, C. K. Prahalad published a book with the same title in 2004.[14] The "bottom of the pyramid" is used by these two professors to denote the huge population whose purchasing power is at the bottom of the population pyramid in the world's economies (especially in the underdeveloped countries and regions). They believe that in traditional business thinking, people at the bottom of the pyramid are excluded from the business map of multinational companies, and the focus is only on the middle class in emerging markets. This is not advisable, because it ignores the huge business opportunities contained in the market at the bottom of the pyramid. In terms of the 4 billion people at the bottom of the pyramid around the world, since their purchasing power parity is less than US$ 1,500, in order to meet the needs of these consumers, the cost of products and services must be

[13]Prahalad, C. K., and S. L. Hart (2002). The fortune at the bottom of the pyramid. *Strategy+Business* 26: 54–67.

[14]Prahalad, C. K. (2004). *The Fortune at the Bottom of the Pyramid*. Upper Saddle River, NJ: Wharton School Publishing.

greatly reduced, which will hence require changes and innovations in product design, business processes, business models and even the whole business. This view is no doubt very insightful because for the first time it brings the Western business system to realize the huge business potential of these bottom markets.

However, it should be pointed out that although in the Chinese market, the "good-enough market strategy" looks similar to the "pyramid bottom market strategy", there are critical differences between them in some aspects, especially in the underlying logic behind the business practice.

Such differences are firstly reflected in the positioning of the target market population. The market strategy adopted at the bottom of the pyramid focuses on those people who are at the bottom of the economic system in terms of their ability to pay, who can be regarded as people who are excluded because of their financial affordability. By contrast, the population targeted by the good-enough market strategy surely covers this group (the price-sensitive consumers), but moreover, they also include those who are in the middle of the market ladder in terms of payment ability (the value-sensitive consumers). Even though there are differences between price-sensitive and value-sensitive consumers in their understanding of value-for-money, yet they all share the purchase behavior patterns clearly driven by their cost-effectiveness considerations.

Differences in the understanding of consumer requirements will also lead to differences in product design focus. In applying the idea of "bottom of the pyramid" into product development practice, most Western multinational companies place more emphasis on low cost and therefore follow the principle of "reduced configuration/simplified version+low price". In contrast, the principle of a good-enough market strategy is reasonable quality plus attractive price. Therefore, in a good-enough market, although low cost is still the necessary competition basis for implementing the market strategy, the focus will be on how to increase the value perception of target users through improving the price–performance ratio instead of merely focusing on low price.

We may compare the Tata Nano, a small car model released by India's Tata Motors Group in 2008, with Haoqing, the newly launched product by Geely in August 1998. Tata Nano, with a market price of only US$ 2,500, was crowned as the cheapest car in the world, targeting the consumer group at the bottom of the market ladder. In order to achieve low cost, designers of Tata Motors adopted the approach of low configuration and simplification, effectively slashing everything from horsepower, interior configuration to safety installations. The car has no air conditioning system, no power steering, no radio, no back-view mirror on the front-passenger side, no side impact beam or bumper.[15] In the case of Haoqing, even as Geely's first car model positioned with significantly low pricing, it still gave much consideration to the bottom line of safety at the beginning of design and kept the car-mounted air conditioning system. The reason was that they believed these factors were the value points to Chinese consumers.

Moreover, in most cases, the local innovators in China's good-enough market will try to bring in some localized innovations into products even during the simplification and low-configuration of the products. These localized innovations can usually be realized at a lower cost yet still address some potential differentiated demands of the target market segment so as to make up for some value excision brought by simplified and low-configuration design, enhancing the product's attractiveness in the market.

The Shanzhai Phenomenon: The Symbiosis of Positive and Negative Factors

With the barbaric and rapid growth of China's mobile phone industry from 2003 to 2009, the copycat phenomenon has drawn a lot of attention. The Chinese *pinyin* for copycat, "*Shanzhai*", has also become a hot word, which even attracted the attention of Western media. In the January 2011 issue of the *Wired*, an internationally renowned science and technology media publication, the Chinese *pinyin* "*Shanzhai*" impressively appeared on its front page.

We can see the development speed and market scale of Shanzhai phones through some data of China's mobile phone market. In 2006, the total shipments of Chinese mobile phones were 480 million units, while the shipments of Shanzhai mobile phones were about 50 million units. In 2007, China shipped 560 million mobile phones, including about 110 million Shanzhai mobile phones (about 70 million for domestic sales with the rest for export). In 2009, the sales volume of Shanzhai mobile

---

[15] Indian Nano car was announced to be suspended in July of 2018.

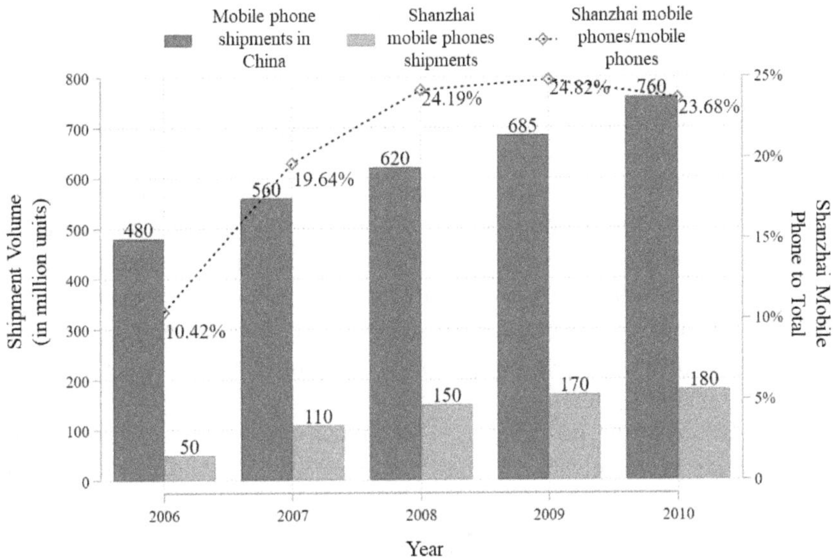

Figure 5.3. Shanzhai Mobile Phone Shipments in China, Year 2006–2010

Source: iiMedia Research.

phones reached 160 million units, an estimated 40% of which were exported (see Figure 5.3). There were even some enterprises, i.e., K-Touch and Gionee, that started with Shanzhai mobile phone manufacturers, who, after years of rapid development, improvement in product quality and transformation into regular operation, became the domestic brands with great market influence at that time.

Public views on "Shanzhai" are very diverse and sometimes contradictory to each other. In most people's eyes, "Shanzhai" is synonymous with low-end, poor-quality and knock-off products. It is criticized mainly because it involves counterfeiting some well-known brands, has poor quality, violates intellectual property rights and evades VAT payment. Needless to say, these problems did exist in the early development of China's local mobile phone industry.

However, other people may hold a view totally different from the negative impression mentioned above. They define "Shanzhai" companies as "enterprises that are not bound by traditional rules and practices but often develop innovative products or business models different from conventional ones". "Shanzhai" is viewed to represent "a novel and radical business innovation model".[16] Therefore, "it is not right and fair to simply classify all Shanzhai mobile phones as 'pirated' or 'illegal' products. No matter such products are viewed legal or illegal, imitated or innovative, they have showcased surprisingly great flexibility and tenacity".[17] It should be pointed out those who hold this view even include some Western researchers or industrial professionals. The emergence of the "Shanzhai phenomenon" in the mobile phone industry has actually catalyzed a profound change in China's mobile phone market, or in a nutshell, it has massively accelerated the mobile phone development speed of all market players, and hence gradually brought about a change in cellphone products from being durable consumer goods to fashion fast-moving consumer goods.

The initial target positioning of Shanzhai mobile phones is much in line with the price-sensitive value-for-money market. And its target customers are mainly the rural population, working population and students with relatively low ability to pay. Geographically speaking, the target consumers are more often concentrated in the markets in the third and fourth-tier cities and the rural areas. These potential consumers are not that fastidious about brand and quality. Instead, they care more about the price in selecting mobile phone products. At that time, the pricing of branded mobile phones was beyond their affordability. For a long time after 2003, the prices of mainstream branded mobile phones were above RMB 2,000, with foreign manufacturers taking a lion's share of this market. In 2005, Nokia was the leader in China's mobile phone market, occupying 27.1% of the total market share, closely followed by Motorola and Samsung, who, respectively, occupied 15.5% and 13% of the total market share of China.[18]

At that time, two important factors triggered a surging in sales of Shanzhai mobile phones. In 2005 in China, Taiwan chip manufacturer MTK (www.mediatek.com) launched the "turn-key solution" for mobile phone design, which fundamentally changed the entry barriers and

---

[16] Johnson, B. (2010). Shanzai! *Wired* UK, December 7, 2010. https://www.wired.co.uk/article/shanzai.

[17] Lee, H., M. M. Tseng, P. Siu, and D. W. Hoyt (2010). Shanzhai ("Bandit") mobile phone companies: The guerrilla warfare of product development and supply chain management. Harvard Business Review Store, March 9, 2010. http://hbr.org/product/shanzhai-bandit-mobile-phone-companies-the-guerril/an/GS75-PDF-ENG.

[18] http://zdc.zol.com.cn/25/251357.html.

product development costs of the industry. In addition, in October 2007, the Mainland abolished the 9-year-long production license system for mobile phones, offering major strong Shanzhai mobile phone manufacturers an opportunity to rise up as regular mobile phone producers, enabling them to get network entry license after submitting their products to the Ministry of Information Industry and Technology for testing. Since then, MTK has been able to achieve rapid development. In 2007, it leaped to become the world's third-largest mobile phone IC design provider, second only to Texas Instruments and Qualcomm. MTK grabbed about 14% of the world market and became the largest IC chip supplier in Chinese Mainland market with a market share of over 40%.

The core of MTK's "turnkey solution" is to integrate all required functions of mobile phones on one chip, thus providing an end-to-end mobile platform, which integrates software, hardware and operating system on a validated mobile phone chip. Such a design can greatly reduce the technical barriers that hinder enterprises with no chip technology R&D capability from entering the chip industry by allowing such enterprises to selectively customize each function module to their products' needs and use those paid integrated functions. This will drastically reduce the R&D cost of hardware manufacturers. Secondly, the development cycle of mobile phones has also been greatly shortened from 6–12 months in the past to 3–6 months or even less now, with the time for technical engineering involvement reduced to just 1 month. Therefore, the speed of market update for Shanzhai mobile phones is very fast, which can better meet the fashion and functional upgrading demands of young consumers in the low-end market.

The chip design architecture of MTK not only contributed to the modularization of product design but also profoundly impacted the modularization process of the whole industrial value chain. With such a technical architecture, Shanzhai mobile phone manufacturers can turn themselves into system integrators. They can carry out their businesses through outsourcing product design, component procurement, assembly, testing, sales and after-sales service with the help of supporting industrial chains. The entire mobile phone manufacturing industry of China achieved high degrees of modularization: (a) MTK occupies the major market share amid all solution providers; (b) Component suppliers were highly concentrated in terms of geographic locations, with a large number of SMEs specialized in making screens, casings, batteries, cameras, storage, headphones, chargers and stylus densely distributed in the Pearl River Delta region; (c) A lot of third-party design enterprises propped up in Shenzhen and Shanghai, which engage in the terminal design of Shanzhai mobile phones (mainly appearance design); (d) Wholesalers bid for different mobile phone models, and those wholesalers with high bids and big volumes finally got distribution rights; and (e) Products were distributed all over China through SME distribution agents, and with the development of the Internet, e-commerce platforms became an important distribution channel for Shanzhai mobile phones.

In this case, the production of Shanzhai mobile phones began to adopt a lean development and manufacturing mode. Often, Shanzhai mobile phone manufacturers will conduct some preliminary market surveys, and then, based on feedback from the sales channels, they test product acceptance by delivering product prototypes to the sales channels. On this basis, manufacturers finalize the functionality design of mobile phone products and select the solution provider to design the integrated solution for the concerned mobile phone. They either test the solution themselves or commission it to a third-party testing agency and then provide feedback to the solution provider for further improvements. Then, orders are placed in sales channels, and phones are assembled, manufactured, delivered and sold. This whole process is very efficient, and because of the flexibility of the whole system, it can quickly respond to fast market changes.

In addition to the consideration of product development speed, in terms of the design of mobile phone products, some micro-innovations are often introduced after analyzing market demand and benchmark products, so as to provide diversified functions, such as super-long standby, dual-card & dual-standby, loudspeakers (for noisy scenes), and even a terminal to receive analog TV signals. In other words, the whole product development mode is fast in pace, dense in parallel work, and is market driven rather than technology driven, with the purpose of greatly improving its efficiency.

From the perspective of the whole industrial value chain, we can also see innovations at the business model level. One of the cores of the Shanzhai model is the benefit-sharing model along the industrial value chain, for instance, the relationship between manufacturers and distributors. Manufacturers complete product assembly and obtain a relatively stable profit share, whereas the retailers need to buyout the mobile phone product and set the price on the premise of assuming sole responsibility for their own profits and losses. In this way, out of the motive of making profits, distributors will be more willing to give feedback about the market demand information to the manufacturers as soon as possible, and also will be more willing to allocate the channels' marketing resources to the sales of Shanzhai mobile phones. In a sense, this benefit-sharing model is much more efficient and flexible than the traditional hierarchical mobile phone distribution channel model in operation back then.

This also indicates that the connotation of "Shanzhai" is far more complex than it seems or the stereotypes in most people's mind. In reality, the "Shanzhai phenomenon" possesses both positive and negative facets. What we need to focus on is if we accept it as a phenomenon, how can we extract its positive facets and apply them to the development and innovation practice of enterprises or industries, and try our best to mitigate the possible negative impacts.

It's worthwhile to point out that China may not be the pioneer of Shanzhai-styled innovation. Historically, there was an IT company that successfully established its business success through Shanzhai-styled innovation, which is Dell, an American computer company that was founded by Mr. Michael Dell in 1984 and went public on NASDAQ in 1988. Dell behaved differently from other companies in American IT industry at that time, because it did not try to meet the market demand through advanced technology and epoch-making products, but actually catered to the unmet market needs brought about by high product pricing through their cost-effective products. The market discovered by Dell has almost all the elements of the "Shanzhai phenomenon" elaborated above — substantial unmet market needs, relatively mature and highly modularized technology, business innovation model with efficiency and cost advantages (such as the direct sales business model of Dell), and the support from a well-established industrial value chain.

Dynamic Shift in a Good-Enough Market

With many product segments in China's domestic market developing into the stage of saturated growth, enterprises in these fields will inevitably need to compete with enterprises in other competitive saturated markets if they want to grow. To a great extent, consumption upgrading will re-energize these saturated markets to become stock growth markets. In this case, enterprises need to adapt to this trend in terms of their good-enough competition strategy, and dynamically move their value-for-money position up along the market ladder. If they simply stick to their original value-for-money position, they may lose the growth opportunities. This is precisely the reason why MI's mobile phone was increasingly challenged by Huawei, OPPO and Vivo in China's domestic market. Because MI's extreme cost–performance strategy at that time did not suit those consumers who had higher requirements for brand image and product positioning. Especially in the value-sensitive good-enough market, with the general trend of upgrading consumption in China, dynamic changes occur in both demand side and supply side. If an enterprise holds a static idea about its positioning in a value-sensitive good-enough market, it will face the risk of losing its original market as time goes by. However, MI's mobile phone products can still achieve great success in the Indian market even though the positioning strategy in China's domestic market is replicated. In 2019, the market share of MI's mobile phone in India reached 29.7%. This is because the current Indian market is similar to the past Chinese market in terms of value-for-money preference of consumers, in that the major markets in India are price-sensitive value-for-money markets. According to data from Counterpoint, India's total mobile phone shipments reached 330 million units in 2018, of which that of smartphones accounted for only 44%. In the Indian market, the functional mobile phones still occupy a large part. This is very similar to the initial stages of the rise of China's price-sensitive value-for-money market.

OPPO and Vivo are just examples telling a different story. Although OPPO and Vivo achieved great success in the Chinese market, they encountered some problems in the Indian market. In the early stages of their entering the Indian market, they adopted a marketing and sales strategy similar to that adopted in China's domestic market. However, the difference between Indian market and Chinese market rendered this replication strategy invalid. In the Indian market, 78% of smartphones are priced between $159 and $200, indicating a price-sensitive value-for-money market. Until 2018, smartphones priced over $500 accounted for only 3% of the total number of smartphones in the overall market. In China's domestic market, the main models of OPPO and Vivo are mostly priced between RMB 2,500 and 3,500, indicating a more value-sensitive good-enough market. What is equally important is that when lower pricing is adopted to adapt to the enterprises' price positioning in the Indian market, it means that the sales channel distributors cannot get as attractive profits as that in the Chinese domestic market. Therefore, OPPO and Vivo had to adjust their strategies in the Indian market. For this reason, OPPO established an online brand "Realme" in the Indian market, which adopted a market strategy that is very similar to the practice of Xiaomi in the Indian market in terms of marketing, sales strategy and offline experience stores. In addition, they also re-positioned their products developed for the value-sensitive market. In September 2019, OPPO even released its Reno 2 in the Indian market. It was the first time that OPPO's flagship product appeared in China's domestic market after it was first launched in the Indian market.

Compared with the value-sensitive good-enough market, the price-sensitive good-enough market is different in the degree of dynamic change. Although both of them demonstrate dynamic changes with the progress of time — which is reflected in the upward migration of enterprises along the market ladder and the changes of corresponding value demand points, where the upward migration of value-sensitive markets will be relatively more dramatic, in that the target users will have higher requirements for product quality and performance improvement. This means that for those value-sensitive positioning enterprises, they need to be fast in capability enhancement with more focus on developing capabilities related to quality and functional performance of their products.

If we stretch our temporal horizons across time, we may find some clues about the future of China's good-enough market by observing what had happened in Japan since the 1990s. From 1992 to 2017, 8 of the 20 best-performing companies in Japan's stock market were from the consumer industries, and half of them adopted "value-for-money" strategic positioning.[19] To a certain extent, this reveals that the good-enough market will become a sustainable business growth opportunity for enterprises in the long term. With the development of China's economy and the gradual increase of Chinese people's income level, the dynamic change of the cost–performance positioning will accompany the process of consumption upgrade, generating dramatically huge market demand in this process.

[19] http://www.p5w.net/weyt/201808/t20180812_2173981.htm.

Chapter 6

China's Advantages in the Field of Complex Product Systems

What Is a "Complex Product System"?

As a well-known saying goes, a falling leaf heralds the coming of autumn. Most often, the trend is hidden in subtle trivialities.

Similarly, if we want to roughly tell the overall strength of a country's manufacturing industry, we can observe it through some "windows" — the competitiveness of a country's manufacturing industry in the global good-enough market, the country's dominant status in the global technology chain, and its degree of maturity in sophisticated product systems. These "windows" provide us opportunities to observe a country's manufacturing strength from different aspects.

The so-called "complex product system" (CoPS) mentioned here is a concept firstly proposed in the 1990s by M. Hobday, a professor of Brighton University, UK. It refers to products, systems or infrastructures with the following characteristics[1]:

(a) The product architecture is hierarchical and systematic, which requires the integration of a large number of components, modules or subsystems;
(b) Such products, systems or infrastructures involve many technical fields and require the integrative engagement of extensive expertise

[1]Hobday, M. (1998). Product complexity: Innovation and industrial organization. *Research Policy* 26(6): 689–710.

and skills, which are therefore featured with dense technology elements, expensive R&D cost and challenging technical barriers;

(c) The products and industrial organizations have salient features of modularization, and involve complex collaboration between various components suppliers;
(d) High customization degree that requires frequent in-depth interactions with users;
(e) These complex product systems are often capital-intensive during the whole process from manufacturing to application;
(f) The concerned backbone enterprises need to have high levels of system integration capability, that is, the ability to integrate product modules across organizational boundaries and technical domains.

Why can a country's competitive advantage in CoPS reflect the competitive strength of the whole country and its manufacturing sector from the macro scope? The following are the reasons, which are closely related to the aforesaid characteristics of CoPS.

CoPS plays a key role in modern industry and economic progress.[2] Some typical complex product systems include high-speed railways, large aircrafts, large air separation equipment, mobile communication equipment, etc. Specific products provided by manufacturers are also important components of industrial or economic infrastructure. Therefore, the advantages in CoPS will indirectly affect the degree of perfection of a country's industrial and economic infrastructure and its comparative efficiency advantages in global competition.

In any country that enjoys certain advantages in global competition in a specific category of CoPS, there must be local leading companies with comprehensive strength in this field. This is also an inevitable result brought about by the characteristics of CoPS. As CoPS integration providers, local leading enterprises need to have all-around strength in multiple technologies, and strong integration and control capabilities of operations and management. The existence of these system integrators will effectively facilitate the gradual formation of a relatively robust industrial

[2]Hobday, M., and H. Rush (1999). Technology management in complex product systems (CoPS): Ten questions answered. *International Journal of Technology Management* 17(6): 615–638.

system and a strong ecosystem in the local market.[3] And this will further enhance the country's global competitiveness on CoPS. In that sense, in CoPS's ecosystems, there is an interactive and interdependent relationship between system integrators and other players within the industrial ecosystems.

It's believed that the more dominant Chinese companies are in system products and brand influences, the stronger the Chinese upstream domestic component industry will be. Among the top 100 global auto parts suppliers released by *Automotive News* in 2017, there were only five Chinese companies. By contrast, with strong advantage in global market competition, China's household electrical appliance industry realized the localization of almost all the related auto parts. This finding is generally reasonable. But we still need to figure out the causal relationships. Literately, whether the strong local auto parts industry passes on its advantages to the local leading product integrator, or whether it is precisely the strong local leading product integrator that nurtures the strong and robust auto parts industry. In addition, this also reflects a fact that the automobile industry is far more sophisticated than the household electrical appliance industry in terms of the technical diversity, components quantity and supply chain coordination complexity. This strong CoPS attribute enables the local leading enterprises with product and brand advantages to play a vital role in uplifting the entire local industrial value chain.

Another key reason why CoPS can be used as the touchstone of a country's comprehensive strength in a certain field is that it can test whether the whole industrial chain has any weakness in technology, supply chain, capability set and management system. Those weak points and bottlenecks will impede the whole industrial system from establishing global competitiveness in quality, cost and flexibility. This is different from the case in the conventional product field, where core enterprises can easily overcome the aforesaid shortcomings through vertical integration, or buffer these bottlenecks through market positioning and

[3] This does not mean that these complex product system integration manufacturers will not carry out configuration of the global layout and integrate and utilize the globally distributed capabilities and resources; if purely out of considering transportation costs (related to geographical distance), coordination costs (affected by institutional and cultural distance), and timely response efficiency, etc., at least a certain number and scale of industrial chain segments will be deployed in the local market.

advantages in their internal capabilities. However, the CoPS in the modern industry is highly dependent on the collaboration across organizational boundaries, which requires the whole industrial system to simultaneously improve its competitiveness and technical level.

Technology Decomposition Under Complex Product System

In the preceding chapters, we discussed learning by decomposition in the general sense, illustrating its critical role in reducing the difficulty of technology assimilation, improving the efficiency of technology learning and solving the cold start problem of technology absorption. Then, if applied to CoPS, how will learning by decomposition be accomplished?

A common mechanism of learning by decomposition is like this. The Chinese enterprises start with the production subcontractors of the foreign leading enterprises, dock into their global production networks, and gradually increase their degree of participation. This illustrates a direct path for Chinese enterprises to learn and master international advanced technology and management experience, which are necessary for them to enter high-value-added markets.[4] There are two typical ways to gradually increase the depth of participation in the production network: supplying components and modules and even final products to core enterprises. Take Hangyang, a company established in 1950, as an example. The company has now developed into the largest air separation equipment manufacturer in the world, with its domestic market share in air separation equipment remaining above 50%, and its output and sales ranking first in the world. In 1993, Hangyang participated in the joint project bidding and system design of Stewart-Warner Company. With the support and guidance of its foreign partners, Hangyang mastered the sophisticated heat exchange calculation methods of key design technologies for ethylene cold box, and improved its manufacturing capabilities through formal and informal learning in production process, design process and quality control system, etc.

At the same time, in their initial stages of capability development, the enterprises only need to focus their attention on a specific module and unit

[4]Child, J., and S. B. Rodrigues (2005). The internationalization of Chinese firms: A case for theoretical extension? *Management and Organization Review* 1(3): 381–410.

technology in complex product systems, so the technical complexity in learning is greatly reduced. However, it should be pointed out that in the process of learning by decomposition, internal R&D of the enterprises still plays an indispensable role, because internal capabilities can help enterprises improve their efficiency in learning by decomposition, and also increase their chance of continuing to embed and participate in the global production network of leading foreign enterprises. Otherwise, as the system integrators, foreign companies will flush out those suppliers who fail to keep up with the improvement of system efficiency in the process of continuous optimization of global production network. In some cases, some Chinese enterprises will even adopt the strategy of parallel development of technology in order to maximize their learning efficiency in technology decomposition. For example, Hangyang has cooperatively designed and produced 8 sets of molecular sieve absorption devices for Linde's large-scale air separation plant system and has independently designed and produced several sets of molecular sieve purification and absorption devices for some Chinese local customers. Due to some differences in equipment requirements between local Chinese customers and foreign customers, enterprises need to tailor their design to the local demands, doing this greatly uplifted the design capability and production experience of Hangyang. After that, Hangyang completed design improvement of its molecular sieve absorption device in an innovative way, which supports plug-and-play and makes field validation test unnecessary.

Universities and research institutions, as intermediaries of technology decomposition, can greatly mitigate the potential negative impact of technology gap within the technology ladder. In the past, the economic and technological catch-up experiences of many newly industrialized countries have shown that universities and independent research institutions are important participants in supporting the technological catch-up process.[5] Universities, scientific research institutions and industrial enterprises form a complementary relationship in reverse engineering and secondary innovation. They divide their roles, where universities and research institutions carry out applied research and initial development activities that require complex knowledge base, while enterprises use their own manufacturing experience and market understanding to complete subsequent downstream development activities.

[5]Mazzoleni, R., and R. R. Nelson (2007). Public research institutions and economic catch-up. *Research Policy* 36: 1512–1528.

The history of China's development of large-scale ethylene cold box technology can be traced back to 1971. Back then, China's Ministry of Machine Building, Ministry of Chemical Industry and the Ministry of Petroleum Industry launched a joint technology development project that aimed to develop alternatives to imported large-scale chemical processing systems. The project was participated by industry, university and research institutions, who conducted joint reverse engineering of equipment imported by Shanghai Jinshan Chemical Fiber Factory. The decomposition of the ethylene cold box, one of the key parts of the imported equipment, was commissioned to Hangyang and another institute based in Lanzhou. They were, respectively, responsible for the decomposition of manufacturing and design details. The joint decomposition project failed to yield the expected result due to lack of knowledge about the core technology, the heat exchange calculation method of the plate-fin heat exchanger. Nevertheless, Hangyang accumulated a lot of system design experience from partnering with the research institutes. In 1993, through cooperating with Zhejiang University, Hangyang jointly developed a software package for thermodynamic properties calculation based on a computer-aided design system imported from Stewart-Warner from the United States.

Adaptive adjustment or localized improvement to imported technology is also one of the forms of learning by decomposition. As local enterprises often have a deeper understanding of local market demands and specific production conditions than foreign companies, they can make corresponding product and production process improvements to address the practical issues closely related to the industrial environment encountered by local customers. Moreover, local manufacturers have strong motivation to realize localized supply of raw materials and parts as much as possible. As an example in this case, in 1981, Hangyang imported manufacturing technology of medium-low pressure turbine compressor from Toshiba in the form of technical drawings. On this basis, Hangyang made adaptive improvements to its engineering details of production and technical parameters of products. Naturally, in the design and manufacturing process of complex product systems, due to the technical complexity of the system and the frequent interaction among system participants, unforeseen changes can happen and lead to failed design and manufacturing. However, even so, the failed technology decomposition may still have its positive value as it can help enterprises acquire some specific technical know-how, and to identify, understand and acquire useful external knowledge in the process of their future technology development. In 2001, Hangyang suffered from a failure when it tried to develop ethylene cold box for a large petrochemical company in China. The reason is that the plate-fin heat exchanger of this product demonstrated high working pressure, and since it was quite large in size, almost two times larger than the products Hangyang designed for the metallurgical industry before, it was impossible for Hangyang to refer to any existing experience. After digging into the root cause of the failure, Hangyang found out that the malfunction was due to the incompatibility of the structural design for thermodynamic properties and the structural design of the manufacturing process. In the end, Hangyang successfully mastered the key technical know-how of designing and manufacturing large-scale product systems with complex structures and established general design principles for such product systems.

Another way of learning by decomposition is to gradually expand from peripheral subsystems to core subsystems, or to gradually upgrade from low-end products to high-end products with higher technical complexity. Such gradual expansion can lead to the split of the large technology gap between externally accessible technologies and internally possessed capabilities on the technical ladder into several smaller ones, therefore reducing the difficulty of technical decomposition. In terms of its practice in the ethylene cold box products field, Hangyang started to provide the spare parts of plate-fin heat exchangers to Yangzi Petrochemical since 1992. Between the years 1993 and 2001, it supplied 10 sets of spare parts for 6 domestic petrochemical enterprises and exported 10 sets of heat exchangers to the United States and Canada. As a component supplier, Hangyang has accumulated increasingly rich experience and expertise in designing and manufacturing. Therefore, it decided to venture into the field of system manufacturing. In 1999, with the support of the import substitution policy, Hangyang obtained the opportunity to supply ethylene cold boxes for the ethylene production line expansion project of Yanshan Petrochemical. In 2001, the first complete set of equipment produced by Hangyang successfully passed the on-site full-load test.

The last typical form of learning by decomposition is inter-temporal learning on technical modules or subsystems. Inter-temporal learning means that the technical knowledge and expertise acquired from outside are first stored as the knowledge base of an enterprise, and then reused and improved in its later technical development stages. In 1981, Hangyang introduced the medium-pressure turbine compressor technology from Hitachi, Japan. In 1982, it cooperated with Hitachi to develop and produce compressors for large-scale air separation systems. In 1987, that is, five years later, it signed a technology transfer agreement with German Demag on the introduction of the design and manufacturing technology of medium- and high-pressure turbine compressors of the latter. The knowledge and improvement experience absorbed and accumulated during technology importation provided a critical launchpad for Hangyang to develop new compressor technologies for the 6th and 7th generation air separation units since 1996.

Technology Recombination Under the Complex Product System

In the previous chapters, it is mentioned that learning by recombination can bring enterprises more knowledge creation opportunities and thus help them to establish unique advantages and break the resource constraints that late-comer enterprises generally encounter. It is worth mentioning that learning by decomposition and learning by recombination often interact with and influence each other. They could even concurrently occur in a specific capability building practice. For the sake of better illustration, we regard decomposition and recombination as two independent processes, with the former paying more attention to knowledge acquisition and assimilation whereas the latter focuses on knowledge utilization and creation.

Some previous studies and observations show that most Chinese enterprises focus on the local Chinese market, as their products were first sold in the domestic market but not in overseas markets at least in the initial stages of their development. Between the 1980s and the early 1990s, the Chinese central government emphasized double targets, both in import and export policies, namely, it implemented import substitution policies to develop domestic enterprises' capabilities and export promotion policies to promote economic growth. It's generally believed that the export substitution policy is beneficial to domestic enterprises (especially the state-owned enterprises). However, in some capital and technology-intensive industries, such a policy did not bring the expected advantages to state-owned enterprises. The petrochemical industry is a typical example. Before 1996, all 20 ethylene production lines were imported from abroad. Similarly, in the late 1980s, almost all large domestic steel enterprises were more inclined to import production equipment from abroad. With China's transition from planned economy to market economy, those large state-owned enterprises had to face increasingly fierce competition in the market from private enterprises and foreign-invested enterprises, making cost control increasingly important for them. Between 1991 and 1995, with the deepening of the reform of the economic system, China's central government formulated new investment policies, demanding that all capital investments in engineering projects should come from the domestic enterprises themselves. At that time, the Ministry of Chemical Industry and Sinopec encouraged enterprises to procure Chinese localized equipment in their recombination and expansion projects. So, in 1999, the import substitution was achieved for ethylene production line for the first time. This fully proved that following the changing market demand and varying market competition has an important influence on technology decomposition and recombination. For example, before 2004, as for Hangyang, its sales revenue in the metallurgical industry roughly accounted for 60–80% of its total revenues. Since 2005, with the adjustment of China's energy strategy and the increased market demand for chemical products, the proportion of Hangyang's revenue from selling large air separation equipment in the petrochemical industry continuously increased, accounting for over 50% of its total revenue.

Integrating external knowledge and technology from multiple sources is often the starting point for Chinese enterprises to realize learning by recombination. In the process of technology catch-up, latecomer enterprises have plenty of opportunities to acquire advanced technology and management experience from foreign enterprises through various forms and channels such as observation, imitation, reverse engineering, technology spillover, labor mobility and technology importation. Through competition and imitation among local counterparts and the interaction between upstream and downstream enterprises of the industrial value chain, the knowledge acquisition channels of late-comer enterprises are diversified. For example, in the process of catching-up, Hyundai from R. O. Korea acquired technologies from 26 enterprises from five countries. Such multi-source technology acquisition played an important role in Hyundai Motor's establishment of its own internal capabilities.[6] As latecomer enterprises may be exposed to various similar technologies,

[6]Kim, L. (1998). Crisis construction and organisational learning: Capability building in catching-up at Hyundai Motor. *Organization Science* 9(4): 506–521.

they gradually establish the ability to identify and select their alternative technologies. Furthermore, they can even acquire the ability to develop technologies that are more adapted to local conditions on the basis of similar existing technologies. In algorithm setting for system design on flow and structure, Hangyang has brought in from different foreign partners software packages targeting different technologies. By assimilating, improving and integrating these software technologies, Hangyang has established its own relatively complete product development and design capabilities. Moreover, when acquiring and integrating multi-source technologies, late-comer enterprises can dynamically adjust their resource allocation strategies between internal development and external acquisition based on the changes of market and technology, so as to make better use of opportunities in the environment and reduce the cost of capacity building. In 1991, when Hangyang was preparing to start the development of manufacturing equipment for plate-fin heat exchangers, it learned that Stewart-Warner was planning to sell the design and production technology of plate-fin heat exchangers and large-size vacuum brazing furnaces. In 1992, a technology transfer agreement was reached. Hangyang integrated the imported technology with the technology it had developed internally, greatly improving its design and manufacturing expertise on plate-fin heat exchanger.

Most of the learning by recombination in manufacturing industry requires coordinated development of product design and manufacturing process. Though improvement in manufacturing process is not as highly visible as product improvement to outsiders, the improvement of production processes often occurs more frequently and has very significant impact on product cost and quality. The coordinated development of product technology and manufacturing process is mainly reflected in three aspects. First, due to the close coupling of product design, production processes and the asynchronous development status between them, there are frequent interactions between product innovation and process innovation. When Hangyang cooperated with Linde in designing and producing the 6th generation large-scale air separation plant system, a great deal of effort was made to solve the technical bottleneck in the manufacturing process. Second, the evolution of the technological architecture of the manufacturing process is not only affected by technical factors (for example, product design), it's also influenced by economic factors, especially the adoption cost of new production processes. Some technologies that require large-scale initial investment will only be economically feasible when the production scale exceeds a certain threshold. Finally, in the process of upgrading product design, enterprises need to simultaneously adapt or localize the production process using the imported technology, such as developing some special equipment and testing tools to improve the manufacturing feasibility and efficiency, and formulating some technical standards for new production processes.

Learning by recombination may also involve the integration of internal and external technical processes and standards. The technological learning of late-comer enterprises is not limited to product design and production technology but also involves the assimilation of technical norms and specifications, such as quality control system, design rules and production technical standards. In the process of technology introduction, foreign partners can be very helpful as they can assist enterprises better comprehend the matching of technology and market, provide technical guidance on localization, and even directly dispatch engineers and technicians on sites to help solve technical problems. Messer Group, for example, is a leading industrial gas service provider in Europe that was founded in 1898 and has more than 100 years of experience in industrial gas operations and service provision. In 2002, Messer sold out its air separation system manufacturing business and transformed into a sole industrial gas service provider. Hangyang reached a strategic cooperation agreement with Messer, supplying equipment to Messer in the global market. In 2006, the two companies set up a joint venture. Messer was responsible for providing product specifications, technical standards and technical guidance, dispatching senior engineers to review product design drawings, supervising the manufacturing process of some key components, and providing improvement suggestions and guidance for Hangyang's internal design and production standards. Hangyang fused its internal technical standards to the technical standards introduced from Messer. At the beginning, Hangyang only adopted the technical standards provided by Messer in cooperation projects with Messer, whereas in other projects it still applied its own technical standards. Upon completing every cooperation project with Messer, it would organize a cross-functional internal seminar to summarize and exchange the experience and knowledge gained during the project implementation process. At the same time, a special task force was set up to technically summarize these learning outcomes and integrate the company's own internal technical standards with those provided by Messer. Finally, new technical standards were formed and applied to all projects.

It is also a form of learning by recombination to create new knowledge by reconfiguring and utilizing the internal technical expertise of enterprises. This requires enterprises to recombine their existing technical expertise to capture new products or business opportunities in new markets. Technical expertise recombination means the cross-temporal integration of activated technology and knowledge accumulated in the past with the existing knowledge, or the integration of complementary cross-domain knowledge obtained from various businesses or external sources. When Hangyang was developing ethylene cold box, except technology used for plate-fin heat exchanger, other complementary technologies had already been acquired during the development process of its air separation technology. However, the working conditions of plate-fin heat exchangers used in metallurgical industry are quite different from those in petrochemical industry. The plate-fin heat exchangers in petrochemical industry have to accommodate much higher structural and working pressure. Then, Hangyang replicated its design and manufacturing experience of plate-fin heat exchanger from an existing field in a new application field, and combined it with its newly developed technologies, based on which it successfully upgraded its design and manufacturing technology of plate-fin heat exchanger.

Resorting to External Competence to Accelerate Decomposition and Recombination

Previous studies that probe into the catching-up by the late-comer enterprises mostly focus on how to improve the internal capabilities of late-comer enterprises, highlighting the role of R&D and investment in internal technology of enterprises. We cannot deny the necessity of internal capability development. However, just focusing on the building of internal capability is not conducive for late-comer enterprises to adopt more effective strategies in their catching-up. And it is not quite in accordance with the rapid catching-up experience of the rising Chinese manufacturing industry. The rapid catching-up of Chinese manufacturing industry is not only the result of domestic enterprises' internal efforts in building and upgrading their capabilities but also the result of their effective use of externally accessible capabilities via learning by decomposition and learning by recombination.

As stated in a Chinese classical book by Xunzi, one of the greatest Confucian philosophers, "Those who make use of carriages or horses may not be any faster than anyone else, and yet they are able to travel a thousand miles. Those who make use of boats may not know how to swim, and yet they can go across rivers". Being good at using external resources and capabilities is also a kind of competence that late-comers need to develop.

In the process of China's technological catching-up, we can find three common forms of harnessing externally accessible capabilities for decomposition and recombination.

Government-driven industry–academic joint technology decomposition is an effective institutional strategy. As the technologies, components and modules involved in the technical decomposition of complex product systems are highly diverse, they need to be collectively handled by participants from various fields including industry and academia. This also brings about the issue about establishing an effective coordination mechanism among multiple participants. In the 1980s, almost all industrial sectors in China were initially plagued by poor design and manufacturing capabilities. Back then, Chinese enterprises mostly adopted the method of importing complete equipment sets to compensate for their weak capability in the manufacturing of complex product systems. In 1983, the Chinese government decided to promote the localization of key industrial technologies and equipment. Since then, the "joint technology decomposition" model was frequently used in the field of complex product systems. This model actually has its prototype in the era of the planned economy, during which it was called "joint technical research". However, compared with the previous model, there is an important change in the technology decomposition model, namely, it incorporates the market mechanism into its specific organization and operation. To some extent, we can even describe it as a hybrid of market mechanism (the so-called "invisible hand") and government intervention mechanism (the so-called "visible hand"). The government's role in joint technology decomposition is not a replacement of the market mechanism, but it serves as a complementary mechanism to ensure efficient coordination among participants of joint technology decomposition. The relevant government departments or their agents are responsible for supervising the progress of the joint technology decomposition projects and coordinating the allocation of resources for such projects. They would decide the amount of financial support based on the importance and complexity of the technologies involved. In some cases, government departments will help the participants in technical decomposition find test customers, that is, to launch some "demonstration projects", so as to enable the enterprises to complete their technical decomposition and secondary development in real industrial application scenarios. Such a practice has not only been seen in China but also in Japan and R. O. Korea during their catching-up with industrial technology developments. For instance, if we compare the development project of HJD-04 digital exchange with that of TDX telephone exchange technology and CDMA wireless system in R. O. Korea, we will find that the practices are more similar than different to each other in nature.

Engaging domestic users with high technology maturity in learning by recombination can greatly improve the efficiency of technology recombination. These users can be invited to test use of new equipment, new systems and new processes. The reason why they are willing to try new technological improvements is that they have strong motivation to improve their production efficiency and product quality. For complex product system manufacturers, the test scenarios offered by test users can be used to validate the functionality and reliability of new products. These pilot users usually have clear requirements for addressing some of their specific adaptive improvement needs or solving their long-standing problems. In addition, users will give timely and detailed feedback information during the testing process, which can help technology providers get a clearer direction in product and technology improvement. It is especially the case when those users have purchased advanced foreign system equipment before, for their rich experience in product use will provide more valuable feedback for product improvement. Sometimes, those users can even use their own experience in problem diagnosis to directly help local manufacturers effectively identify and solve the technical problems of their new equipment.

Using knowledge redundancy to reinforce enterprises' abilities in learning by decomposition and learning by recombination is also a strategy that can be adopted. Technology recombination is resource-consuming for enterprises, where redundant knowledge acquisition is deemed to be problematic and therefore to be eliminated. However, in the process of learning by decomposition, cost control and reduction should not be regarded as the most important considerations. On the contrary, some enterprises with successful experience of technology catching-up will intentionally allow knowledge redundancy in technology decomposition and recombination. For example, Hangyang launches a large number of cooperative R&D projects with universities every year, covering aspects ranging from applied research, basic research, design, testing and tool development. In fact, Hangyang was capable of completing some development projects all by itself. Interestingly, it took a parallel development strategy, namely, launching cooperative R&D projects with universities and research institutions while founding an internal team to conduct R&D on selected topics. This approach can make enterprises more effective in assimilating and transferring external technological development results, greatly expanding their knowledge base and scope of internal expertise, which will further enhance their competence in learning by decomposition and learning by recombination.

China's Catch-Up Experience in the Field of Complex Product Systems

The previous sections elaborated on the learning by decomposition and learning by recombination mechanisms of complex product systems at the enterprise level. These mechanisms are of universal significance to the technological catching-up of late-comer enterprises. China has some successful experiences in catching-up in the field of complex product systems from industrial and national levels.

The development of high-speed rail technology, especially in the initial stages, involved multi-source technology decomposition. In 2004, China Railway Rolling Stock Corporation (CRRC) cooperated with German Siemens, Canadian Bombardier, French Alstom and Japanese Kawasaki Heavy Industries in the form of technology introduction to jointly produce 200 km/h Electric Multiple Units (EMUs). Such a practice, on the one hand, enhances China's bargaining power in technology importation. On the other hand, it promotes China's ability in learning by recombination on high-speed rail technology. On this basis, driven by related government agents, China strengthened and utilized its industrial ecosystems featuring industry–academia cooperation, starting to deconstruct the complex product systems such as high-speed rail. On February 26, 2008, China Ministry of Science and Technology and the former Ministry of Railways signed a joint action plan to jointly develop CRH380 with a design speed of 380 km/h. This joint plan involved CRRC, over 500 supporting enterprises, dozens of universities and national key laboratories, which are strongest in related fields. Over 10,000 researchers and scientists participated in the project. By 2011, China had developed and manufactured 17 types of EMUs, which is represented by "Harmony" CRH380 that is based on 4 technical platforms, and constructed the Beijing–Tianjin Intercity High-Speed Railway, Wuhan–Guangzhou High-Speed Railway and Beijing–Shanghai High-Speed Railway. When technology decomposition is completed to a certain extent, technology recombination becomes a natural result. In June 2012, in order to integrate different technology platforms, and also to master the key core technologies, under the leadership of China Railway Corporation, China Academy of Railway Sciences Co., Ltd took the lead and pooled the strength of CRRC Group and related enterprises in initiating the design and development of the 350 km/h China Standard EMU. By the autumn of 2014, the design scheme of the "China Standard EMU Development Project" had been finalized, adopting 254 important standards, 84% of which were Chinese standards. The overall design and key technologies were all independently developed. In June 2017, China Standard EMU was successfully put into mass production and officially named "Fuxing", with all technical indicators reaching the world-class level. As of January 2019, the mileage of China's high-speed rail reached 29,000 km, accounting for over 2/3 of the total mileage of high-speed rail in the world. China has gradually developed into the only country in the world with a complete network of high-speed railway systems.[7] It should be specially noted that China's huge domestic market potential has played an important role in promoting the rapid adoption, improvement and massive commercial application of high-speed rail technology. High-speed rail systems involve not only the application of complex system technologies but also complex management of commercial operations. This makes it difficult for high-speed rail technology to gain development opportunities purely based on market mechanism before the maturity of its technology and management level reach a certain degree.[8] However, the commercial operations of

[7] http://baijiahao.baidu.com/s?id=1641619412752131753.

[8] *The Economist* in the year of 2020 raised a very intriguing question, namely, why China's automobile industry has not replicated its successful catching-up experience in conventional internal combustion engine car industry (see "Poles apart China, America and the planet's biggest break-up", Technology Quarterly | Technology in China, *The Economist*, January 4, 2020). It should be pointed out that from the successful development experience of China's high-speed rail technology, the technical complexity, the accumulation of technology and the substantial investment required for technical development cannot

high-speed rail should never aim at short-term financial returns. From a longer-term perspective, the large-scale application of high-speed rail technology in China will greatly change the whole country, as it will greatly improve the transportation efficiency and significantly promotes the efficient cross-regional mobility of people, thus strengthening the connectivity of Chinese cities and ultimately fueling the development of the Chinese economy.

During the development of COMAC C919, China's first domestically produced single-aisle passenger jet, salient features of industrial-ecosystem-based learning by decomposition and the learning by recombination by system integrators can be identified. Developed by Commercial Aircraft Corporation of China Ltd (COMAC) in 2008, C919 large aircraft is China's first trunk liner civil aircraft with independent intellectual property rights complying with the latest international airworthiness standards. In the development process of C919, the development strategy of "Designed by China, integrated system, global tendered and phased in localization" was adopted, resolving over 100 core technologies including integrated design of aircraft engine. Once again, the joint technology decomposition mode was conducted in the development process of the

explain this well as the long-term resources and time investment necessitated by the technical complexity and technical iteration of high-speed rail technology will at least be higher than that in terms of the automobile technology. There are some important differences in terms of this: First, the number of competitors of China in the development of its high-speed rail technology is relatively limited, with only a handful of participants clustered together, making it easier to adopt the government-led ecosystem-based learning by deconstruction. By contrast, there are a lot of system integration participants in China's automobile industry. Because of the dispersion of resources, the aforesaid model of learning by deconstruction was difficult to be implemented. Secondly, the product volume of the automobile industry is far greater than that of the high-speed rail, which means that catching-up in terms of core automobile components manufacturing not only needs to be based on product technical design, but also requires the establishment of a very strong systematic manufacturing capability, especially that in maintaining the stable quality in mass manufacturing, which usually takes a long enough time to gradually acquire and accumulate, which is often a strong advantage of those global giants in the automobile industry. At the same time, on the demand side, the automobile industry is more affected by market-based mechanisms, so it is difficult for the government to stimulate enough market demand for local participants during the early cold start of catching-up. This is also an important reason why the Chinese government will turn to support the electric vehicle industry in overtaking in corners.

C919 large aircraft in China, with the participation of 22 provinces, over 200 enterprises, 36 universities and hundreds of thousands of industrial professionals.[9] At the same time, based on the independently patented design, COMAC systematically integrated subsystems of various complex product systems of United States companies such as Parker Hannifin (the fuel system and flight control system), Eaton (the fuel and hydraulic transmission system), Honeywell (the landing gear system and starter), Hamilton Sundstrand (the electrical power system) and GE (the flight control system). Its fuselage is jointly manufactured by Chengdu Aircraft Industry (Group) Co., Ltd (the nose), Hongdu Aviation (the front fuselage, middle and rear fuselage), Shenyang Aircraft Industry Group (the rear fuselage and vertical tail), AVIC Harbin Aircraft Industry Group (the wing body fairing and front main hatch), Xi'an Aircraft Industry (Group) Co., Ltd (the middle fuselage, middle wing, slat and flap 2) and other domestic aircraft manufacturers. On May 5, 2017, the C919 test flight was successfully completed.[10]

In the field of new energy vehicles, China also launched its ambitious plans. The field of electric vehicles provides China's automobile manufacturing industry a chance to overtake in corners. In the field of traditional automobile manufacturing, high requirement in technology accumulation makes it almost impossible for late-comers to challenge those industry leaders. Late-comer enterprises face multiple disadvantages in brand, technology, scale and cost. In terms of electric vehicles, due to the change in power unit, the backbone automobile technology shifted from fuel engine technology to battery technology. Moreover, the mechanical complexity of electric cars is much lower than that of traditional fuel-engine cars. According to a teardown analysis of the consulting firm UBS, the electric motor of Chevrolet Bolt is composed of only 24 moving parts, whereas the internal combustion engine of Volkswagen

[9]Baidu Baike, C919. https://baike.baidu.com/item/C919/2400615?fr=aladdin.

[10]To a certain extent, the early civil aircraft technology development attempts of China, such as the trial development of Yun-10 Aircraft in the 1970s (see Figure 6.1), and the development of ARJ21 regional jet started in 2002 and completed in 2015, can be regarded as early attempts of learning by deconstruction and learning by reconstruction, which provided experience in talent training and future development for the subsequent technical development of C919. *Source*: The story of COMAC, August 15, 2018. https://www.jiemian.com/article/2391002.html.

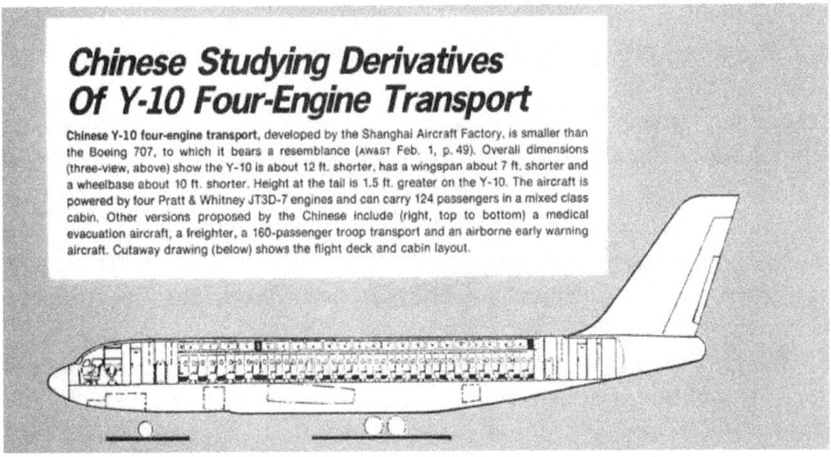

Figure 6.1. Yun-10 Aircraft: Early Efforts of Civil Aircraft Technology Development in China

Source: https://www.jiemian.com/article/2391002.html.

Golf consists of 149 moving parts.[11] However, as a new type of complex product system, electric vehicles need to face the competition of the existing systems, namely traditional fuel engine vehicles, which sets a higher threshold for quality, performance and cost–performance for substantial market penetration of electric vehicles. In this case, it will be very time-consuming to complete the technology shift purely through market mechanism. This is why China has issued a series of industry promoting policies, including giving subsidies, to accelerate the commercialization pace and market acceptance of electric vehicles. However, while allowing government policies to play a role, to avoid the inefficient resources allocation and problems brought about by the excessive influx of enterprises that lack substantial impetus for technological development into the market, the Chinese government has been continuously fine-tuning the subsidy policy in recent years, aiming to catalyze this technology shift process by ushering in market competition. In this process, along with the

[11]Dahl, J. (2018). Why China's electric-car industry is leaving Detroit, Japan, and Germany in the dust. *MIT Technology Review*, December 17, 2018. https://www.technologyreview.com/s/612566/why-chinas-electric-car-industry-is-leaving-detroit-japan-and-germany-in-the-dust/.

development of autonomous driving and Internet of Things (IoT) technology, a new technology recombination opportunity is brought about for the development of new energy vehicle technology on the basis of its original development track, namely, autonomous driving technology is integrated with electric vehicle technology, so as to use China's huge local market scale to stimulate the market demand. Therefore, in the past five years, a large number of start-up companies have propped out in related fields and formed a growing industrial ecosystem in China. This will bring China a very favorable development opportunity and a promising future in the field of smart vehicles.

Seeking technology recombination opportunities based on market needs is another effective strategy adopted by Chinese manufacturing enterprises in many product fields. Market needs that are taken as the starting point of technology recombination can be those unmet needs that have not yet been addressed by the existing products and technologies, or those excluded by the existing market because of the price or capacity restraint. These potential demand opportunities can be readily captured through price–performance strategies. For example, in the process of the long-term evolution (LTE) of mobile communication technology, we can see the long-term coexistence of 2G/3G/4G multi-standards in networks provided by various operators. Global commercial LTE network operators need to operate hybrid networks with multiple standards and multiple frequency bands. Under this circumstance, SingleRAN rose as a timely solution. In 2008, Huawei took the lead in launching the SingleRAN solution, helping operators realize multi-standard converged deployment at the whole wireless access network level from equipment convergence, site convergence to operation and maintenance convergence under different standards. It can help customers to continuously lower the operational and maintenance costs, reduce the difficulty of network construction, and improve network performance and maximize network output value. When the market demand changes, operators can adjust the types of radio frequency modules according to the customer needs, and then flexibly change their service capacity. Secondly, through the modularized and standardized design of radio frequency units, multiple frequency bands using the same standard radio frequency modules are realized, which greatly reduces the machine size compared with the traditional designs, and saves the machine room and sky space needed for equipment installation. Furthermore, the same frequency band can support smooth evolution of multi-module networks, that is, multiple systems can be realized under one frequency band relying on software configuration, without the need to add new hardware completely. After that, in 2018, Huawei released the 5G era-oriented SingleRAN Pro based on its continuous innovation. Such reconstructive innovation based on unmet market demands not only created value for customers but also brought more market expansion opportunities for domestic enterprises themselves.

Generally speaking, for complex product systems, the effectiveness of their technology catching-up usually depends highly on the compounded outcome of many factors, particularly the core performance improvement, the perfection of industrial ecosystem and the time window for catching-up. During a long time in their technological development, if the late-comer enterprises cannot quickly raise the performance of their core technologies to a threshold within a relatively short time window, they will probably lose the opportunity for subsequent catching-up. Take the development trajectory of Loongson[12] for example. Loongson adopted the strategy of independently compiling its CPU source code, and tried to establish a stand-alone ecosystem outside the Intel system and the ARM system. In 2001, Loongson team began to develop Loongson CPU in the Institute of Computing Technology, Chinese Academy of Sciences, and in 2010, Loongson ICT Technology Co., Ltd was established, which began to develop chip products and technologies leveraging market mechanism. In terms of its design principle, Loongson followed the principle of improving the general processing capacity first before enhancing the dedicated processing capacity. It decided to firstly improve the performance of a single core and then consider increasing the number of cores, and to enhance its design capacity first and then resort to advanced technologies. As for the technical level, Loongson learned from Intel's unified system architecture to achieve cross-platform compatibility of operating system, learned the unified application interface technology of Google and Microsoft to achieve cross-platform compatibility of APP, and learned from Apple to sort out and optimize the system (especially the graphics system) centered on user experience, so as to realize the compatibility of operating system with different main boards and upgraded binary CPU, and the overall outperformance of the system compared with foreign competitive products even when each local part is inferior to that of the

---

[12]Loongson's Godson series CPU is a general-purpose microprocessor designed by the Institute of Computing Technology, China Academy of Sciences, which adopts self-developed LoongISA command system and is compatible with MIPS command set.

foreign counterparts. In addition, in terms of chip product technology, it is difficult to achieve the goal of establishing an independent and controllable new system different from the existing technology system without the support of a relatively complete software and hardware ecosystem. It is precisely because of Loongson's continuous trial and error, its efforts to improve the chip performance to catch up with the mainstream CPU technology in the market, and the technical development strategy adopted in its system design, as well as the government's industrial policy support and the gradual formation of the industrial value chain consisting of nearly 1,000 enterprises that Loongson finally established a relatively complete independent and controllable industrial ecosystem.

Chapter 7

The Rise of Internet Companies in China

What Is Behind the Rise of Chinese Internet Companies?

Since this book focuses on the rise of China's manufacturing industry, you may wonder why we discuss the rise of Chinese Internet companies here. This is largely based on two reasons. On the one hand, the rise of Chinese Internet companies, in fact, did play a positive role on the demand side in boosting the rise of the Chinese manufacturing industry. As mentioned in previous chapters, the huge potential market demand is of vital importance for the development of China's manufacturing industry. However, whether such potential market demand can actually drive the development of a manufacturing industry will depend on the extent to which these demand potentials are fully released. In this regard, since China's official access to the Internet in 1994, the rise of Chinese Internet companies, especially the Internet platform providers, has greatly triggered the demand released in the Chinese market, thus promoting the rapid development of "Made-in-China". On the other hand, the development of Internet companies has also played a role in empowering industrial development on the supply side, promoting the improvement of the efficiency of the manufacturing industry as a whole. Especially after 2018, with more and more attention paid to the industrial Internet, the Internet has accelerated the trend of "Made-in-China".

As the rise of China's manufacturing industry, the rise of Chinese Internet companies has been equally impressive. According to the 2018 Internet Trends Report by Mary Meeker, who is known as "Queen of the Internet", 9 out of the 20 largest Internet companies in the world by market capitalization are from China, while the remaining 11 are all from the United States.[1] On February 26, 2019, App Annie, the leading global provider of mobile data and analytics, announced the top 52 publishers of 2018 (selecting the revenue leaders in the top two app stores Google Play and App Store). 11 Chinese companies were included in the list, among which Tencent had been ranking first for three consecutive years, while NetEase ranked second in year 2018.

What is more, in some Internet-based areas, the business models of Chinese Internet companies were replicated by European and American companies. In an article titled "Bike War: How Silicon Valley is Copying Chinese Innovation", according to a report by TechCrunch, Spin, an American startup, had attempted to replicate the models of Chinese bike-sharing brands OFO and Mobike in the US market.

If we could travel back to the late 1990s, and imagine ourselves viewing the current technology for the first time, we would be amazed at the achievements made by Chinese Internet companies nowadays, because those "super apps" that Chinese consumers are very accustomed to every day such as WeChat, Alipay, Tmall and Taobao were not born until 1998. When Taobao first appeared in 2003, most Chinese consumers still had doubts about online shopping. Before 2011, we had not sensed the influence of WeChat on our information communication based on social networking. However, these applications have now penetrated into the daily lives of the Chinese urban residents and become an indispensable part, changing the way of life and work.

The arrival of every new era will force people to cast away something they are accustomed to, nudging them to gradually learn to embrace changes which will later become what they are used to.

Then, what factors have fueled the rapid rise of Chinese Internet companies?

---

[1] https://www.sohu.com/a/233843839_808479.

Advantages of Network Effect Brought by Market Size

If the huge domestic market has brought great growth opportunities to China's manufacturing industry, it has also endowed China's Internet firms with the fundamental conditions for rapid growth. However, market size operates differently in these two industries.

As we know, the network effect is of great significance to the growth of companies under the context of the Internet. Especially for those Internet companies providing platforms, the network effect on the demand side means that the value that the users can obtain from specific products and services will depend on the number of its users. The larger the user base or the number of network nodes, the higher the value that can be obtained by a single user or network node. For example, due to China's huge population base, many platform enterprises acquired users at relatively low cost in their early stages of development. Moreover, even in their initial stage where they could only concentrate their limited resources on segmented user needs, they still obtained their needed initial scale from the potential huge user base. For instance, when Tencent QQ first competed against Microsoft's MSN, it tried to shun away from the advantageous business of MSN that targets business scenarios by focusing on non-business scenarios with younger generations as their target group, from which they still acquired a huge user base.

By now, the development of China's Internet has yielded an amazingly huge size of user base. As of December 2021, the number of netizens in China reached 1.032 billion, up by 42.96 million YoY. The Internet penetration rate reached 73.0%. The number of mobile Internet users in China reached 1.029 billion, up by 43.73 million YoY over the end of 2020. The proportion of Internet users using mobile phones to access the Internet reached 99.7%. The number of online shoppers in China reached 842 million, up by 59.69 million YoY over the end of 2020, accounting for 81.6% of the total netizens.[2] This huge scale of Internet users provides a natural advantage for Internet companies to capitalize on the network effect.

To a great extent, the development of China's Internet industry is highly dependent on the well-established Internet infrastructure. The huge

---

[2]See the 49th Statistical Reports on Internet Development in China released by China Internet Network Information Center (CNNIC) on February 25, 2022.

potential user base and the massive demand to be realized have attracted substantial investments in the Internet industry. In turn, the large size of China's Internet user base has effectively reduced the cost of building and maintaining Internet infrastructure. As for the residents of China's first- and second-tier cities, they may even find it handier and cheaper to use Internet apps in China than when they travel in Europe or US.

The Shift of Market Ladder and the Realization of Opportunities

In the development of China's Internet industry, the market ladder has been an essential booster. From both static and dynamic perspectives, we can analyze how the market ladder functioned to spur the dynamic competition and rapid development of Chinese Internet enterprises.

The concurrence of huge market scale and market gradient makes it easier for start-ups in the field of consumer Internet to identify their own sweet-spot market positioning and target customer groups. On the one hand, such a market with above features can help start-ups in the consumer Internet field avoid head-to-head competition with the existing enterprises. On the other hand, it also helps them focus on specific market segments to provide products and services with differentiated advantages so as to quickly obtain revenue streams to support their further development. For example, we would often cite the case of differentiated positionings by Kuaishou and Tik Tok. Although they are often lined out for comparison, they adopt different user positioning strategies. Tik Tok mainly targets young people in first- and second-tier cities, while Kuaishou targets the so-called "small-town youngsters" in third- and fourth-tier cities or even below. Due to the differences in target groups, they also share different values. While Tik Tok mainly tries to enrich the consumption experience of content consumers, Kuaishou values diversification, popularization and decentralization in terms of content producers, attempting to meet the needs of users for "recording and sharing".

The dynamic changes in the market ladder also bring Chinese Internet companies more opportunities to expand their scale and scope. With the upward shifting along the market ladder, the business of Internet companies can capitalize on the released incremental demand to continuously break the glass ceiling of their growth in both revenue and coverage area. An example in this case is Taobao.com, a subsidiary of Alibaba. It has been expanding its scale in e-commerce transactions and seller base in recent years, penetrating even into the rural areas where e-commerce was underdeveloped. According to the China Taobao Village Development Report (2014–2018), Taobao Villages[3] are highly densely distributed in the eastern coastal areas at large, showing a trend of exponential growth in certain regions. In 2018, the number of Taobao villages in Zhejiang Province accounted for 36.6% of the national total, while that in the 6 coastal provinces (Zhejiang, Jiangsu, Fujian, Guangdong, Shandong and Hebei) accounted for over 95% of the national total. Such a geographical distribution can be attributed to the nature of e-commerce. In essence, e-commerce is very much dependent on infrastructures in three aspects: information flow, capital flow and logistics, while most often infrastructure in these three aspects is more developed in economically developed areas than in underdeveloped areas. This distribution pattern also shows that even nowadays when e-commerce is highly developed, due to people's lower acceptance of e-commerce and the insufficient infrastructure in economically underdeveloped areas, a large gap across regions may still exist, but the gap will gradually be narrowed with the passage of time.

Specific Advantage in Internet Cost of China

As mentioned in the preceding section, among the 20 Internet companies with the largest market value in the world in 2018, 11 are from the United States and the rest from China. This brings about two interesting topics for discussion — why is Europe absent from this ranking? And why is China doing so well? We need to compare the United States, Europe and China together, so as to better explore the possible answers to these questions.

In China, Internet companies need to complete trial and error in a very short period of time to improve their products, services and business models so as to adapt to the uncertainty and dynamics of China's market environment. Therefore, the cost of trial and error will directly affect the speed of evolution and possibility of success of these Internet companies. It must be admitted that in China the supervision of data and privacy in the Internet industry has been relatively loose. The first reason for this is that

[3]Taobao Village refers to a village where the number of active online stores reaches more than 10% of local households and the annual transaction volume of e-commerce surpasses RMB 10 million.

the Internet develops at a very fast speed and the government lacks governance experience. The second reason is that the government hopes to boost innovations in this field with loose supervision. Although costs may inevitably arise as the result of loose supervision, which is especially true for individual consumers who may bear certain risks and costs due to data and privacy issues, the rapid development of the Internet industry has indeed brought many conveniences and benefits to life and work of the Chinese people. In fact, to a certain extent, the development of the Internet industry in the United States has also benefited from relatively loose supervision of data and privacy. By contrast, Europe adopts much stricter regulations in this aspect. The most typical reflection is the General Data Protection Regulation (GDPR) stipulated by the European Union. This Regulation was approved by the European Parliament on April 14, 2016, and was officially enforced on May 25, 2018. According to the regulations, the maximum fine for law-violating enterprises can reach as much as €20 million or 4% of their global turnover, whichever is higher.

The relatively low trial and error cost is also a result of the high tolerance of Chinese consumers, who have gained excellent user experiences due to the development of Internet applications and therefore tend to be more tolerant when the Internet governance environment is being improved.

If we compare the development of China's Internet industry with that of the United States, one factor that needs to be highlighted is the drastically different innovation directions in the development of the Internet industry in the two countries. We know that e-commerce has played an important role in the application of the Internet for a long time. And the development of e-commerce is highly dependent on the development of information, payment and logistics infrastructure. In the United States, thanks to its longer development period, high-level economic development and relatively sound economic infrastructure, Internet companies can very much focus their attention and resources on their own areas of expertise in the process of their development after the start-up stage. Besides, they can provide products and services efficiently with the help of relatively better external information, payment and logistics infrastructure and third-party services. However, it's a different story in China. In the early development of China's Internet industry, the infrastructure of information, logistics and payment was quite under-developed. Therefore, many Internet companies had no established infrastructure to rely on to seek development opportunities but had to set their own development direction toward developing better infrastructure. In other words, the entrepreneurial and innovative opportunities privileged to many Chinese Internet companies were precisely due to such imperfection or bottlenecks of the external environment. For example, a very important reason why Alibaba decided to set up Alipay was the distrust between sellers and buyers in e-commerce transactions back then.

Another difference between US and China is the cost of logistics services. The development of American e-commerce depends on the logistics cost advantages of the 2B (to business) side, that is, the efficiency advantages of large-scale logistics. However, the picture in China is very different. In China, as the development of e-commerce occurs mainly in the domain of consumer Internet, with the continuous growth of e-commerce scale, the cost of 2C (to consumer) side logistics (the end logistics) has been continuously declining. This is, on the one hand, related to the large population base and density of many cities in China, while on the other hand, it is related to the relatively low labor cost of logistics distribution in China. According to a research report of Guotai Junan Securities, taking Yunda Express as an example, between 2013 and 2017, its business volume surged from 1.1 billion pieces to 4.7 billion pieces, the per piece transportation cost via trunk line decreased from 1.93 yuan to 0.94 yuan, and the per piece transshipment cost via trunk line decreased from 0.69 yuan to 0.39 yuan. Perhaps China's 2B side logistics is far less efficient compared with that in developed countries, but China is building an advantage that even developed countries can hardly replicate in end side logistics.

The varying conditions between countries can also explain some intriguing questions related to e-commerce development status. For example, we usually believe that products that are more standardized and less demanding in user experience are more suitable to be sold via the Internet. That's why Jeff Bezos decided to sell books and music records when he founded Amazon. According to this business logic, clothing products, especially women's garments, seem to be not suitable for e-commerce. However, judging from the development of e-commerce platforms such as Taobao and Tmall, the sales of clothing category, especially women's garments, has grown rapidly in the e-commerce domain. This is largely due to the incomplete retail infrastructure of China and the low efficiency of the supply chain back then. Therefore, the online channel has obvious advantages in efficiency and cost compared with the existing offline channels in China. Especially in some cases, online channels can be used to efficiently digest the inventory of offline stores. In contrast, in the US, compared with the existing conventional channels, the emerging e-commerce channels do not enjoy such significant advantages in price and efficiency.[4]

"Waterloo" of Western Internet Companies in the Chinese Market

In terms of degree of success, compared with other industries (such as electronics, machinery and other manufacturing industries), the operations of European and American Internet companies have not been quite successful in China. Over the years, we have witnessed many American Internet companies gradually make strategic retreats from the Chinese market. For example, as one of the world's largest Internet companies by market value, Amazon maintained its dominant position in the US e-commerce market with a market share of 47% in 2018. However, Amazon announced that it would stop providing seller services to third-party sellers on Amazon China website on July 18, 2019. We should know that Amazon once had a glorious history in the Chinese market — since it acquired Joyo.com from Lei Jun at a price of US$ 75 million, it continuously expanded and occupied a lion's share in China's B2C e-commerce market, and its market share in China once reached 15.4% in 2008.

Some opinions attribute this type of failure to differences in government regulation and cultures. However, Professor Feng Li from Cass Business School, City College, University of London, pointed out that might not be exactly the case — "Because in some other countries, such as Indonesia, Thailand and Saudi Arabia, despite strict government regulation and cultural differences, Internet companies from Europe and America can still achieve great successes, just like Google, which still holds 90% market share in search engine segment in these areas".[5] Even if one attributes the failure to the lack of in-depth understanding of the Chinese market by foreign enterprises, it is hard to convince all of us, because these

[4]Chinese E-commerce PK American Ecommerce: What is the difference? Cifnews. July 9th, 2014. https://m.cifnews.com/Article/9981?ivk_sa=1024320u.

[5]Li, F. (2018). Why have all western internet firms (WIFs) failed in China? A phenomenon-based study. Academy of Management Discoveries. DOI: 10.5465/amd.2017.0102.

Internet companies from the United States can simply hire senior managers from China to handle business in the Chinese market. Therefore, there must be some more critical systematic factors that lead to this problem.

China's Internet industry is featured with rapid development and turbulent changes. On the one hand, the demand of Chinese consumers changes very quickly. Take the download and installation of apps and use of data on smartphones as an example. Chinese netizens are more open to new apps, but they are equally fast in abandoning apps as well. The per capita number of app installations in China is as high as 38, but at the same time, up to 43% of apps in China are only used once, while the proportion in the United States is only 25%. Only 15% of apps in China are used more than 10 times, compared with 37% in the United States. On the other hand, a study conducted by Boston Consulting Group (BCG)[6] in 2017 pointed out that the rapid and changeable characteristics of China's Internet market are also closely related to the leaping growth opportunities in the Chinese market. In developed countries, the progress brought about by the development of the Internet has been gradual, usually in a way that an industry gradually upgrades on the basis of the original sound foundation. However, when China entered the Internet era, the market maturity of some industries was low, and many market demands could not be met by existing industries, with a lot of market gaps existing. In this case, the application of the Internet has addressed many hard-to-break industrial pain points, so those enterprises that cut into the market with the help of the power of the Internet have the opportunity to grow by leaps and bounds, and even surge to become the dominant players in some areas.

This means that in order to be successful in the Chinese market, either foreign or local enterprises need to conduct highly efficient decision-making and operations so as to better adapt to this fast-changing market. For foreign Internet companies, it is necessary to realize more localized operations and decision-making authorization, otherwise their whole system will not be able to keep up with the pace of local competitors.

Unfortunately, however, from the actual tactics of many foreign Internet giants who have met their "Waterloo" in the Chinese market, they seemed to have come short of doing it the right way. To a great extent, this is because these Internet giants from the Western world were shackled by

[6]Boston Consulting Group (BCG), a global management consulting company, is the world's leading business strategy consulting organization with customers in all industries and regions.

their past victories, often over-stubbornly insisted on simple replication of their previous successful experience at home in the Chinese market, overlooking the unneglectable impact from the different market situations beneath the surface. For example, since Amazon entered the Chinese market, it has been trying to replicate its path to success in its local market, insisting on allowing no e-commerce advertising across the globe and focusing its major resources and attention on logistics and warehousing. Doug Gurr, president of Amazon China, admitted in an interview that it took Amazon a long time to realize that copying the American Amazon model in China does not work.[7] Kaifu Li, the former president of Google Greater China, also mentioned that "American companies ... they won't invest resources (in the Chinese market). They have no patience. They also do not allow the Chinese teams enough freedom, which makes them unable to match up with China's top entrepreneurs (also the world's top entrepreneurs)".

This idea of simple replication also reveals the lack of profound knowledge of these foreign Internet companies about the differences of the Chinese market. The appointment of their Chinese business management team also somehow reflects this. For example, since the departure of a Chinese President Hanhua Wang in 2012, Amazon China has experienced three presidents in seven years, among whom Steve Frazier, Doug Gurr and Zhang Wenxiang (a Chinese American) are non-Chinese. Kaifu Li also mentioned in 2018 that "Google China is a branch company of the world's most famous Internet company with great brand advantages. However, as for adapting product forms to Chinese users, its bond with the headquarters in the Silicon Valley has become a stumbling block".[8] Google's headquarters in the Silicon Valley was considered to have no knowledge of search habits of Chinese users and to be not willing to make any necessary strategic adjustments to realize the localization of products.

For many Internet applications and services, the special behavior patterns of Chinese users require highly localized product development strategies. As indicated in an example cited by Kaifu Li illustrating the huge differences in habits of using search engines between Chinese and American netizens, Americans regard search engines as the yellow page, who only check the top-ranking results and will leave the page after

---

[7]https://m.jiemian.com/article/3055423.html.

[8]https://m.jiemian.com/article/3059554.html.

clicking one of the links, while the Chinese netizens are accustomed to taking search engines as "shopping malls", who check through all results one after another displayed on the page and wish to keep the main page of the search engine after one of the links is clicked. Yizhi Dong, a lawyer who has specialized in the Internet field, mentioned a story about Kaifu Li in one article titled "Waterloo of Western Internet Giants in China. Why?" Mr. Li once said: "The fundamentally different user attitudes and usage habits should push those Western Internet giants to adapt their products based on the specific needs of Chinese users. That is why I suggested Google to allow an exception by following Baidu, adapting its products to realize one new window by one click. However, the change of core products requires a lengthy review process at the company headquarters, as the added code "branch" will increase the difficulty of maintenance". "The headquarters has always rejected to have too many code 'branches'. Whenever we wanted to develop a new feature, we have to fight a tough battle against the headquarters, which only worked to slow our pace and exhaust ourselves. Many employees of Google China are tired of fighting with the headquarters and left in frustration".[9] Ming Li, Yahua Tang *et al.* also mentioned in an article titled "15 frustrating years: Waterloo of Amazon e-commerce business in China" that "I spent several months before finally getting my proposal of product adaption approved. During this period, Baidu has won more users with its more localized product". "It may take us one or more months to develop a program, for any modification on the apps of Amazon does not involve just a single country but the globe".[10] Amazon China is also faced with similar problems, where any tiny change may have to go through a lengthy organizational decision-making process.

Coincidentally, a similar situation occurred in the "do-or-die battle in the Chinese market" between Tencent QQ and Microsoft MSN. For MSN, the offline message feature invented by QQ was not difficult to realize technically. In fact, MSN's China R&D team already proposed this in as early as 2005. Yet, the proposal failed to make it even on the meeting table of MSN headquarters. It was not until 2008 that the Microsoft headquarters approved the development of this feature. However, the best time window had already been missed.[11]

[9] https://m.jiemian.com/article/3059554.html.

[10] https://m.jiemian.com/article/3055423.html.

[11] https://zhuanlan.zhihu.com/p/31465260.

Of course, the attempt to adopt a universally applicable management mode to manage the business operation in China has its objective reasons. From the perspective of strategic intention, to Internet giants from Europe and America, their home market is the focus of their business operation and competition. By contrast, their entrance into the Chinese market was very much an exploratory investment. Their business in the Chinese market may only account for a minor part of their global business deployments which was not big enough to attract the attention of the company's senior management team. Whereas to Chinese Internet companies, for a long time, the Chinese market means everything to them, perhaps being even their only market territory. This huge difference in strategic attention allocation between senior management teams will surely result in different strategic choices and behavior patterns. Internet companies from Europe and US are more inclined to continue using their established management systems and processes to manage and control their business operations and decision-making in their global market (including the Chinese market), because such practices are thought to be able to help them reduce operating costs and control potential risks in such a "highly uncertain" market as that in China.

More importantly, similar to the situation in the manufacturing industry, the competition in China's Internet industry is very fierce. This is certainly due to the fact that the highly segmented nature of the Chinese market itself has produced a lot of entrepreneurial space. However, more importantly, with the development of China's economy, a torrent of capital (including foreign capital and domestic capital) flooded into the field of venture investment, causing many Internet companies to adopt similar growth strategies, namely, the strategy of "cash-burning" (i.e., to directly use the invested money in buying traffic and user scale) with an attempt to break the critical mass and survive in this fierce business competition. The competition was much more intense than that in the United States where the Internet economy is highly developed, at least in many niche segments. Due to the uncertainty and the importance of speed for survival and competition, Chinese Internet companies lay heavy emphasis on the rapidly iterating micro-innovation mode. These micro-innovations include localized innovations according to the characteristics of the demands in the Chinese market and their process innovations centered around the value chain business.

Under such circumstances, the foreign Internet companies venturing into the Chinese market seemed to be not well-prepared for such fierce competition. This is also why Professor Feng Li, Chair of Information

Management of Cass Business School of City University of London, cited the inability to cope with extreme competition as one of the important reasons for the foreign Internet companies to fail in the Chinese market. In order to cope with this kind of competition, the Chinese enterprises adopt an innovation strategy as described in a famous saying, "crossing the river by feeling the stone", namely, to realize rapid improvement through continuous trial and error, because the dynamic changes of market demand and competition make it difficult to manage and deal with it completely with formalized rules and systems.

The Rise of Industrial Internet

The mutually reinforcing consumer Internet and industrial Internet means a lot to the future of China's Internet industry. If the greatest development opportunities of China's Internet industry from 1994 to 2018 have been driven by the consumer Internet, then the next wave of development will center around the industrial Internet. This is because with the development of consumer. Internet in recent years, except in a few vertical niche markets, a relatively solid and less changeable market structure has come into being, with the growth largely depending on stock growth rather than incremental growth. At the same time, the potential of consumer Internet in propelling efficiency improvement through market competition has been relatively fully unleashed. The further improvement of efficiency has been increasingly dependent on the development of industrial Internet and its empowerment to consumer Internet.

In 2018, the concept of industrial Internet attracted enormous public attention. One of the most important reasons is the fact that Tencent and Alibaba, the two most important giants in China's Internet business landscape, expressed great interest in the development trend of industrial Internet from the perspective of company strategies. As an example, Huateng Ma clearly stated in an open letter published on October 31, 2018, that "The first half of the battle of mobile Internet is coming to an end, and the prelude of the second half is slowly unfolding. The main battlefield of the Internet industry is shifting from the consumer Internet to the industrial Internet".

To a great extent, the great attention on the industrial Internet is the result of the following background factors. First of all, with the intensifying competition and the gradual forming of the Internet industry landscape, people started to see the waning of dividends of consumer Internet. Typically, in either online or offline scenario, the cost of customer acquisition or traffic is becoming more expensive. In some cases, the cost of conducting business online is even higher than doing it offline. That's why we can see that some enterprises (even those with strong Internet genes), after their traffic attracting front shifted from offline to online, are now returning to the offline or online and offline mode.

Secondly, the development of consumer Internet both brings opportunities and raises requirements for the development of the industrial Internet. If enterprises want to identify, capture, match and meet users' needs efficiently, they will need the empowerment from the industrial Internet so as to eliminate the bottleneck within value chains and further improve the efficiency in value creation. For example, in November 2017, ONECONNECT, an associate of China's Ping An Insurance, launched Gamma, a one-stand intelligent loan solution platform orienting small- and medium-sized financial institutions, which is built with intelligent channel management system, intelligent input configuration platform, anti-fraud platform, intelligent micro expression facial review auxiliary system, customized scoring card, intelligent risk control engine and Gamma intelligent loan all-in-one transaction terminal. As the core link in the intelligent loan solution, Gamma intelligent micro expression facial review auxiliary system, based on micro expression recognition technology, captures the subtle expression changes of customers in real time through remote video to alert fraud risks based on intelligent judgments. In this regard, the development and gradual integration of technologies such as IoT, AI and big data supported the development of the industrial Internet and opened up more diversified opportunities for the possibility of value chain combinations and innovation directions.

In the development of the industrial Internet, "data" are of fundamental importance. On the one hand, data are the underlying factors affecting the quality of decision-making. On the other hand, information asymmetry and data opacity in industrial value chain have always been important constraints to efficiency improvement of industrial value chains. However, a common misunderstanding in the past has been that many enterprises held a view of pure technology determinism, and wishfully believed that as long as they invested in these data technologies, they could solve the existing low-efficiency problems. Such views ignored two important facts. First of all, in theory, data technology could bring more diversified data to enterprises. However, the increase of amount of data does not necessarily promise good results. If the data cannot be interpreted to output tangible practical significance, they will fail to help enterprises improve the operational and decision-making efficiency. Therefore, when constructing a digitized system, the priority is to determine what kind of data enterprises need to solve the bottlenecks and problems that constrain their efficiency improvement, and also what ability they would need to interpret the significance of these data from the perspectives of technology and management. In addition, with data acquiring increasing importance, the distribution and sharing of data in the industrial value chain may change the distribution of controlling powers among participants in the value chain or ecosystem. This will cause some gaming behaviors in data generation and sharing, and even make data transparency amid participants completely achievable. However, due to asymmetric distribution of benefits, such data assets are not efficiently utilized, as in many cases, it is difficult to interpret the fragmented data, or too often the efficiency of data interpretation cannot keep up with the pace of industrial development. Therefore, only by integrating these fragmented data assets into an integral piece can we assist all participants of the industrial value chain in better providing high-quality services to their end users via eliminating those efficiency bottlenecks, and ultimately co-sharing the value increment created.

Chapter 8

Multinational Corporations: Role Change from "Teacher" to "Peer"

Challenge Launched by "Students" to "Teachers"

For many years, Western multinational companies have been enjoying enormous advantages in the Chinese market and thereby achieved huge successes. This is certainly because they have well-established advantages in branding, capital, management experience, core technology, etc. that the Chinese local enterprises could hardly compare with in the early stages of their development. Besides, because these multinational companies all operate globally, they can effectively integrate resources across the globe and flexibly adjust their market strategies and resource allocation according to the changes in market demands across countries. In a sense, they can couple their own capital and technological advantages with the huge market potential and low-cost manufacturing of the Chinese market, so as to compensate for their lack of in-depth understanding of the Chinese market in the early stages of their entry into China.

The product development strategy of Western multinational companies in the Chinese market has been called a "glocal" strategy. The word "glocal" is coined by combining the two English words global and local into a new one. It's used to indicate that enterprises operating internationally need to demonstrate global thinking and behavior as well as target the local market contexts.

More often, the glocal strategies of Western multinational companies could come in three forms.

The first is to develop localized products targeting the Chinese market, which are usually sold only in the Chinese market. The purpose of the strategy is to leverage the existing advantages of multinational companies in branding and technology, and translate such advantages through capturing the demands in the Chinese market. This strategy has been largely effective in the early stages of China's market operations. Yet, the gradual upward migration of local enterprises along the catch-up ladder bring certain challenges to the Chinese enterprises. Multinational companies need to build certain low-cost manufacturing capabilities, and to be more agile in product development and operation decisions. Otherwise, their existing market advantages will be easily removed by local competitors. In addition, when this strategy is adopted, the connection between business operations in the Chinese market and that in the global market is relatively weak, which is not conducive to the synergistic effect brought about by global resources in the long run.

Second, developing and designing products adopting a globally unified standard, and then putting them into the Chinese market directly or after some minor changes. We have to admit that this strategy is conducive to taking full advantage of reduced cost brought by economies of scale, and can harness the absolute advantages of corporate image and brand to cultivate and capture the market when the Chinese market is relatively immature. However, with the development of the Chinese market, some challenges may arise. For example, there may be some localized specific needs in the Chinese market, which cannot be fully met by globally unified product design. In addition, Chinese enterprises adopting cost-effective competition strategy will offer products with reasonable quality and attractive price that constitute a low-cost substitute for multinational products and services.

Third, to develop products in China, and then graft or integrate such products into the global market. In this case, an important prerequisite is that the China subsidiaries have acquired relatively mature product R&D capabilities, and are capable of developing products that meet the global technical standards. With the increasing efficiency of Chinese local enterprises in improving their capabilities, Western multinational companies are often concerned about possible knowledge leakage.

Particularly, as Chinese local enterprises gradually establish their own resources and competence base, their advantage in their deep understanding of the Chinese market will gradually become obvious. Coupled with their advantage in flexibility, Chinese enterprises began to move upward on the market ladder in the local market and inevitably ran into the direct competition with foreign multinational companies. In fact, in many fields, Chinese enterprises have risen beyond the pure-sense imitators or followers, whose strength is even strong enough to erode and shake the once unchallenged dominant position of multinational companies in the Chinese market. As reported in the *Financial Times*, Paul Polman, CEO of Unilever, mentioned that they are faced with more and more challenges from the fast-growing local companies — "Most of our competitors in the emerging markets are regional enterprises".[1] According to a survey, 73% of the executives of large multinational companies claim that in emerging markets, local companies are more competitive than multinational competitors.[2]

Household appliances market may be one of the most challenging market areas for multinational companies from Europe and America, whether it's the color TV sets market, air conditioners market, or microwave ovens market, which was even true in the 1990s, when the Chinese local enterprises were just regarded as low-cost competitors, who did not compose a real threat in the targeted market segments of multinational companies. Nowadays, the multinational companies have to fight a tough competition against Chinese enterprises in the global market and even have to sell off some of their household appliances business to the Chinese competitors. For example, Haier, which started to produce refrigerators in 1984, has become a most famous household appliance brand in China and occupies 8.3% of the global market as one of the largest refrigerator manufacturers in the global market. Although the data of Haier's global market share does not seem that dominant, it is already a very outstanding market performance given such a highly fragmented world market of refrigerators.

Consequentially, multinational companies need to complete two interrelated tasks in the Chinese market: how to effectively compete with local competitors and at the same time efficiently tap into the growing opportunities of emerging economies.

---

[1]Daneshkhu, S. (2014). Stiffest competition from local business, says Unilever chief. *Financial Times*, July 30, 2014, p. 1.

[2]Chin, V., and D. C. Michael (2014). 2014 BCG local dynamos: How companies in emerging markets are winning at home. The Boston Consulting Group, July 10, 2014, p. 6.

Glocalization of Multinational Corporations: Experience from Philips

Philips's involvement in the Chinese market can be dated back to the 1920s. In 1985, Philips established its first joint venture in China, Philips Beijing Co., Ltd., which officially made the first step of "In China, for China". In the next 30 years, Philips successfully synchronized its corporate development to the rapid growth of China's economy. In order to better integrate into the Chinese market, Philips relocated its regional headquarters from Hong Kong to Shanghai in 1996. Three years later, Philips (China) Investment Co., Ltd. was founded. In 2010, Philips elevated the status of the China market as another "home market" besides the Netherlands.

China's market is changing rapidly, and consumers' needs become more and more diversified. Closer to the market, faster in R&D and better in efficiency are the goals of Philips's R&D reform in China. The success of "GoPure Car Air Purifier" R&D project exemplified the R&D system transformation of Philips. With the maturing of the conventional automotive lighting technology such as LED, Xenon and other technologies, the market begins to become saturated. On the one hand, Philips needs to find new business growth points in automotive lighting. On the other hand, it needs to expand the automotive after-sales market from the existing car lamp segment. Therefore, Philips has newly established the Mobile Business Unit, which is affiliated to the Automotive Lighting Business Division. According to the tradition of Philips's R&D system, most product R&D is a "closed door" work by the Philips Research, which was informed of product need by a business department. The decisions about the product were made by Philips Research instead of by the market department or business department. If there is any feedback on customer's demands, it is usually first sent to the relevant development department of Philips, and then the development department contacts Philips Research for product R&D or improvement. In this process, Philips Research is somewhat isolated from the market. Because Philips researchers are only responsible for R&D, and are seldom connected with the market, they are less sensitive to market demand or product pricing. It is often the case that the new technology developed is either difficult to produce or too expensive to be implemented. The newly established Mobile Business Unit hopes that their first project will be successful. Therefore, in order to speed up the R&D progress, it was decided from the very beginning that the marketing department and sales department, which are closer to the market, would join in the meeting summoned in the Philips Research. Therefore, market research and technical feasibility analysis are conducted along with R&D work. The "Car Air Purifier" was decided to be the first new product of the Mobile Business Unit, with the project named "GoPure". Compared with Xenon lamps, which experienced an over-10-years-long research, the "Car Air Purifier" project took less than 2 years to complete the whole process ranging from proposal making, project establishment to the market launch. Moreover, through the innovation of purification materials, the purification performance is two times better than that of similar products. Nowadays, an "end to end" process is pushing the "Car Air Purifier" to the market. And such a process has been widely adopted inside Philips.

The project of "Car Air Purifier" does not only mean a successful transformation of the R&D process, but also an attempt in product development and market promotion. The idea of this project started from the attempt to respond to China's air pollution issue, which has been the focus of attention in recent years. If an air purifier is installed inside the car, it can purify the air and reduce the pollution caused by the interior decoration of the car. Nevertheless, after the successful product development in the Chinese market, this product can also be sold to other countries outside China. Air pollution also exists in many big cities in Asia. So car-air purifiers can be directly extended to these markets. In the European market, air quality issue may not be as serious as that in China. However, in Europe pollen allergy is quite a common issue, which even induces asthma in severe cases. Therefore, Philips Research started from the consideration of "how to prevent pollen allergy" and found that if the filter of a vehicle purifier is slightly modified, it can be used to filter pollen and responds to the needs of consumers in the European market.

In addition to air purification, food safety has become a key research direction of Philips since 2009. "Soy milk maker" products, which were originally developed for the Chinese market, were promoted into the European market after some modification. Basically, the idea of soy milk maker originated from the Chinese market and was put forward by some business groups after referencing the supporting data from GFK, a German consumer research company. It is not a tough decision to make as the soy milk maker market had been existing in China for 7 or 8 years by then. It's such a huge market that even if Philips could only grab a few percentage points of market share, the sales generated thereby will be enormous. Related quantitative research shows that for soy milk makers, consumers are more concerned about reducing soybean dregs, easy cleaning and good taste. Philips has also conducted product development based on such market needs.

After its launching in the China market, the product entered the European market in a new form and was sold as a soup maker in this new market. Europeans don't have the habit of drinking soy milk, but they love drinking thick soup. Researchers in Philips noticed that soy milk maker can heat up beans and water while chopping them, which are the two basic functions needed for a soup maker. The soy milk products of Philips happen to have both functions. At the same time, many surveys have found that about 25% of Chinese users will directly put beans into the machine (without soaking them in water for 8 h in advance). This will give high requirements on the power of the motor, which needs to match with the power required for processing a large amount of raw materials such as radish and potatoes. Therefore, Philips sent soy milk maker back to Europe and hired soup experts to customize localized recipes for it.

In order to make the best soup, corresponding improvements need to be made in the heating curve and cutting process. Because the product was originally designed for making soy milk, not for making soup, this brought challenges to the manufacturing process. One obvious difference is that making soy milk would require strict time-control to inhibit the activity of some stomachache-causing enzymes. However, this is not much needed in making soup, though it can be easily adjusted through modifying the software. Another challenge is to ensure that the products originally developed in China can also meet European standards, such as being BPA-free, and can at the same time work normally under slightly higher voltage levels. After the product was launched in the European market, consumers were quite satisfied with the soup maker products. In addition, the newly launched machines were also very easy to clean. However, Philips also received feedback from customers complaining about the small capacity of the machine. The capacity of 1 L to 1.1 L is big enough for making soy milk at home. However, when making soup, people tend to make more soup and store it in a pot at low temperature to be served one to two days later. Before that, people used to break the raw materials with a manual blender, put them in a pot and heat it on fire. Based on the feedback, Philips made some product adjustments. At present, their soup makers are being sold in France, Holland, Belgium, Germany, Argentina and Turkey.

Another similar example is the noodle maker products. With the development of China's economy, China's middle class has been rising in their numbers and affordability. Their cooking habits are quite different from those of Westerners. Based on this, Philips launched a survey called "New Value Space", focusing on discovering new products and new ideas that are not available in the market at present but would be highly appreciated by customers or that can address consumers' unmet needs. The issues consumers are concerned with have become the anchor of Philips's voyage for their new product development. Philips found that Chinese people eat noodles a lot and very frequently. And Chinese consumers want to have a household electrical equipment to make home-making noodles less difficult than it is now. Philips Kitchen Appliance seized this opportunity and made the business plan and sales forecast of noodle makers. After evaluation, this plan was given a higher priority, and then the domestic household electrical appliance research and development department developed a noodle maker which was greatly welcomed by Chinese consumers. The products were planned to be sold online over a period of two weeks, but were sold out within just a few days. A full control of the noodle ingredients by customers is a great advantage of the homemade noodles compared with the ready noodles sold in the market. In other words, it means greater food safety for customers. Another advantage is the versatility of the machine. After adding flour, water or egg juice, it can make noodles with different shapes and widths within 15 min. The third advantage is that the produced noodles are very fresh. They are made with good quality flour, clean water and fresh eggs, which are therefore not easy to spoil.

Similar to their soy milk makers, Philips also brought their noodle makers to the international markets. Their first market outside China was Japan. With a rich culture in noodle making, Japan's consumers like eating Udon noodles, buckwheat noodles and hand-pulled noodles, each of which has a different shape and requires different raw materials and production processes. Philips tried to further understand and study these characteristics. It found that Japanese customers pay great attention to the mouthfeel and taste of noodles. They can easily distinguish good noodles from bad noodles. Therefore, Philips improved the production process and added the link of noodle curing onto the mixing and extrusion processes. In addition, due to the different agricultural production processes, the quality of Japanese flour is also different. Philips improved the molding abrasives to meet the actual needs of Japanese consumers. In addition, in the product test, it also found that it's important to Japanese consumers if the noodle maker can be cleaned within one minute. This is mainly because Japanese consumers like to place the noodle maker besides the rice cooker and bread maker, both of which can be cleaned quickly because of their Teflon surface. Philips also made further modifications to the molding grinding tool based on these market needs.

Behind the Chinese Market Strategy

The glocal strategy of Western multinational companies in the Chinese market is not as simple as it seems. Behind their glocal decision, there are a lot of things to be considered. There are also many factors impacting the decision-making of the executives of those multinational corporations.

First of all, multinational companies need to consider what kind of industries or market areas the Chinese local competitors would be more likely to seek growth opportunities and realize their catch-up? Because in those areas, it is easier for Chinese local enterprises to make use of the particularity of the market to gradually build up resources and necessary competence base, and it may be a wise choice for multinational companies to avoid competing against Chinese enterprises or to establish partnerships with them in such areas. Take Philips as an example. Traditionally, Philips's strong in-house R&D capability enables it to handle almost all its development work. However, the fierce competition from local competitors has mounted up pressure on Philips to reduce the production cost of energy-efficient fluorescent lamps. Many local Chinese companies use manual labor to make these lamps, while Philips adopts a fully automated production mode. Thanks to the lower labor cost in China, local competitors can significantly reduce the production cost of each bulb by 1.5 to 2 Dutch guilders. It is almost impossible for Philips to compete with these new competitors in cost. Therefore, Philips changed its original close-loop production system and decided to subcontract the bulb orders to the local Chinese manufacturers and share its production processing with them. Such a decision encountered great controversy and difficulty at first, because it would simply lead to the closure of their factories in Holland and Poland.

Generally speaking, according to the catching-up experience of Chinese manufacturing industry in the past, when a specific industry or market segment possesses the following features at the same time, it is more likely for Chinese local enterprises to achieve rapid catching-up: (a) As far as the market itself is concerned, if there are huge discrete unmet needs in the market, then the Chinese local enterprises can more easily find market spaces to avoid competing against multinational companies; (b) When the technology concerned is relatively mature and stable[3], with less frequent change in the direction of technology development, and the product or technology is highly modular-based, the Chinese local enterprises will have a longer time window for learning, and can harness the advantages resulting from technology decomposition and recombination; and (c) A complete and relatively mature modular-based supply chain to support product manufacturing or service provision has been formed in the Chinese domestic market. This means that local enterprises can access the robust ecosystem to compensate for their lack of resources or internal competence, so as to react to any market changes with high agility.

Of course, the above three conditions may also change with time. Specifically speaking, technology maturity and stability may not always constitute a favorable condition for the catching-up of Chinese local enterprises, which is especially the case as evidenced in the catching-up experience of Chinese manufacturing industry. In the emerging fields such as new energy vehicles, big data and artificial intelligence, in recent years, Chinese local enterprises have gained many opportunities to overtake in corners. To a great extent, this is related to the fact that Chinese enterprises have reached a certain stage in their own capacity development in recent years. In other words, the larger the technological gap between Chinese local enterprises and Western multinational companies, the more important the maturity, stability and modularity of technology will be for realizing successful catch-up. However, with the narrowing of the technological gap between Chinese local enterprises and multinational companies, if Chinese local enterprises have successfully equipped themselves with technology and product development technological capabilities, they often could find some business opportunities in those emerging fields (or the fields where there is a high level of uncertainty and fast speed in technology development). Because in this case, the knowledge and technical expertise gradually accumulated by Western multinational companies over a long time may not be extended to the new technological

[3]Brandt, L., and E. Thunb (2016). Constructing a ladder for growth: Policy, markets, and industrial upgrading in China. *World Development* 80: 78–95.

development trajectory, so different competitors almost return to the same starting line.

Proactive migrating downward from the original high-end positioning in the market ladder is also an option that multinational companies can consider. On the one hand, the good-enough market that is positioned comparatively lower on the market ladder is of certain attractiveness itself. On the other hand, the proactive downward migration can also play a strategic role to counter-strike or deter the continuous upward migration of the local enterprises. Gadiesh *et al.* described the business example of GE Healthcare. In order to expand the sales of Magnetic Resonance Imaging (MRI) equipment in the Chinese market, GE has developed lite version MRI for hospitals in second- and third-tier Chinese cities, making its price more attractive to users. Moreover, this strategy will not affect GE's existing high-end market. Instead, it can serve to dampen the threat from continuously upward-moving local Chinese enterprises. Such value-for-money product attempt was even replicated and proved successful in the Indian market.[4]

Naturally, deep insights into the needs of the Chinese market and the ability to capture them via localized designing have become a critical cornerstone for multinational companies. A.O. Smith has achieved great successes by taking advantage of the above-mentioned qualities in the Chinese market. A.O. Smith positions its water heater business as a B2B business in the United States, taking business users as the main targeted customers. However, in the Chinese market, it positions its water heater business more as a B2C business, selling products directly to the end users. Therefore, its gas water heaters, water purifiers and air purifiers sold in the Chinese market are all developed by its R&D team in China based on the characteristics of the Chinese market demand. For example, they noticed that Chinese consumers like drinking hot water and have very diversified demands. Especially for families with children, the traditional method to get hot water is very troublesome, since they need to first get some fresh water, then boil the water, and then pour the boiled water back and forth in two containers to cool it, which may some times take more than half an hour. Consumers want to get purified hot water that is adjusted to their expected temperature directly, so as to shorten the waiting time for reconstituting powdered milk or making tea. Therefore, in

---

[4]Gadiesh, O., P. Leung, and T. Vestring (2007). The battle for China's good-enough market. *Harvard Business Review* 85(9): 80.

AWE 2018, A.O. Smith launched a water purification hot water tap based on the consumer needs.[5] Wei Ding, president of A.O. Smith China, said: "Since the establishment of our factory in China in 1998, we have never air-dropped any products directly from overseas market to the Chinese local market. We forged our own core technology and a lot of locally developed innovative technologies, all of which were the brainchild of A.O. Smith China R&D team based on the needs of the Chinese market. There were not many foreign-funded enterprises willing to establish such a large-scale localized R&D team. A.O. Smith insisted on doing this and did it from the first day. That's why our product technology is getting stronger in problem solving. When we started, we only hired 30 engineers, which has surged to 500 engineers nowadays and will continue to increase to over 800 in a few years. We are advancing with the times. Many foreign-funded enterprises are either weak in sense of localization or institutionally handicapped to conduct localization, with their overseas headquarters taking the total control. This may lead to their failure to study the local market and loss of many opportunities".

Embracing the Internet is also a good strategy for the consumer markets. In recent years, the volume of e-commerce transactions has been growing in China. Chinese consumers are getting more used to shopping online. The existence of the Internet has greatly boosted the exposure of brands and products to potential customers, helping multinational companies secure growth in their China business. According to the financial report of L'Oreal Group in 2019, L'Oreal's turnover in the Chinese market increased by 32% year on year, among which the sales from e-commerce channel soared by 43.7% year on year. In 2019, Jean-Paul Agon, CEO of L'Oreal Group, revealed in an interview with the *Financial Times* that the contribution from the online sales channel of L'Oreal China has reached 35%, which is way higher than that in other markets, with the same figure as 15% in the UK, 11% in the US and only 4% in its home market in France. The Chinese market contributed about 85% of L'Oreal's growth.[6]

[5]Ding, W. (2018). Sina Home, former senior vice president of A.O. Smith: Adhere to localized R&D and only solve the professional category of users pain points, November 18, 2018.

[6]Yang, Q. (2019). About 85% of L'Oreal's business growth comes from the Chinese market. How does L'Oreal plan to sustain it? Jiemian.com, July 12, 2019 (https://m.jiemian.com/article/3303783.html).

Challenges That Must Be Faced

In the 1960s and 1970s, the competition creed held by many multinational companies was "Capture US market share, capture the world". Because the US market represents the market with the highest requirements on quality, technology and brand reputation. If a company's products can maintain continuous development in this market, it is enough to prove its competitive strength. However, now, the Chinese market, especially the mid-end Chinese market, is becoming the touchstone of multinational corporations' dominance and competitiveness.[7]

Under such circumstances, multinational companies are facing a series of challenges that have occurred and that are taking place in the Chinese market. Traditionally, the core of competition from multinational corporations has been "global consolidation", which is even true in the Chinese market. However, with the increasing importance of the Chinese market in the business map of multinational corporations and the growing share taken by local enterprises in the market, multinational corporations need to change their previous globalization strategies and embrace a new mission, that is, "localized consolidation + global adaptation".[8]

More specifically, how to redefine the relationship between local R&D and global management has become the first issue that Western manufacturing multinational companies need to think about. Because the standard process established within multinational companies for the purpose of their global consolidation is prone to bring about potential conflicts in managing localized R&D. Philips China tried to transplant its air purifier products to the automotive industry by launching "Automotive Air Purifier". This idea was immediately welcomed by some car manufacturers. Honda tried to customize this product and made it a big selling point for new cars. However, Honda and Philips disagreed on the installation site of the purifier within the car. According to their experience, Philips's global R&D headquarters proposed to put the purifier on the dashboard, car roof or back seat. This decision was rejected by Honda as it would incur the redoing of the collision test which would significantly increase the cost and time. Because Philips Global Research has the final

[7]Gadiesh, Orit, Philip Leung, and Till Vestring. "The battle for China's Good-Enough Market." Harvard Business Review 85.9 (2007): 80.

[8]Santos, J. F. P., and P. J. Williamson (2015). The new mission for multinationals. *MIT Sloan Management Review* 56(4): 45–54.

decision power, even if Philips (China) Research that is entrusted to develop the "automotive air purifiers" found the decision of the headquarters does not meet the actual customer demands, they can only forward the customer feedback to the headquarters without any direct response. As a result, the stalemate between the global R&D headquarters and Honda lasted for over a month. In the end, during a business trip to attend a meeting in Shanghai, Benjamin Azoulay, vice president of Philips Automotive Lighting and general manager of Philips Mobile, flew to Honda in Japan with the members of the "Automotive Air Purifier" project team. After being briefed and explained the customer's needs, Benjamin Azoulay finally agreed on the customer's requirements and immediately gave the green light to the project. Three weeks later, the project team submitted a commercial proposal to Honda, which would have taken at least 3 months under the normal feedback process. The relinquishment of rigorous control power throughout the system and the omission of intermediate reporting and communication links is rewarded with substantial increase in information accuracy, efficiency and speed. This also means that multinational companies need to redefine the role of local R&D in the global R&D system. When entering the Chinese market, multinational companies often start from selling products designed earlier in the developed markets. Nowadays, there are more and more innovation opportunities in the Chinese market. Compared with application-oriented R&D, more opportunities arise from R&D activities oriented to fundamental research. To multinational companies in China, the seamless docking of these two R&D systems will bring them both opportunities and challenges.

How to reach a balance between product quality, price and market response is also an important challenge for multinational companies. With its growing weight in the Chinese market, good-enough market is becoming a market that Chinese local enterprises and multinational companies in China can't afford to ignore or lose. For multinational enterprises positioned in the high-end market with little variations, they have to adjust their original positioning in order to adapt to the rapidly changing value-for-money market, which will require relevant adaptive changes in their product development and business operation systems. The rapid changes in the Chinese market require enterprises to respond quickly to market demands. For multinational companies that follow standard procedures, it might be relatively longer for them to respond to the Chinese market. With more price-sensitive consumers, the Chinese market often requires multinational companies in China to provide products with balanced quality and price when they find low-cost alternatives. For example, foreign consumers tend to use three-headed shavers, which would cost at least RMB 700 to 800. It's already too expensive for Chinese consumers who just need a product that can remove the beard without paying a premium price for it. In order to meet Chinese consumers' demand for low price, Philips launched two-headed shaving products whose cost is only about RMB 200 to 500 and that can not only cater to consumers' demands but also ensure the company's profitability requirements. This product is not only launched in other developing countries such as those in Asia (the local residents in these areas have beards that are similar to that of the Chinese), but also into the American market. In the United States, Philips built its product image as being "young", which made the product popular among the young people (such as high school students with fewer beards).

To some extent, the good-enough market is becoming increasingly significant from the strategic perspective. The biggest challenge is not only the development of products and technologies but also the adjustment of production and operations. This kind of challenge will even occur in the whole company's culture and business philosophy. As Jean Vacalopoulos, general manager of Philips LED global R&D department, mentioned in an interview with Philips China, a big challenge is to make the company's important stakeholders agree to produce and sell value-for-money products — as you know, for years, Philips's company motto has always been providing the "best" products.

Another pressing challenge that has become more and more urgent over time is the competition for talents from the Chinese market. This is actually a new problem that arises with the passage of time. For many years, with competitive salary and welfare level, perfected management system and superior image in the market, multinational companies have become the priority for many local talents when making their career choices. Even for a long time, being able to work in a multinational company was regarded as the best form of recognition for a fresh graduate's ability. However, time is changing many things and refreshing our perceptions. After investigating 411 multinational companies, Bain and American Chamber of Commerce in China jointly released the 2018 China Business Climate Survey Report. According to the survey, half of the companies surveyed have at least 10% of their global income from China. It is found that although multinational companies used to be the most attractive employers in the past, they are now often at a disadvantage in the local talent competition, losing to some local start-ups and medium-sized enterprises that provide faster and more attractive career development opportunities. According to the survey, 45% of respondent foreign companies think that domestic competitors are more attractive to job seekers. This ratio was higher than only 36% in 2016. In addition, 1/3 of the foreign companies surveyed complained a higher talent attrition rate in 2017 over that of 2016. And competition from domestic enterprises has been an increasingly weighted causal factor for them. Our field study into Philips China in the same period also showed similar results. Compared with other institutes of Philips around the world, Philips (China) Research was a late-starter that is challenged with insufficient ability and technology and high-quality talent pool of the R&D team. In the past, China's talent market was not mature. Although new talents can be attracted, they are often not of high quality. Nowadays, the Chinese talent market is gradually maturing, but companies have to face fierce competition from the world's top 500 enterprises in local talent recruitment. In other words, although the supply of talents is increasing, the demand is also increasing. With the rapid development of China's information technology industry, the demand for talents in software and hardware development is growing rapidly. Moreover, Chinese information technology enterprises can also provide more attractive remuneration to talents, which further raises the cost of talents recruitment to multinational companies in China. In recent years, with the commercial application of the Internet, the progress of cross-border competition and service-based manufacturing, more and more traditional business models are being significantly changed. Competition also becomes more international. How to ensure the supply of high-quality talents and compete with newcomers in the market on talents and products is a great challenge for Philips (China) Research.

Chapter 9

Rules of Survival in the Chinese Market

Capturing the Unmet Market Needs

To survive and prosper in the Chinese market, enterprises need the wisdom for survival and the courage for competition.

We can summarize some survival rules, but it doesn't mean that they are axioms and the ultimate truth. Although these rules have been tried more or less by many enterprises, they are more rules of thumb which can help participants in the market better understand the competition they face and the principles they need to think about, thus improving their survival probability in the Chinese market and the probability of successfully capturing market opportunities.

These rules can be sub-divided into nine tenets as follows:

a. Capturing the unmet market needs;
b. Building strength on low-cost manufacturing capabilities;
c. Integrating localized innovations;
d. Seeking a delicate balance between low cost and reasonable quality;
e. Harnessing the power of business model innovation;
f. Maintaining fast response to the market;
g. Exploring game-changing business opportunities;
h. Leveraging glocalization advantages;
i. Never stop running.

Let's start with discussing the first tenet, i.e., capturing the unmet market needs.

Identifying and capturing the existing but unmet market needs is a precondition for all rules of survival in the Chinese market. In terms of the process of catching-up by local Chinese enterprises, a big gap exists between such enterprises and Western multinational companies in product technology and design, so it is necessary for them to avoid direct competition with Western multinational companies. At the same time, local enterprises have a natural advantage in understanding the needs of the Chinese market. Therefore, they can combine their understanding of the market with their dimension-reduction technology imitation of multinational companies' products.

For example, in the 1980s, China's automobile industry mainly focused on the production of government-procured cars, while entry-level private cars for Chinese families were still quite scarce. As a result, some joint ventures and automobile brands emerged, including the household car models SAIC Santana and Tianjin Charade.

"With Santana, we can go anywhere". This was an almost household slogan in China at that time. In 1983, Santana, the first joint venture car by Shanghai Auto and Volkswagen, went off the line in Anting, Shanghai, and entered into mass production in 1985. It became popular as an entry-level family car because it was cheap in maintenance, easy to repair, of durable good quality and affordable in price. Charade, another household car brand in China back then, was the first hatchback introduced in the form of "Complete Knocked Down" (CKD for short) and put into production in September 30, 1986. In 1985, Tianjin Automobile Industry Corporation signed an agreement with Daihatsu of Japan to introduce Charade, the second generation Daihatsu car launched in Japan in 1983. Although the above two family-car models were only entry-level products, Santana was priced at RMB 200,000 at that time whereas Charade cars were priced roughly at RMB 130,000, which was still expensive for Chinese family users at that time. Geely Automobile, which was founded in 1997, aimed at entry-level consumers in China, and its pricing was merely between RMB 30,000 and RMB 57,000, which was much lower than the price of many joint venture automobile brands back then.

Of course, such unmet market needs not only stay at the price level, but also include those niche market needs that are not covered by existing products or brands. For example, Wahaha based in Hangzhou started mass production of "Future Cola" in May 1998. Because Coca-Cola and Pepsi-Cola have formed strong brand influence in first- and second-tier cities, Wahaha's Future Cola turned to small towns and rural areas where the local consumers were not aware of those big brands. This helped Future Cola become the third-ranking brand in China's soft drink market at that time.

The fast development of Pinduoduo also proves the great potential of such unmet market needs. As a social e-commerce platform established in September 2015, Pinduoduo had the number of its registered users exceed 100 million in September 2016. Its monthly GMV exceeded RMB 1 billion, and its average daily orders exceeded 1 million. According to data released by UBS, as of the end of 2018, the number of annual active users on Pinduoduo reached 418 million, making Pinduoduo the No. 2 e-commerce platform in China. The number was only second to the 636 million of Alibaba and surpassed the 305 million of JD.COM in the same year.

Some enterprises have made mistakes in capturing unmet market needs. For example, Nokia sensed the potential commercial value in China's value segment, so it launched Nokia Asha 210 mobile phone model in July 2013 with a market price of RMB 559 and the product design featuring full keyboard layout and dual card & dual standby, which were widely adopted in the Chinese market. To cater to the preference of users in the Chinese market, the product also was preinstalled with popular applications such as QQ, WeChat and Sina Weibo. However, this mobile phone model failed to achieve the expected success, despite its design tinged with the characteristics of the Chinese market needs. There are two reasons that can explain this result. First is the pricing. Due to the simplification of performance and functions, this mobile phone model has no advantages in cost–performance when compared with the low-end Chinese mobile phone products with the same prices. Secondly, the full-size keyboard design does not conform to the Chinese users' habits. Because such a price targets low-end users, whereas the full-size keyboard design mostly attracts those middle and high-end business users with good education backgrounds (see Figure 9.1).

Figure 9.1. Nokia Asha 210 Mobile Phone (Launched in 2013)

Source: QWERTY-packing Nokia Asha 210 goes official, 24 April, 2013, https://www.gsmarena.com/nokia_announces_qwertypacking_asha_210-news-5908.php.

Building Strength on Low-Cost Manufacturing Capabilities

Low-cost manufacturing capability is the foundation of almost all competitive strategies in the Chinese market. This is because, on the one hand, the good-enough market is of great significance to competitors in the Chinese market, and it can even be said that "the winner of the good-enough market wins the whole market". And the good-enough strategy must be based on low-cost manufacturing capabilities. On the other hand, with the improvement of their capabilities, Chinese local enterprises will try to move up on the market ladder. Therefore, foreign multinational companies that only pay attention to the high-end market are often faced with the cost control pressure brought about by intensifying competition. **It is not easy to materialize the advantage of low-cost manufacturing, for it cannot be achieved simply by resorting to China's low labor cost advantage.** Moreover, throughout the different development stages of

China's manufacturing industry, the advantage of low-cost manufacturing will vary along with the change of competence status and competition focus.

At the toddler stage of China's manufacturing industry, when introducing advanced production equipment and manufacturing processes, some enterprises with certain capability level will consciously analyze the whole production process. After that, they will not completely introduce the whole fully automatic production lines or directly copy the production technology of foreign counterparts, but will replace some of the production links that could have been completed automatically with manual methods without compromising too much on production quality, which can greatly reduce their investment costs. This can be seen in the early stages of many joint ventures or local enterprises, for example, in the importation of Shanghai Bell's production line, or in the early semi-automatic and semi-manual production line adopted by BYD and Geely Automobile. We can call this production method a "hybrid production system", which can keep high production flexibility while keeping the advantage of low cost. This is especially suitable for the competitive Chinese market.

In the process of adjusting and optimizing the production process, some local Chinese enterprises have even gradually established their very strong core capability, that is, the capability of integrated design of the production system. They not only could integrate different-sourced production technologies and equipment into one system, but could also make continuous improvements on some equipment and tools, or even manufacture some key equipment themselves. Although this ability needs to be built up in a gradual way, once it is established, it will bestow enterprises' unique competitive advantages that are difficult to be imitated by their competitors.

If we want to really understand the low-cost manufacturing capability of Chinese enterprises, we cannot just focus on the standalone manufacturing capability of enterprises, because many enterprises' low-cost manufacturing capability is actually based on the embedded ecosystem. Take the *Shanzhai* phenomenon we discussed earlier as an example. More than 30,000 upstream and downstream enterprises on the mobile phone industry value chain clustered on North Huaqiang Road in Shenzhen City, covering almost all market segments ranging from design and solution provision, component procurement, assembly and production, testing, packaging, distribution and after-sales services. This atomized industrial ecological structure allows those seemingly "micro" individual enterprises to unify into one with extreme balance in efficiency and flexibility. It is like in a beehive, though each individual bee looks very weak, when they form a whole on the basis of division of labor, they can achieve their goal of group survival with high efficiency, and can effectively cope with the dynamic changes of the environment, thus in a group sense, they realized "big" based on "small".

In most cases, the unity of individuals into an organic whole is the mixed result of a specialized division of labor based on market mechanism and a long-term cooperation based on relationship mechanisms. That is to say, on the one hand, these interconnected individuals use the market mechanism to establish a contract-based division of labor and cooperation relationship, ensuring the relatively high coordination efficiency between them. On the other hand, opportunistic behaviors and short-term behavioral tendencies that may exist under the market mechanism need to be buffered or even eliminated through the long-term relationship between core enterprises and partners (including suppliers). Especially, many activities to improve efficiency and build capabilities require substantial long-term investment with the nature of sunk cost, whereas pure market mechanism may greatly defuse the motivation of such investment.

That's why some Chinese manufacturing enterprises are gradually changing their strategy from vertical integration to system integration over time, that is, the core enterprises as the system integrator function similar to a platform or a connection hub, which efficiently matches and allocates various resources on the supply side based on discrete demands on the demand side. Therefore, when these core enterprises provide products and services to the end users, a large number of value-generating activities along the industry value chain are performed by external suppliers and partners. And the competing relationship between suppliers, the long-term relationship between core enterprises and suppliers, and the cooperative relationship between suppliers and core enterprise's competitors will co-exist.

Integrating Localized Innovations

A stereotype held of China's manufacturing industry is that innovations seldom occur in China's manufacturing industry, so that the competitiveness of the industry is mostly attributed to low prices.

If we carefully observe the designs that have gradually become standard configuration in the market, especially when compared with the equivalent products in European and American markets, or when we compare the products provided by local enterprises with those provided by European and American enterprises in the Chinese market, we will find quite a few unique value designs in the Chinese market (at least in the beginning, for we need to consider the case when such product designs eventually become the product attributes of products of European and American enterprises in the Chinese market).

A typical case could be the super error correction function of DVD players. Before the year of 2000, the quality of video discs in the Chinese market was often defective, so the discs would easily get stuck in the process of playing, which would influence the user experience. In view of such specific needs of the Chinese market, some domestic VCD and DVD player manufacturers designed the so-called "super error correction" function to address this issue. In terms of the technology realization path, the general solution is to address it from the hardware or the software level. At the hardware level, by increasing the power of the optical pick-up head, the corresponding information can be read despite the tainted or scratched marks on the disc. On the software level, using a player processor, the decoding program is solidified, and fuzzy decoding automatically complements missing codes between associated codes, with skipping of unrecognized code, so that users can get a better viewing experience.

Another typical localization innovation is the dual card & dual standby technology of mobile phones. Dual card & dual standby has become the standard configuration of Android phones in China. However, back in history, it was Nokia that firstly developed the "dual card" technology. And it was Coolpad, a Chinese mobile phone manufacturer, that really realized the co-existence of "dual standby" function and "dual card" function. At the end of 2005, Coolpad released a smart dual standby mobile phone named "Coolpad 728", which became the world's first mobile phone with "dual card & dual standby" function. It's attractive to Chinese consumers mainly due to two reasons. First of all, by supporting dual cards, it enables users to separate work and life or other different usage scenarios using just one mobile phone, making it much competitive in both cost and easy-to-carry feature compared with the case when two differently numbered mobile phones are used. Secondly, in an age when the early mobile communication service providers in China charge high in voice call services and Internet services, such a feature allows users to take advantage of service packages from different operators, which reduces the total costs of users in short messages, voice calls and Internet access. Such tactics can be regarded as a kind of "arbitrage behavior" that takes advantage of the services provided by different operators.

Interestingly, the value positioning of this dual card & dual standby design has actually dramatically changed in recent years. At first, Coolpad 728 was priced at RMB 1,780, which was relatively high for a domestic mobile phone model back then. Therefore, dual card & dual standby technology became a value-based selling point, attracting a large number of buyers. Subsequently, with the rise of China's "*Shanzhai* mobile phone" industry, these low-end mobile phone manufacturers saw the market demand potential of dual-card & dual-standby function, thus gradually turning this design into a must-have feature of *Shanzhai* mobile phones, and even setting for Chinese consumers a stereotype that mobile phones with dual-card & dual-standby feature design are low-end mobile phones. Perhaps this is why Apple didn't launch iPhone XR and XS Max with dual card & dual standby design into the Chinese market until September 2018. For Android phones in almost all Chinese markets, dual card & dual standby has become a must in product design.

Such examples can be found in various industries and product fields in the case of both consumer goods and industrial products. That is why an article titled "A CEO's guide to innovation in China" published in *McKinsey Quarterly* in 2012 mentioned that many executives from developed countries misunderstood the phenomenon of "*Shanzhai*" and thought that it was only a simple copy of innovations from other markets. Although such a practice does exist, the products developed based on the *Shanzhai* model actually contain many product features specially developed for the Chinese market scenario.[1]

Seeking a Delicate Balance between Low Cost and Reasonable Quality

In 2008, Interbrand Consultancy conducted a survey of more than 700 business professionals on their perceptions about products made in

[1]Orr, G., and E. Roth (2012). A CEO's guide to innovation in China. *McKinsey Quarterly*, February 2012.

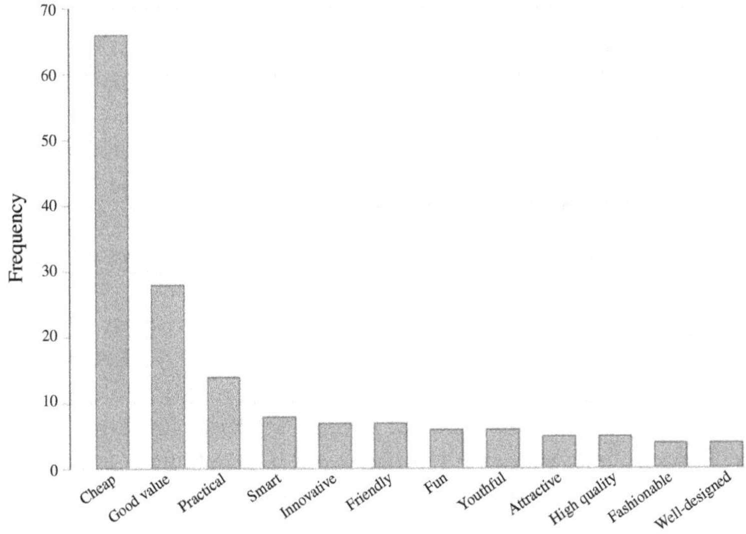

Figure 9.2. Western Consumers' Perceptions about the Image of Made-in-China Products

China.[2] As indicated by the survey results, "cheap" and "good value" were more frequently mentioned than other key words when the respondents were asked about their perceived image of Chinese products. By contrast, such words as "high quality", "fashionable" and "well-designed" were the least mentioned. Although the results may be affected by the limited respondent sample size of the survey, they still reflected, to some extent, the prevailing view around the world about Made-in-China at that point of time (see Figure 9.2).

As mentioned above, good-enough market plays a very important role in the rise of China's manufacturing industry. Especially in the early days, price-sensitive cost-effective positioning was the starting strategy adopted by Chinese enterprises when they were relatively weak in competence, which brought Western consumers an impression that Made-in-China products are cheap and value-for-money.

There is no doubt that Made-in-China will never stop at this. When Chinese manufacturing enterprises acquire certain level of technology, quality and capability, they will naturally move upward on the market

[2]Ding, Q. (2008). Branding their way to a better future. *China Daily*, December 19, 2008. www.chinadaily.com.cn/bizchina/2008-12/19/content_7321731.htm.

ladder and penetrate into the value-sensitive good-enough or even premium markets. This may explain why the frequency of the words "smart" and "innovative" in the aforesaid survey was much higher than that of the other words.

With the rise of Chinese leading enterprises in various fields, the world's views on Made-in-China will gradually change in the foreseeable future. It is like once before the 1960s, Made-in-Japan was regarded as the synonym for "cheap and fine", and it was not until the 1980s that Made-in-Japan gradually took on the image of "high quality". This change essentially reflected the improvement of the competitiveness of a country's manufacturing industry as a whole in the global market. Adrianne Jeffries,[3] an investigative reporter of The Markup, mentioned in a market survey in 2007 that most American college students surveyed believed Nokia (Finland) and Samsung (Korea) were both Japanese brands. This also indirectly proved that, due to the reputation of Japanese manufacturing, Western consumers have already recognized the quality level of Japanese products and might subconsciously associate any high-quality products they don't know well with Made-in-Japan (if such brands are not familiar ones in their home markets).

If measured by market share, some Chinese enterprises have become global leaders. Yet, it goes without saying that the overall image of Made-in-China still needs to be continuously improved, and it will take time for Made-in-China to be associated with "high quality". To truly achieve this goal, China's manufacturing industry will need to gradually establish global leadership in quality, design and brand.

And here are the questions that need some serious thinking. Does high quality have to be reflected in higher market prices? In the process of establishing a global image of "high quality", can the enterprises choose to keep their advantages through their positioning of value-for-money for a relatively long time? In retrospective review of the development of Western multinational companies, we would often subconsciously assume that the selection of the strategy of high quality, high price and high gross margin is an inevitable trend. As a Chinese enterprise that has achieved the greatest successes in the journey of globalization and technology leadership, Huawei answers the question in a way that might help us think

---

[3] Jeffries, A. (2013). Make way for Huawei: Can the Chinese smartphone company buy its way into America. *The Verge*, July 15, 2013. https://www.theverge.com/2013/7/15/4514086/make-way-for-huawei-us-push.

deeper about this question. The average annual net profit margin of Huawei from 2008 to 2017 was about 8.48%. With advantages in superior technology and market monopoly, leading companies in the high-tech industry are often privileged with a profit level that is impossible to achieve for conventional enterprises. On the surface, Huawei's net profit margin data seems to be mediocre and fails to match with its leadership position in the global telecommunication market. But there is no doubt that Huawei is already the most competitive company in the global market in terms of product quality and technical level. In fact, such a profit level just mirrors Huawei's dominance in the whole industry, that is to say, any enterprise that intends to challenge Huawei's position in the industry would have to meet two criteria — it is able to survive with a net profit margin of as low as 8% and it has the same or even higher level of management efficiency compared with Huawei. It is very difficult to simultaneously meet the above two conditions, especially for those publicly listed competitors, as they have to grapple with the pressure of short-term financial performance imposed by the capital market when they attempt to copy Huawei's extreme cost–performance strategy.[4]

Harnessing the Power of Business Model Innovation

Business model defines the reproducible and sustainable business logic and operational mode for enterprises to create, deliver and capture value. If the classic competition mode in the industrial era is to focus on products, with the advent of the Internet era, considering the great advantages of the Internet in promoting information flow and resource aggregation, the probability of business model innovation has greatly increased, which becomes an important business power. Moreover, with the empowerment of the Internet, business model innovation is more powerful than in any preceding era. It has the power to destroy the previous dominance of the existing business models and the power to create a new competition landscape for those pioneering innovators.

[4]As a non-public company, Huawei's top management team can decide to invest a lot of capital and resources in capability building and other links that need strategic patience, even if such investment may erode its profitability in the short run or even bring losses in a relatively long period of time. In other words, those executives only need to be responsible for the long-term value creation for the company instead of short-term financial pay-off for shareholders.

Although business model innovation does not need to be confined to the catch-up scenario faced by the Chinese manufacturing industry, when it involves good-enough product factors, it can bring amazing opportunities to Chinese enterprises as late-comers to achieve stunning growth.

The development of China's mobile phone industry vividly demonstrates the role played by business model innovation throughout the evolution of this industry. The development experiences of mobile phone producers like K-Touch and MI all illustrate this point.

In April 2002, Beijing K-Touch was established. In October 2004, K-Touch launched TY300, its first branded mobile phone that is 100% independently developed by itself. In February 2006, K-Touch was granted the GSM/GPRS/CDMA mobile phone production license by China National Development and Reform Commission (NDRC). Merely one year later, it rose up to become the champion in China's domestic mobile phone sales. This rapid success is partly credited to the continuous efforts K-Touch staged in product development, and is partly contributed by its brand-new business model. Different from the traditional practice of focusing the mobile phone sales mainly on first- and second-tier cities at that time, K-Touch Mobile focused its products on mobile phone users in third- and fourth-tier cities. More importantly, traditional mobile phone sales are completed through pyramid-shaped multi-layer sales channels. Under this model, mobile phone manufacturers can get 20–30% of the profits in the industrial value chain, but they need to bear the cost of promotion and inventory, and the end retailers can only get an average profit share of 5%. By contrast, K-Touch eliminated the intermediary channels, and instead directly linked with end retailers in third- and fourth-tier cities, adopting a buyout system in cooperating with these end retailers. That is to say, it sold K-Touch mobile phones to retailers at a fixed price. And retailers can decide on their own final selling price and thus secure a sales profit rate of 40–50%, which is much higher than that in the conventional mode. As a result, the retailers are highly motivated, and they can take over the burden of product promotion and inventory from K-Touch. This sales model not only helps all participants in the business model get more benefits than that from the traditional model, but it also ensures higher efficiency in operations along the whole value chain.

MI Mobile Phone was established in 2010. Its rapid rise can be first attributed to its anchoring of the "unmet market needs" as the starting point of all its business logic — consumers want to get an extremely powerful mobile phone hardware with a reasonably affordable price tag. In addition, behind all its "Internet thinking" is its stress on pursuing the ultimate user experience. As quoted from Jun Lei, the founder of MI, to pursue the ultimate user experience, MI needs to "drive itself nuts and drive its competitors to the dead end". We can deconstruct "ultimate" into various aspects.

First of all, ultimate experience should be reflected in the "focus" on product and value positioning. MI puts a lot of stress on its hardware that is "born to fever", and consciously leads its consumers to compare the functions of its hardware products with the benchmark products (MI selected Samsung Galaxy series as its benchmark). The logic it wants to reinforce is also quite straightforward, namely, to meet the customer's requirements about hardware performance similar to that of benchmark products at halved price. In order to continuously boost users' "value perception", MI continuously updates its hardware configuration, its software system and its interface.

In this process, XIAOMI's product development follows the pattern of "micro-innovation based on fast iteration", namely, it makes minor adjustments to the previous products, and based on timely market feedback, it makes further adjustments. Products of XIAOMI have to pass closed testing before they are officially launched. At first, the products will be offered for use to a limited number of people, and then they will be made available to the public when certain conditions are met. In this development mode, when the product is still immature, the initial test is crucial. And through continuous improvement, product cost could also be reduced.

On the basis of its product positioning, XIAOMI adopted hunger marketing strategy in constructing its business model. To a great extent, this is not only because of the limited production capacity of its supply chain, but also because it needs to achieve break-even through such a mode. Earlier when each millet product was launched, the price might have even been lower than its cost. However, the cost can be rapidly reduced once the products are sold in vast numbers. Moreover, the hardware cost itself by nature shows a downward trend. Such an approach of bridging the current cost gap through future returns demonstrates forward thinking, which can achieve break-even as soon as possible by increasing the flow rate of the installation base. It's different from traditional business thinking, in that when handling business in the traditional way, people would lower inputs in order to realize break-even faster.

Maintaining Fast Market Response

The rapidly changing feature of the Chinese market has become a reality that enterprises competing in this market must try to adapt to. Such rapid change is partly due to the dynamic changes brought about by market competition. Behind the fast-growing economy is the rapidly surging purchasing power of Chinese consumers. Therefore, many enterprises are often featured with strong opportunity-led tendency in their growth model. They are highly sensitive to external market opportunities and are able to capture the emerging growth opportunities through rapidly changing their products and services. Because Chinese enterprises have gained strong fast imitation ability over the years of their development, and because of the low entry barriers in many industries, if enterprises cannot respond to the market quickly, the market opportunities will not be as profitable as it used to be or even disappear when a lot of competitors and imitators flood into the market.

From the perspective of external environmental factors, the environmental dynamics the Chinese enterprises are faced with are not only a result of the cut-throat imitation and competition among enterprises but also the volatile institutional environment. Such institutional uncertainty can come from the frequently adjusting of policies and regulations in different economic development stages. It's also likely rooted from the so-called "institutional voids" (which is particularly true for some new phenomena and new problems, where the system design often lags behind the practice). It should be pointed out that in the Chinese market, the institutional defect does not always bring about additional risks or costs, it can bring an opportunity for some enterprises. For example, in the early development stages of e-commerce, the institutional voids privileged the e-commerce enterprises back then with faster development opportunities.

Market responsiveness of local enterprises not only carried great significance in the past era, it also has significant impact under the current trend of consumption upgrading. In June 2018, the report "Buyers' Consumption Upgrade, Market Growth Rebound" released by Kantar Worldpanel and Bain & Company showed that local brands achieved a sales growth of 7.7% in 2017, which contributed 98% of the growth in China's fast-moving consumer goods market, whereas the sales of foreign brands only increased by 0.4%. Bruno Lannes, a global partner of Bain & Company and one of the co-authors of the report, pointed out that "there are multiple reasons behind this, but one of the main reasons is that local enterprises are faster in speed and agiler in operation mode. This is very crucial for the rapidly changing Chinese consumer goods market".

To rapidly respond to the market, Chinese enterprises have adopted various strategies for adaptive exploration in different industries. In the process of scale expansion by enterprises, the existence of economies of scale makes it possible for them to improve their efficiency, which often requires a centralized management mode. However, rapid response to market changes requires enterprises to have a high degree of flexibility, which is very dependent on the decentralized management model. Therefore, enterprises need to reach a balance between centralization and decentralization in designing their management mode. Take RT-Mart, the local supermarket chain, as an example. In 2010, RT-Mart achieved a revenue of RMB 40.4 billion, surpassing Carrefour to become the No. 1 in the Chinese retail department store industry back then. In choosing a business model, Mingduan Huang, the founder of RT-Mart, did not adopt Wal-Mart's centralized management mode or Carrefour's decentralized mode (that is, local operations under a store manager). Rather, he adopted a "middle way" between the two, that is, the headquarters is responsible for opening new stores, purchasing and distribution, whereas individual stores decide on their own product pricing, membership management and in-store exhibitions.[5]

Some enterprises are also fully capitalizing the empowerment by the Internet to balance ultimate efficiency with flexibility of the operating system. As the Internet celebrity economy becomes a growing hot spot, some garment factories have begun to embrace this opportunity. Due to the fashion-following and fast-moving characteristics of clothing products under the Internet celebrity mode, time or speed has become an important factor to define product value for customers. For example, in a garment factory in Dongguan, its online celebrity can even attract 800–1,000 orders per day, and the supply cycle can sometimes be as short as 7–10 days, which presents great challenges to the factory. As a result, in terms of management, the factory put delivery time as a priority that is more important than price and quality. Accordingly, the company has established a profit-sharing mechanism for employees to stimulate their initiative and enthusiasm. In terms of the management mode, efficiency

[5]Li, R. (2018). Wong Ming-duan of RT-Mart: Won all competitors but lost to the times. Sohu, January 14, 2018. https://www.sohu.com/a/216664907_675092.

management is strengthened by the quantitative indicators of floor space efficiency and manpower efficiency, project team mechanism is adopted to obtain better internal operation flexibility, and long-term cooperation relationships with some subcontract factories are established to secure the flexibility and adaptability of the supply chain to address fluctuating demands.

Exploring Game-Changing Business Opportunities

In the Chinese market, the ambitious enterprises will never be satisfied with being just the followers of upward migration on the market ladder. Instead, they are constantly seeking game-changing business opportunities and opportunities to "corner-overtake" the leading companies in their business fields. Such game-changing business opportunities are related to the change in the technology paradigm in many cases. Because the change in the technology paradigm will destroy the competitive advantage base of the existing leading companies to a great extent, and open a new time window for late-comer enterprises to catch up with the technology. For example, from the figure from some highly cited papers, we can see that China has developed rapidly in the field of artificial intelligence, and is constantly narrowing down the gap between itself and the United States (see Figure 9.3).

In terms of the impact of the change in the technological paradigm, we can first look at an example related to Japanese enterprises, namely, the challenge by the quartz watches to the mechanical watches. In 1880, P. Curie (husband of the great Madame Curie) and J. Curie first discovered the piezoelectric effect. Then, it was not until 1967 that Switzerland developed the world's first quartz electronic watch. However, Swiss watch manufacturers were not optimistic about the market potential of quartz watch technology back then. Seiko from Japan, however, was able to discern what others could not. Believing that this new technology would have a good market prospect, it decided to invest in the quartz technology. In 1969, Seiko launched the world's first quartz watch named "Quartz Astron". Soon, Japanese watch manufacturers started mass production of quartz watches. Inoue Tatsuhiko (2014) once pointed out that, from Swiss mechanical watches to Japanese quartz watches, we can see the redefining of the product value. Swiss mechanical watches were once regarded as the icons of "time precision". With the appearance of quartz

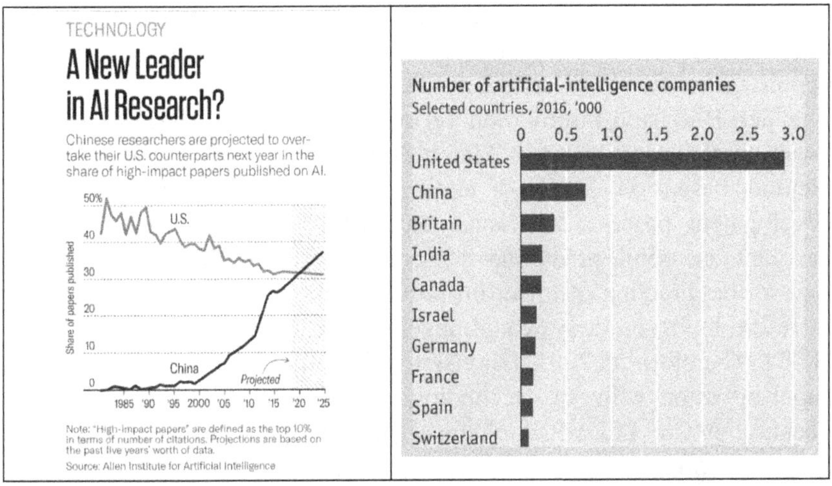

Figure 9.3. China's Rapid Development in Artificial Intelligence

Sources: Harvard Business Review, July August 2019, p. 27; Artificial intelligence: Algorithm Kingdom. *The Economist*, July 15, 2017, p. 49. Allen Institute for Artificial Intelligence. Race of the Machines, Press report; Wu Zhen Institute.

watches, time precision became a synonym for quartz watches. More importantly, while Swiss mechanical watches occupy the high end in the whole market ladder, quartz watches are able to achieve time accuracy with lower costs. Consequently, Swiss mechanical watch producers were forced to redefine their product value from the perspectives of fashion and design.

When the underlying core technology of the entire industry is facing the change in technology paradigm, such episodes occur repeatedly. The late-comers can change the existing pattern of the industry by redefining the product value and market positioning. Founded in 2001, Hikvision adopted a value proposition of supplying leading video products and professional industrial solutions to the world. Since 2011, Hikvision has become the leader of the global video surveillance industry. In terms of market share, it has been the global market leader in the security and video surveillance business. The reason for its success is it successfully captured the market opportunity in the video surveillance during the transformation from analog technology to digital technology, which enabled it to change from a mere market follower to a market leader. In the era of analog technology, European, American, Japanese and Korean enterprises have established a very strong technology and market base, leaving not much opportunities for Chinese enterprises. The predecessor of Hikvision, Zhejiang Hikvision Information Technology Co., Ltd., began to develop video compression board in March 2000, adopting reverse engineering method based on MPEG-1 coding and decoding standard. In its development process, Hikvision successfully foresaw the technology development trend, predicting that compression algorithm will advance toward the direction of lower bit rate and less hard disk occupancy, and therefore the technology would develop from MPEG-1 and MPEG-4 to H.264. Therefore, in 2001, Hikvision Information and Gong Hongjia, an angel investor with key technologies, co-founded Hikvision Digital Technology Co., Ltd, which obtained the exclusive right to use video and audio compression and decompression software technology based on H.264 standard and the exclusive right of running compression and decompression software technologies on DSP chip. After that, Hikvision launched DS-4000M compression board based on MPEG-4 standard in 2002 and DS-4000H compression board based on H.264 standard in 2003 (H.264 became a standard technology in the industry thereafter). In 2004, Hikvision expanded vertically along the industrial chain, transforming itself from an R&D-based manufacturer of compression boards to an R&D-based manufacturer of digital monitoring products. It launched DS-8000HC embedded hard disk video recorder based on H.264 algorithms. When the new generation video coding standard H.265 met application requirements, Hikvision further launched its self-developed Smart265 coding technology, which was fully compatible with H.265, and, at the same image quality, it reduced the amount of data by at least 30% compared with when using H.265, and 70% compared with when using H.264. This greatly reduces the cost of video transmission and storage, making products and solutions of Hikvision more competitive in the market.

When capturing game-changing business opportunities, due to the important role of technology leap, enterprises need to build their internal capabilities on the new technology track. The efficiency of technology learning and the effectiveness of technological capability building are indispensable key foundations. However, for Chinese enterprises, their manufacturing capability with high efficiency, flexibility and low cost is often not easy to be perceived, but it constitutes another important power for them to gain competitive advantages. When talking about the field of security and video surveillance system, Jon Cropley, chief analyst of video surveillance in IHS Markit, pointed out in 2016 that "There has been a rapid downward trend of equipment price in recent years. The average price of global network video surveillance cameras has dropped from US$ 500 in 2010 to less than US$ 130 in 2015. Manufacturers from China can often gain market share by offering much lower price than their Western competitors".[6]

This is also evidenced by the competition of a Chinese company DJI in the unmanned aerial vehicle (UAV) industry. In 2016, *Time* released the list of "the 50 Most Influential Electronic Devices in human history". In this list, there are many epoch-making electronic products that we are so familiar with, i.e., iPhone, Polaroid camera, Sony Walkman, Nintendo Game Boy game console and Nintendo Wii game console. Among them, the only product produced by a Chinese enterprise is "DJI Phantom UAV" (which ranked 46th). In the early days, UAV was only a professional tool or a technical toy for a few geeks. When it started its business in 2006, Shenzhen DJI Innovation Technology Co., Ltd. began to ponder on how to turn UAV into a consumer product. This requires redefining of the product's value proposition. In 2012, DJI launched Phantom UAV, which became the industry benchmark as a consumer-grade UAV. As DJI UAV has a large share in the American market, it will inevitably be challenged by UAV manufacturers from the United States. *Forbes* published an article in 2016, analyzing the failure of 3D Robotics, an American drone company. Founded in 2009, 3D Robotics[7] was the largest consumer drone manufacturer in North America at that time. In April, 2015, it launched its first mass market-oriented UAV. Due to production delay, numerous component problems and competition from DJI's UAV products, 3D Robotics finally announced it would exit UAV hardware manufacturing and only provide software development services for UAV manufacturers. Colin Guinn, the former chief revenue officer of 3D Robotics, explained the company's failure in this way, "We realized that as a software-centered company based in Silicon Valley, it is difficult for us to compete with a

[6]Lai, J. (2016). a&s Global Security Top 50: Price competition accelerates industry convergence. a&s, November 24, 2016. http://security.asmag.com.cn/news/201611/89562.html.

[7]Chris Anderson is one of the co-founders of this company. He had been the chief editor of the famous tech journal *The Wired* in the United States and also the author of the best selling book *The Long Tail*.

powerful manufacturer based in China that adopts a vertically integrated mode [referring to DJI]" Actually, the market price of Solo, a 3D Robotics' UAV equipped with universal joint and GoPro camera, was over $1,700, while DJI Phantom 3 Pro suite with the same configuration was only priced at $1,300, which further dropped to only $1,000 in 2016.[8] This fully shows that in the value-sensitive good-enough mass market, competition does not only involve technical factors, but also requires very powerful low-cost manufacturing capabilities as the foundation.

Leveraging Glocalization Advantages

The leading local enterprises are not satisfied with their success in the local market, as they have weathered through the fierce competition in the local market and gradually built up confidence in their own capabilities. Such enterprises often boast broader global horizons and the desire to pursue territorial expansion.

In seeking expansion into overseas markets, these leading local enterprises consider the domestic market and overseas market not as separate ones but as an integral whole — supporting their international expansion with their development in the domestic market, whose growth can be thereafter pulled by the development in the international market. To realize this, it is an inevitable option for them to replicate or transplant their localization experience accumulated in the Chinese market to overseas markets. The replication strategy often starts from seeking value-for-money needs in overseas markets. A report in the *Financial Times* on September 24, 2004, described two examples of Haier's capturing of two segmented needs in the US market. Haier developed a mini refrigerator with a folding desktop for student consumers in American market, because when visiting students' space-tight dormitories, Haier's product designer found that some students would put a wooden board on two mini refrigerators to serve as a desktop. Another example is its double-layer freezer. It's often described as "the only freezer with drawer design in the world" — the upper part of the freezer allows users to fetch frozen items by flipping the lid as in the traditional design, whereas the lower part has a drawer that can be pulled out. In this way, people (especially for elder

[8]Kathy (2016). How did America's best drone company lose to DJI. guancha, February 13, 2017, https://baijiahao.baidu.com/s?id=1547869311315962&wfr=spider&for=pc.

people) can conveniently take out frozen items from any position in the freezer.

Huawei advanced its international development following a very similar starting logic. From 1995 to 1998, the competition landscape of China's domestic communication equipment market experienced a tectonic shift. This was partly due to the financial crisis that shrunk the international market demand, forcing many large multinational companies to buffer the impact of the recession by competing in the Chinese market. At the same time, it is also because more than 400 local communication equipment manufacturers flooded into the Chinese market. Such an increasingly saturated domestic market, and the underutilized production capacity Huawei had heavily invested in, in a sense, drove Huawei to start its internationalization process. Of course, it's also much credited to the strategic vision of Zhengfei Ren, the founder of Huawei. As early as in 1994, Zhengfei Ren said that "10 years later, the global communication industry will be dominated by few leading players, and Huawei will be one of them". In 1999, Huawei's overseas sales accounted for less than 4% of its total sales. By 2005, Huawei's overseas sales exceeded its domestic sales revenue for the first time. In order to replicate and transplant its local market experience, Huawei began to focus its internationalization in developing countries and emerging markets. Zhengfei Ren said in a speech that "When we planned to internationalize, we found all fertile lands have been occupied by Western companies. Only those desolate, barren and undeveloped places bear the opportunities for our expansion".

Even when expanding into developed countries, Huawei chose to first start from those niche markets and small-size customers that were neglected by global giants. Huawei took the initiative to find some small-size operators, identify and satisfy their unmet needs with the most value-for-money products and fast response services possible. Evoxus, for example, a small British telecommunication company, needed to compete with telecommunication giants such as British Telecom (BT), so it urgently needed to save investment costs and reduce operating costs. Hence, Evoxus chose the equipment and services provided by Huawei.

How to integrate the resources and capabilities of local and overseas operations under the glocalization mode is also an important issue. For these Chinese leading local enterprises, their resource integration involves how to integrate overseas resources with local resources and how to integrate resources in multiple overseas markets. The former usually takes the form of the combination of the low-cost manufacturing advantages and value-for-money market experience accumulated in the local market with the technological assets in overseas markets. In 2011, Peter J. Williamson, a professor of Judge Business School, Cambridge University, and Anand P. Raman, chief editor of the English edition of *Harvard Business Review*, mentioned that as domestic consumption becomes more and more important to China's economic growth, many Chinese enterprises' overseas mergers and acquisitions (M&As) are not necessarily only for accessing overseas markets, but sometimes for better strengthening of their position in the Chinese market. For example, after Geely acquired Volvo, it announced that it would combine Volvo's technology and design know-how with China's local manufacturing capacity to better serve the Chinese market, and to uplift Volvo's global sales through the sales growth in the Chinese market.[9] Moreover, because markets in developed countries are more mature than the Chinese market, there exists a time lag in terms of product needs and technological development. Chinese enterprises can carry out R&D and technology acquisition overseas, then transplant the developed products to the local market for localized adaptation, and then, finally provide value-based good-enough products to the local market through low-cost manufacturing. Huawei has even evolved to a stage that it has the global R&D network serve as its ability enabling system for its glocalization. It has established across the globe 16 R&D centers and 31 cooperative R&D centers, and more than 200 cooperation projects were initiated with universities until 2020. The core principle of location selection of these overseas R&D centers is to make full use of local technology and talent advantages. For example, Huawei established a software R&D center in Bangalore, India, a micro-design and quality control center in Japan, and an aesthetic design R&D center in Paris, France. Another consideration for selecting the location of R&D centers is to be close to competitors, which is why R&D centers are also set up in Holland, Finland and Sweden.

In the process of harnessing the advantages of glocalization, Chinese enterprises have to improve their management system. Those global talents attracted from abroad will change, in many ways, the strategic thinking pattern and management style of Chinese enterprises. Huawei attracted an army of foreign senior management talents during its

[9]Williamson, P. J., and A. P. Raman (2011). How China reset its global acquisition agenda. *Harvard Business Review*, April 2011, 109–114.

years-long market operations. The examples include Colin Giles, former president of Nokia China and former global executive vice president (who later served as executive vice president of Huawei's consumer business), and John Suffolk, former chief information officer of the UK government (who later served as Huawei's global Internet security director), Laine-Ylijoki Tommi, former senior director of global supply chain management of Nokia, Sony and Ericsson (who later served as president of Huawei's consumer business integrated delivery department), Abigail Sarah Brody, former design director of Apple (who later served as chief user experience designer of Huawei's Consumer BG), and Joonsuh Kim, former creative director of Samsung (who later served as vice president of Huawei's mobile phone design). Huawei also implements a post-rotation system to bring its local managers and employees who have been honed in overseas operations back to the local market, bringing in best practices and breaking and updating existing rigid management rules within the organization as much as possible. For example, in 2005, Huawei had many of its provincial sales representatives in the Chinese market replaced by managers with overseas operation experience.

Never Stop Running

Run! Forrest! Run!!!

Perhaps many of us still remember this sentence that Jenny shouted at Forrest Gump in the film *Forrest Gump*. At hearing it, Forrest Gump started his running and never stopped running, both on the road and in his life journey.

Never stop running forward. This implies a headstrong spirit triumphing over any environment changes, regardless of good or bad times, success or failure.

If we cast our sight on what is happening in the Chinese market, we will find that only those enterprises that never stop their footsteps can survive and develop continuously in this drastically changing market. For them, every pinnacle they climb up is just another starting point of their journey to come.

One self-evident reason why tireless running is regarded as one of the survival rules, even the most fundamental one, in the Chinese market is that ever since the beginning of the market economy and globalization in China, the market competition landscape has never stopped changing. Profound changes have been seen in the market needs, competition landscape and institutional evolution. Therefore, even if some competitive advantages could be established in the previous time points, most of these advantages cannot be sustained, and the competence established based on such advantages can be destroyed by the tide of change.

Therefore, in the past few years, we have witnessed the rise of many Chinese local enterprises, and also the disappearance of many once brilliant enterprises in the historical timeline and even in our memory. Even for Western multinational companies, their success in entering the Chinese market and their advantages in the local market are not enough to ensure their continued success in the Chinese market, and some of them even have to withdraw from this market in the face of fierce competition from Chinese local enterprises.

For many Chinese enterprises that have secured the leading status in China's domestic market, this kind of tireless running is of special significance. Because in many industries, we can see that among the local leading enterprises in a given industry, those enterprises ranked first and second are sometimes from the same city. For example, Hikvision and Dahua in the field of video surveillance are from Hangzhou, Zhejiang, and Zoomlion and Sany Heavy Industry in the field of construction machinery are from Changsha, Hunan, Tianneng Group and Chaowei Group in the new energy battery industry are from Changxing, Zhejiang, and Runtu and Longsheng Chemical in printing and dyeing industry are from Shangyu, Zhejiang. This is the result of the so-called "intra-city competition effect".

The fact that competition in the same city can push those industry leaders to continuously improve their capabilities can be attributed to the following factors. First, when the enterprises are located in the same city, the competition between them is more explicit and easier to be observed by both sides, so the pressure brought about by this competition is more direct. What is more, consumers will compare them consciously or inadvertently. Second, it is easy for them to imitate and learn from each other, because in this case, geographical factors are no longer the main obstacle to the diffusion of information and knowledge, and knowledge spillovers through the flow of personnel are more likely to occur. This will force enterprises to spend more efforts and resources on seeking differentiation, whether at the product level or at the technology base and capability level. Such differentiation under the trend of convergence will greatly promote the development of core competences of both parties in the long run.

In addition, for those industry leaders, their strength also depends on their efficient supply chain and industrial ecosystem to a great extent. Competitors in the same city can promote the formation of a relatively complete industrial ecology and supply chain in the local area more quickly, and can realize the sharing of cost of establishing the industrial ecology and collective assets. In fact, a certain competition and cooperation relationship is also formed within the industrial ecology, which will also promote the efficiency of the whole industrial chain.

Chapter 10

The Future of Made-in-China

History Is a Pathway to the Future

Everything in the past is just a preface.

To examine the innovation path that Chinese enterprises are experiencing and will experience, we may need to think from a broader perspective. Seen from a longer historical period, those countries and regions that have experienced the transformation of their role from imitators to innovators (including Japan and R. O. Korea) can give us some insights about the innovation path. In the past, these previous followers in technology and economy have experienced the same development path, namely, from building advantages in low-cost to building advantages in value-for-money. Later, with their global reputation established, they finally successfully associated their domestic manufacturing with high-quality products.

From the sanctions against ZTE in 2018, to a series of suppression efforts against Huawei from the US government in 2019, to the case when many Western companies (such as producers of Google's Android system and ARM's chip design) suspended the contracted technical support to Huawei's business, all of this sends out a wake-up call to Chinese people about the possible escalation of trade conflicts between China and the United States. Moreover, such conflicts came in new forms that China has never seen before.

So, how to decipher this string of incidents and other phenomena centered on the China–US trade conflict? Looking back into the history of human society, perhaps the first things we see are those events that keep happening repeatedly. However, these recurring incidents are often not isolated, but are like dots scattered discretely on the canvas of time, which make up a whole picture when all these points are connected with lines. In fact, the US government's suppression against Huawei did not start recently. The curtain was drawn back since 2008 when the US government rejected, in the name of "national security", the bid of Huawei and Bain Capital to acquire 3Com. Although Huawei has made many attempts and efforts to enter the US market, it ultimately failed because of the administrative intervention and blocking from the US government. Moreover, to see through the surface of an event, its better to view the standalone event against a bigger backdrop.

It's not wise to be arrogant to believe that China can already fully compete with Europe and the United States in both technology and industry in the global competition. At least so far, the United States is still the country with the most powerful technical and economic influence and dominance at the top of the industry pyramid. It must be admitted that there is still a big gap between China and the United States in basic research and core technologies.

However, we should not belittle ourselves. We cannot deny that China has made huge efforts and progress in many technical fields, and realized breakthroughs and achievements in some local fields (especially in industrial applications). Particularly, we cannot deny the unremitting efforts of Chinese enterprises, countless scientists and engineers over the past 40 years. It is precisely their dedication and efforts that have shaped China's manufacturing industry today and even China's future. In a special report released by the *Economist* on innovation in emerging markets in 2010, Goldman Sachs estimated that China would account for 36% of the world's incremental GDP between 2000 and 2030.[1] More importantly, although there are still many weak points in China's high-end manufacturing, China already deserves the title of the world's only super industrial power straddling over the high-end, mid-end and low-end market segments.[2] As a matter of fact, the rise of Chinese companies has aroused the concern of more and more multinational companies. However, such

---

[1]The world turned upside down. *The Economist*, April 17, 2010. A special report on innovation in emerging markets.

[2]N. Ning (2018). The road-map of Chinese manufacturing upgrade: From system design to localization of components, February 26, 2018.

concern is itself a signal indicating Chinese enterprises are constantly gaining in competitive and technological strength.

In light of the current status of China's overall manufacturing industry, China's real advantage still does not lie in R&D and design, but its strong manufacturing capacity (with a fine balance in scale, fast response and quality, supported by an efficient self-contained industrial chain). In July 2019, McKinsey Global Institute released its report "China and the world: Inside the dynamics of a changing relationship", pointing out that the McKinsey Global Institute's (MGI) new China–World Exposure Index showed that China's dependence on the world has declined, particularly in terms of trade, technology and capital. This reflects China is somehow transiting into a development mode driven by domestic demands. Meanwhile, as pointed out in "Globalization in Transition: The Future of Trade and Supply Chain", another report released by McKinsey Global Institute in January 2019, the trend also reflects the fact that China's local supply chain is maturing day by day. Value-for-money will continue to serve as the most important source of China's strength and competitiveness over the long run. In light of this, how to exquisitely balance product quality and attractive price will become an important direction of China's innovation endeavors. In this regard, even if Chinese enterprises continuously build up their own capabilities and expertise in R&D and design, they can never play down the significance of manufacturing capacities to the development of their competitive advantages.

The external environment of Chinese enterprises' innovation is undergoing great changes. With the gradual implementation of the policy of de-capacity and de-leverage, compounded with the gradually climbing operation costs, Chinese enterprises are faced with the need to move up the market ladder. Meanwhile, as Chinese enterprises are already facing the pressure from global competition in many industries, how to secure a more favorable position in the global value chain is also emerging as a pressing issue that they need to focus on and solve. This also adds further pressure on Chinese enterprises to innovate. China's manufacturing industry must (since there is no other option) gradually establish its competences in R&D, design, core technology and core links of industrial value chain. For those Chinese enterprises that have gone further on the journey of innovation, they will try to leverage the power of innovation to build their own advantages in the global industrial value chain and grow into truly global companies and innovators. They have ambitious goals.

Next, we can ruminate over the issue of craftsmanship. As we know, with the transforming and upgrading of China's manufacturing industry, more and more industrial professionals have started to rethink some unresolved issues of China's manufacturing industry, one of which is why China's manufacturing industry is relatively short in craftsmanship as compared with Japan and Germany. Although different people may interpret craftsman spirit differently, they would generally agree on describing craftsmanship with such words as focused, persistent and perfection-seeking. In employees of Japanese and German manufacturing enterprises, we can see the full embodiment of craftsmanship. However, some people attribute craftsman spirit to the influences of different national cultures, which does not seem to hold. If we refer to Chinese ancient classics, two books are quite peculiar, namely *Mengxi Bitan* (by Kuo Shen from Northern Song Dynasty) and *Tiangong Kaiwu* (by Yingxing Song from Ming Dynasty, about Chinese technology in the 17th century). These two classics are partly the miniature of the consummate technology perfection-seeking spirit of ancient Chinese craftsmen and professionals. Therefore, looking back into the Chinese historical tradition, there is always a cultural pedigree of craftsmanship. Then, why is China viewed to be short of craftsmanship when it has done such an excellent job in manufacturing scale and global influence over the decades-long development of its manufacturing industry since its reform and opening-up? Largely, the answer to such a question lies in the characteristics of China's industrial structure. As for the manufacturing industries of Germany and Japan, the industrial structure carries marked features similar to that of mature economies, namely, a highly concentrated industry with a handful of giant enterprises (or leading enterprises) holding the majority of the market share. Under such an industrial structure, most enterprises adopt one of the two survival modes: choosing niche segments or different geographical areas to avoid directly competing against leading enterprises in the mainstream market, or becoming the suppliers of these leading enterprises to nestle in their industrial value chain network. No matter what choice they make, under the pressure of competition, they need to be highly focused, either on niche market segments or links in an industrial value chain, and constantly seek to consummate the business and technology integration. Otherwise, it will be difficult for them to survive for a long time. However, China's industrial structure is very different. For some industries, even when they have been developing for a long time, they still remain fragmented or less consolidated as compared with that in developed countries of Europe and America. Meanwhile, China has experienced an unprecedentedly massive, rapid and lasting economic growth in the past decades, which has offered enormous business growth opportunities to Chinese enterprises. Under such circumstances, Chinese enterprises tend to be more occupied by the external business opportunities and tend to overlook refining the internal management or making long-term investments to develop internal capabilities. Therefore, the expected behavioral patterns of concentrating, focusing and perfection-pursuing can only be observed in a few Chinese enterprises (including some hidden champions). Of course, looking into the future, it's foreseeable that craftsmanship will gradually become more common in the Chinese manufacturing industry. On the one hand, China's manufacturing industry will gradually catch up with that of Western developed countries and develop an increasingly mature industrial structure. On the other hand, with the gradual slowdown of China's macroeconomic growth, Chinese enterprises will be forced to pay more and more attention to the organic growth driven by capacity improvement.

Awakening of Individualism Amid Consumption Upgrade

The past five years saw the changes in the driving force of China's economic growth. As we know, from the perspective of macroeconomics, consumption, investment, import and export and government procurement can be the short-term driving forces to powerful economic growth. Different from the previous eras when investment and government procurement served as the principal driving forces, in the past five years consumption has become a leading force for steady development. As indicated from the data of the National Bureau of Statistics of China, during the past five years the contribution from consumer expenditure to China's economic growth has surged from 47% in 2013 to 64.6% in 2016 and even further to 76.2% in 2018.

Behind the fact that consumption emerges as a major driving force of China's economic growth is consumption upgrading catalyzed by the rising disposable personal income of Chinese residents. The mega-trend of consumption upgrading is also profoundly alternating the competition focus in the Chinese market and the foundation of enterprise competitiveness. It means that Chinese consumers will no longer appreciate only the low-price attractiveness. Instead, they have begun to attach more importance to product quality and brand value, gradually shifting from pursing tangible value to intangible value. In this context, the competitive positioning of Chinese enterprises is gradually changing from attractive low-price to value-for-money positioning. This can be observed in the changing consumer behaviors in many product fields. In 2019, the average selling price (ASP) of MI's smartphones in Chinese Mainland and overseas markets increased by 13.3% and 6.7%, respectively, compared with that in the same period of last year. The sales revenue of middle- and high-end smartphones priced over RMB 2,000 accounted for 32.3% of that of all MI's mobile phone products.

Consumption upgrade means that it will bring larger consumption demand at the macro level. The estimation of McKinsey predicted that by 2020 "mainstream consumers" will account for 51% of China's urban population, which will cover up to 167 million households and nearly 400 million people.[3] Such "mainstream consumers" will rise up to be the backbone consumers in China, whereas those price-sensitive value consumers will involve 116 million families and 307 million people, all of whom will become the target customers of value-sensitive and price-sensitive good-enough markets.

More importantly, the awakening of Chinese consumers' individualism has become a matter that deserves really serious attention from enterprises, especially those stressing on brand value.

Once upon a time, the needs of Chinese consumers were highly homogenized. People born in the 1960s and 1970s may still remember clothes with monotonous color and style that Chinese people used to wear. Back then, almost every Chinese family would buy similar products at about the same time, though such items may have changed from the "old three items" (watch, radio and bicycle) to the "new three items" (Color TV, refrigerator and washing machine).

Chinese people's emotions and attitudes toward the Spring Festival Gala represent a symbolic epitome mirroring the changes of the times. In 1983, when the Spring Festival Gala was first presented to audiences by China Central Radio and Television General Station (CCTV), it immediately became one of the centerpiece shows of the Spring Festival, the most

[3]Atsmon, Y., and M. Magni (2012). Meet the Chinese consumer of 2020. *McKinsey Quarterly*, March 2012. https://www.mckinsey.com/featured-insights/asia-pacific/meet-the-chinese-consumer-of-2020.

important festival for Chinese people. It soon became the must-have event on Chinese New Year's Eve. To the audience living in the 1980s and 1990s, the Spring Festival Gala became, in a sense, a key collective ceremonial event for the Chinese New Year's Eve. To them, the Gala brought them joy and beautiful memories. At that time, people never gave a bad remark about the Spring Festival Gala. However, since around 2010, the Spring Festival Gala has been subjected to more or less "criticism" from the audience. It should be pointed out those latest sessions of Spring Festival Gala can easily dwarf its predecessors in terms of the available star resources, production cost, sound, lighting and electronic technology and the production cycle of programs, all of which was unimaginable in the past. If so, why does the audience still complain so much about it? This is not (at least not entirely) a problem of program production itself, but is caused by the changing trend of the times, that is, the awakening of people's individualism nowadays — in most cases, it has become increasingly unrealistic to continue using such repetitive or homogeneous products to address the current diversified needs.

This shift has even significantly impacted the market strategy options of luxury brands. For many years, luxury brand manufacturers cared less about the forthcoming Internet era. They wishfully believed that the Internet era would never fundamentally change consumers' taste preference and buying patterns related to luxury brands. For a very long time, luxury brand manufacturers were skeptical about the feasibility of e-commerce in luxury goods business. They were primarily concerned that if they participated in the e-commerce business that features price competition, it could damage their brand image. They questioned whether the consumer experience traditionally provided through offline channels could be realized through online channels. If they developed their businesses online, would it have a negative impact on the sales channels of stores that they traditionally relied on? As more and more luxury brand manufacturers realize that the younger generation has different characteristics from their previous generations, they begin to adapt themselves to the changes of the times. Just as what Sandeep Seth, the global CEO of SK-II, said when explaining the relationship between "change" and "unchanged" of SK-II's classic products: "High-quality products and services are the foundation of our brand, and it is the creed that we will never change ... As for brand reform, we hope to create a new consumer experience based on consumption views and habits of different times, such as our future experience store project that we launched in order to cater to the preferences of young people who love digitalization and interactivity. Millennials redefined the meaning of "luxury goods" — luxury goods are not those produced by machines in a repetitive way, but those that always arouse curiosity and surprise".[4]

The Millennials and Generation Z[5] have been emerging as the main force of consumption, which is a huge variable in this era. Most of them are born in the "cradle" of the Internet Age and are thus the natives of the Internet Age. The overwhelming yet highly fragmented information in the Internet environment and the increasingly influential social networks have enabled key opinion leaders (KOLs) in social networks to outperform traditional media advertisements to exert more influence on Millennials and Generation Z in their interpretation and selection of brands. Meanwhile, in terms of demand side, Chinese consumers are increasingly diversified in their preferences and individualized in their tastes. When surveyed about the reasons for buying international brands, more than 60% of the respondents said that it was because "international brands are a way of self-expression".[6] In this era of advocating self-expression, all enterprises and brands need to make efforts to adapt to this changing trend. Just as luxury brands fear being "no longer young", no brand wants to be marginalized in the future competition.

The Ongoing "Downward Market Penetration"

For many years, we have often been biased when discussing the market and consumer needs because we often unconsciously ignored the fact that the people from first- and second-tier cities can only represent a small portion of China's vast population base scattered around its immense market ladder. According to the "2018 Civil Affairs Development Statistical Bulletin" issued by the Ministry of Civil Affairs of the People's Republic

---

[4]Szubrycht, A. (2017). What Millennials & Gen Z expect from modern luxury brands? May 9, 2017. https://www.linkedin.com/pulse/what-millenials-gen-z-expect-from-modern-luxury-brands-anna-szubrycht.

[5]There are different opinions on the specific time division between The Millennial Generation and Z Generation. It is more common to define millennials as people born between 1980 and 2000; Generation Z refers to people born after 2001. See: https://www.chicagotribune.com/nation-world/ct-gen-z-millennials-20180820-story.html.

[6]Achille, A., A. Kim, L. Qin, and F. Poh (2018). Six new trends of Chinese fashion consumers. McKinsey, June 1, 2018. http://www.sohu.com/a/233668039_165955.

of China, as of the end of 2018, China has 34 provincial administrative regions, including 4 municipalities directly under the Central Government; 333 prefecture-level administrative regions, including 293 prefecture-level cities (including sub-provincial cities); and 2,845 county-level administrative regions, including 382 county-level cities, 1,329 counties and 117 autonomous counties. That is to say, a large number of consumers in China are in towns and rural areas outside first- and second-tier cities.

In recent years, the trend of permeating into the lower market segments along the market ladder was referred to as “market sinking” or “downward market penetration”. On the macro level, it often refers to the expansion of target consumers of products and brands to consumers in the markets of third- and fourth-tier cities or even below, where either in terms of consumption scale or growth speed, huge market potential has been gradually exposed. The consumers within the sinking market are often labeled as “living outside the Fifth Ring Road” or “small town youth” in the new media. In fact, as a rising new consumer group in Chinese domestic market, they share the same aspiration for better lives as those consumers in first- and second-tier cities, who only differentiate themselves by their consumption behavior patterns. Such differences will determine enterprises’ product value positioning and strategy choices if they want to better capture the huge business opportunities contained in these sinking markets.

Several compounding factors are the reasons for the occurrence of market sinking and its explosive growth in recent years. First, more and more enterprises find their current market segments too competitive as many markets have been largely saturated in both territories and user base, which makes it more difficult for them to scour new growth opportunities in such old markets. That’s why they are often pressed to explore new incremental growth opportunities to avoid the potential impact brought about by the ever-increasing competition in existing markets. No doubt, market sinking is logically reasonable, as it could funnel in more incremental growth opportunities. It could expand the existing customer base and transplant the existing products and services into the newly explored sinking market after some trimming and transformation. It’s predicted by the forecast released by McKinsey and Morgan Stanley that by 2030, China’s personal consumption will increase from RMB 29.6 trillion in 2016 to 65.3 trillion, and over 66% of the growth will come from the sinking market.

Secondly, there are a lot of unmet needs in the sinking markets. With the development of the economy and the increase of disposable income, greater demand for higher quality of life than before emerge the sinking market. In light of this, although market sinking is more often described from the supply side, if viewed from the demand side, it is in essence a consumption upgrade in the sinking market.[7] However, compared with first- and second-tier cities, there is still a remarkable gap in the supply of products and services in the sinking market, both in terms of product options and product quality. Traditionally, the consumption needs in the sinking market are mostly met through localized offline retail businesses, primarily in the form of grocery stores and small shops. The new retail business forms such as Freshhema.com, which can be found in first- and second-tier cities, are rarely seen in the sinking market.

In recent years, the accelerated sinking of China's e-commerce giants has also promoted the rapid release of demands from such markets. The third-tier, fourth- and even lower-tier cities have become new battlefields for Chinese e-commerce giants. For example, as of the end of March 2019, the monthly active mobile users of Tmall of Taobao reached 721 million, which increased by 104 million year-on-year over that of 2018, and its annual active consumers reached 654 million, an increase of 102 million over the same period of 2018, 77% of whom came from third- and fourth-tier cities and rural areas.[8] By the end of June 2019, the number of online home appliance stores in JD.COM exceeded 10,000, with their customers distributed in 25,000 townships and more than 600,000 administrative villages around China. As e-commerce relies heavily on efficient

[7]In this regard, the idea that simply regards market sinking as a signal of consumption degradation is biased. Because, although those marginalized consumption demands gradually released with the developing economy and the rising income are often regarded as the slim version of the core market demand, for those consumers in the sinking market, the new demands they released are substantially improved if compared with their own original demands. Besides, such demand is also constantly expanding in its scope (i.e., consumers become accustomed to goods and services that used to be beyond their consumption choices). This clearly carries the characteristics of consumption upgrading. It also verifies a point I expressed earlier: it's often very difficult to describe a phenomenon happening in China in one word, as the Chinese market could often take on multiple attributes at the same time.

[8]Tao, L. (2019). The Chinese e-commerce business in financial sheets: Giants strive for downward penetration whereas new players are running with scissors. The 21th Century Economic Report, May 22, 2019.

logistics, payment settlement and sound internet infrastructure, these e-commerce giants have promoted the formation and upgrading of these commercial infrastructures in the process of their continuous expansion. Besides, the relatively low labor cost in the sinking market is a very favorable factor for controlling the last-mile logistics distribution cost.

Compared with that in first- and second-tier cities, consumers in sinking markets certainly demonstrate a different profile. Although they cannot compare with consumers in first- and second-tier cities in terms of absolute income, they are stronger in marginal propensity of consumption, which is especially true for consumers in third- and fourth-tier cities. Thanks to the more affordable local housing cost, education cost and living cost in small towns and rural areas, consumers in these areas are more willing to spend on consumption. According to the China Consumer Confidence Index Report issued by Nielsen, in 2018, consumer confidence is the weakest among residents of first-tier cities and is much stronger in residents of third-tier cities and rural areas, which also proves the above-mentioned point.

For those enterprises embracing the sinking strategy, they might be rewarded with lower market development costs. This is because since consumers in the sinking market are still gradually establishing their brand awareness, they are relatively short of product and brand awareness, and have not yet formed stable personal brand preferences, hence their product purchasing behavior can be easily influenced by media and advertisements. At the same time, with the continuously deepening penetration of the Internet, the power of social networks cannot be ignored. This is largely due to the slower work pace there than that in the first- and second-tier cities, which allows the residents more leisure time and lower time cost. Therefore, they are privileged with low costs in maintaining their social networks. This is why the life of people living in the sinking market areas tend to be more like that in the traditional acquaintance society of China, where the social network people needed to maintain were relatively small in scale, but closer in terms of interpersonal relationships. It is precisely because of this that Pinduoduo, Tik Tok and Kuaishou managed to realize fast selling of products by tapping into interpersonal social relations in the physical world, primarily in the third-, fourth-, and lower-tier cities and towns.

It should be pointed out that market sinking came in hand with the mega-trend of consumption upgrading in China. It is precisely because of the lasting consumption upgrade that demands of all market ladders have been continuously released. In other words, China's market sinking takes place along the entire market ladder, not just in some local areas. The lower end of the market ladder is more likely to experience brownfield growth, while the upper end of the market ladder is more likely to experience greenfield growth. According to the research report "New Trends of China Consumers: Three Motives Shaping New Consumer Groups in China" jointly released by BCG and Ali Research Institute in May 2017, China's personal consumption has been growing between 2016 to 2021 by USD 1.8 trillion, 75% of which were contributed by consumers from the emerging middle class to the upper-middle class or above, whereas 46% of which were contributed by consumers from cities below the third tier. In addition, in the "Insight Report on the Sinking Market" released by Alimama Insight Lab in August 2019 (see Figure 10.1), it's pointed out that the gross merchandise volume from the sinking market grew much faster, with 77% of product categories demonstrating faster turnover growth in third-tier cities and below than in first- and second-tier cities. The explosive growth of the sinking market is result of consumer population increase and consumption upgrading. According to the report, for 84% of product categories surveyed, their consumers in tier 3–6 cities outnumbered that in first- and second-tier cities. And 61% of product categories have higher average transaction value in third- to sixth-tier cities than that in first- and second-tier cities. In addition, in March 2018, Taobao launched Taobao Uland, while JD.COM launched JD Groupon to fend off the Pinduoduo, a new e-commerce player rising from the sinking market. It was found that 78.3% of the users who uninstalled Pinduoduo App turned to Taobao, whereas 50.3% of the users who uninstalled Taobao App turned to Pinduoduo. That is why we often say that "Tmall is an upgraded version of Taobao, while Pinduoduo is a sinking version of Taobao". The above figures reflect a trend of the concurrence of consumption upgrading and market sinking.

There are two important cores to decipher the value demand of the sinking market. One is the pursuit of value-for-money by the sinking market. Of course, there are two kinds of value-for-money markets, that is, the price-sensitive type and the value-sensitive type, which are classified based on the disposable income level of people in the market and their degree of awareness about product quality and brand value. In some sinking markets, these two sub-types could co-exist or even cover the same consumer population at the same time. Another value core is the pursuit and yearning for better life quality. Sometimes, what people are pursuing

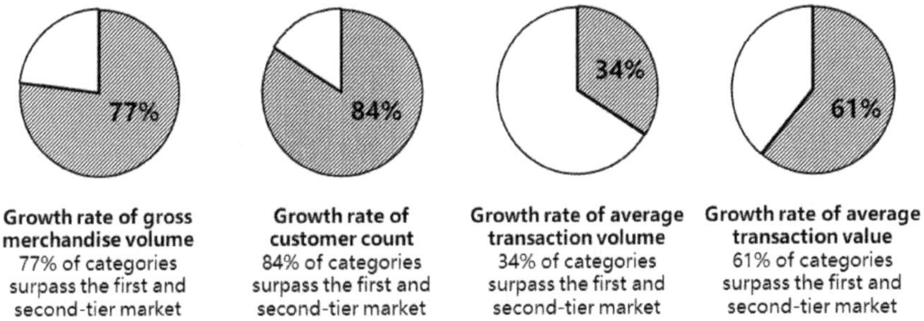

Figure 10.1. Fast Growth of Chinese Cities below Tier 3

Source: Alimama Insight Lab, Sinking Market Insight Report, August 2019.

is not just a product, for a product is actually just a carrier conveying what people value in their mind. Therefore, after penetrating into the sinking market, many consumer products convey people's admiration for a certain lifestyle and quality of life. Just like in the 1990s, parents and children in the first- and second-tier cities regarded dining at McDonald's and KFC as a kind of self-indulgence and reward beyond their daily routine. Yet, nowadays, for first- and second-tier city residents in China, it has become no more than a routine consumption behavior.

Time is changing a lot of things, but surely not people's aspirations for quality of life. Nowadays, McDonald's, KFC, Starbucks, Haidilao, etc., which used to be found only in larger cities, have a presence in many small counties. Before they know it, people living in small counties gradually develop the habit of buying their daily necessities in supermarkets where online payment methods like Alipay and WeChat payment have become a routine. Likewise, they visit the e-commerce platforms to explore new products and brands that they have not heard of before and are amazed. To these people, those products and services are more than what they seemingly are. In fact, more importantly, they represent a new way of life. Many foreign brands are also trying to capture this incremental growth opportunity. For example, Lego from Denmark, the much-beloved childhood toy to many children in first and second-tier cities, has accelerated its expansion in China since 2016. After opening three direct brand flagship stores in Beijing and Shanghai, it opened Lego toy franchised stores in nearly 30 second- and third-tier cities across China, with plans to open another 140 stores more. Even before that, Lego Education had already entered the sinking market in China through opening franchise stores.

Can the Labor Cost Advantage Sustain?

Chinese Premier Keqiang Li gave his preliminary diagnosis about China's economy at a government meeting summoned in October 2015, saying that "China's economy is in the painstaking process of shifting from the old economic growth driver to a new one". After that, the phrase "new growth drivers" began to formally appear in the speeches of national leaders and government work reports. What is the background for proposing the concept of new growth driver? We can try to interpret it from the following trends of changes.

First, the "re-industrialization" of developed countries will change the pattern of global manufacturing. Since 2000, the whole world is facing a mega trend of "re-industrialization". In the past, considering the migration of labor costs, developed countries have long been outsourcing manufacturing to overseas countries. After 2000, more and more developed countries began to rethink the hidden danger in "hollowing-out the manufacturing industry", particularly the United States, which made a lot of adjustments and proposed "re-industrialization" since 2005. This signified the triumphant return of manufacturing on government's agenda in developed countries. Of course, for developed countries, "re-industrialization" not only means to restart the manufacturing industry, but to harness the new developing trends and new drivers to realize the smartization, Internet-bonding and high added value of the high-end manufacturing sector. In the past 40 years of reform and opening-up, China's manufacturing industry has benefited from industrial globalization. "Re-industrialization" of developed countries will inevitably collide with the rising manufacturing power of China, forcing Chinese enterprises to transform and upgrade their development model.

Second, the economic development trajectory of developed countries has proven that, with the development of the national economy, the increase of GDP often benefits more from high-end manufacturing and less from low-end manufacturing. This is because the rising economic development level will lead to the upward shift of labor costs, which will accordingly reshape the manufacturing modality that adapts to the new paradigm. It means that the key factors driving the rapid development of

China's manufacturing industry are inevitably changing. Over the past 40 years, the rapid development of China's manufacturing industry has been benefiting from the low-cost labor force and the imitation advantage enjoyed by late-comers. However, in the future, it will be more driven by technology, R&D and innovation. And the changes in economic environment and competitive environment will also alternate the way Chinese enterprises establish their global competitive advantages.

Many years before the pressure of transformation was first felt, traditional labor-intensive industries had already initiated their adjustment. Take the textile industry, a typical labor-intensive industry, as an example. Since 2005, China's textile industry has sped up its transfer to Vietnam, Cambodia and other Southeast Asian countries. At first, it was just a sporadic act of individual manufacturers. However, it laterally evolved into a common act of enterprises on the industrial value chain: textile and garment OEM enterprises (such as Shenzhou International and Jasan Group) made successive deployments in Southeast Asia. Before long, upstream enterprises in cotton yarn, printing and dyeing and fabric business quickly followed suit (such as Huafu Color Textile, Blum Oriental, Weixing Co., Ltd. and Lutai A, etc.). The initial motivation of production capacity transfer might be more out of the consideration of labor cost, proximity to the market and preferential policies of the host country. However, in recent years, concerns about trade wars and tariff barriers have also become important driving factors.

What we need to consider here is not only the gradual loss of cost advantage in the global value chain but also the impact of the rising labor cost on Chinese enterprises in the local market. Recently, driven by gradual implementation of policies on de-capacity and de-leverage that are compounded by the rising manufacturing costs, Chinese enterprises face the pressing need to change their market positioning. At the same time, as Chinese enterprises are already facing the pressure of global competition in many industries, how to seek a more favorable position in the global value chain is also a problem that Chinese enterprises need to focus on and solve. This will also bring new pressures to the innovation drive of Chinese enterprises.

"China Corporate Social Security White Paper 2018" mentioned that 53% of all enterprises surveyed had their labor cost accounting for over 30% of their total cost. 16.27% of them have their labor cost taking up 50% of their total costs. In the case of Haidilao, according to its 2018 annual report, its labor cost in 2018 was RMB 5 billion (29.56% of its total cost), while its annual operating income was RMB 17 billion. It's the reason why Haidilao started to develop an automated service solution. Even for Internet-based companies like Luckin Coffee and Meituan, their labor costs have, respectively, accounted for 45.05% and 56.83% of their total costs.

Evidenced by the macro-level data, China's population growth has remained low since 2000 (see Figure 10.2), while the number of its working-age labor has been in decline after reaching its peak in 2010 (see Figure 10.3). This also confirms that the growth modality featured with the cliche labor-intensive industries is difficult to sustain. But does this mean that China has completely lost its labor cost advantage?

Industrial transformation and upgrading have been proposed many years ago, and are not new topics. However, when revisiting China's economic growth, we will realize that China is already at a critical junction point. There is no doubt that China's manufacturing industry is now

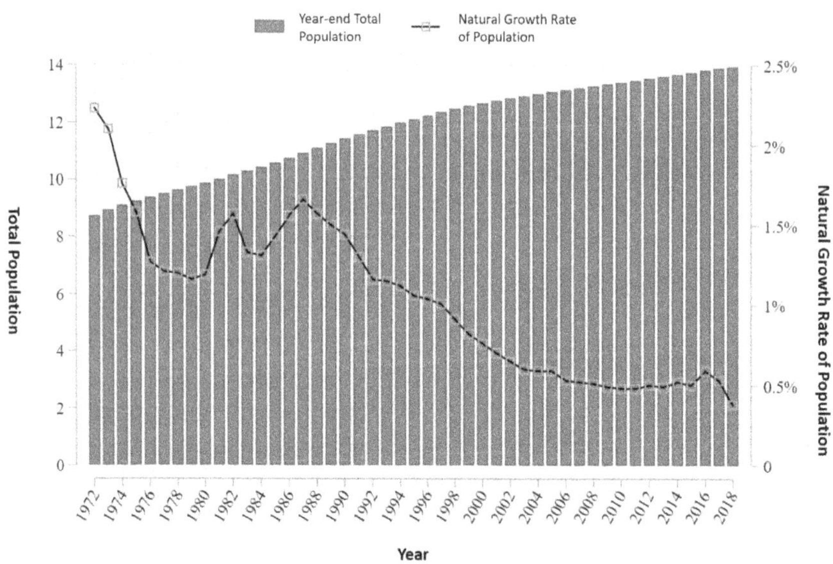

Figure 10.2. Population of China: 1972–2018

Note: The population data in 1981 and before were based on household registration statistics. The data of 1982, 1990, 2000 and 2010 were the estimations based on the census data of that year. Data of other years are estimated from the annual population sampling survey. Active servicemen are included in the total population and the population breaks down by sex, and they are also included in the urban population when it is broken down by the urban and rural population.

Source: China National Bureau of Statistics.

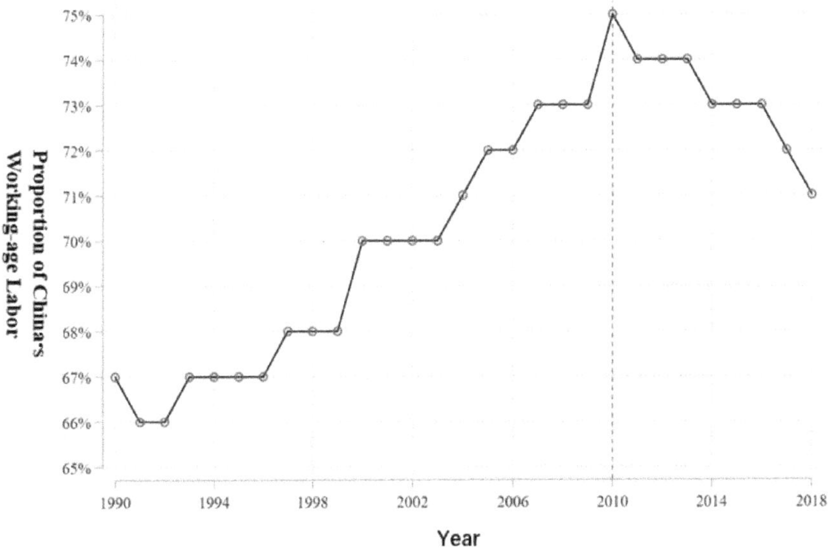

Figure 10.3. Proportion of China's Working-Age Labor Force: 1990–2016

Source: China National Bureau of Statistics.

struggling with the loss of its traditional competitiveness due to the rising labor costs. However, in the past, when talking about China's labor advantage, our focus was often on low-end labor force. When discussing the vanishing demographic dividend, people are more concerned with the evaporation of low-cost labor force, mainly the labor-intensive labor force. However, observing from a broader perspective, we will find that China has produced from its higher education system a huge number of college graduates every year over the past two decades (see Figure 10.4). These laborers who continuously transfuse into the economic system are very different from the high-intensity manual laborers that China used to build its manufacturing advantages on in the past. These college graduates were referred to as the "knowledge workers" by Professor Peter Drucker, the father of modern management. Actually, for China's manufacturing industry, the real problem it faces is that the industrial structure it established in the past is more like a human capital structure with manual workers as the core. Thus, it has become a great challenge for the Chinese manufacturing industry to transform the old industrial structure into a new one that can give full play to the cost advantages (or more exactly speaking, in cost and skills) of its knowledge laborers. In a sense, if China can

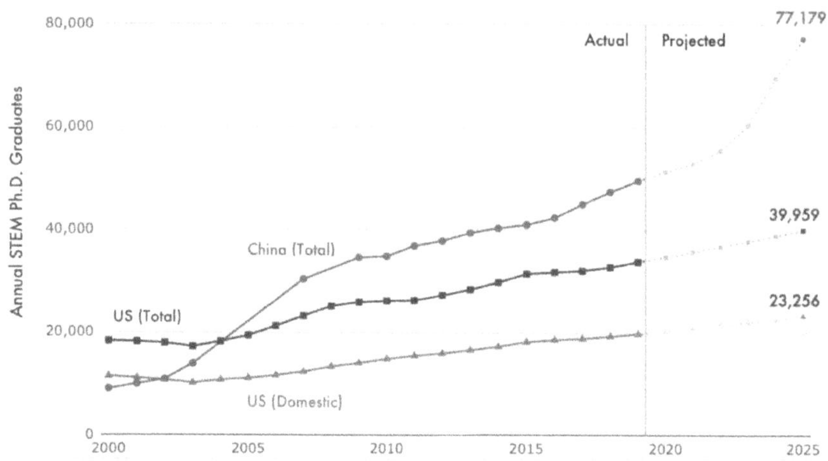

Figure 10.4. The Numbers of Annual STEM (Science, Technology, Engineering and Mathematics) PhD Graduates for China and US

Source: Zwetsloot, R., J. Corrigan, E. Weinstein, D. Peterson, D. Gehlhaus, and R. Fedasiuk (2021). China is fast outpacing US STEM PhD growth. Center for Security and Emerging Technology, August 2021, p. 2. National Center for Education Statistics' Integrated Postsecondary Education Data System (IPEDS) for U.S. data, Ministry of Education for Chinese data.

complete such an upgradation and transformation of its industrial structure, it means that the cost advantage of China's manufacturing industry will take a new form, bringing China the next golden decade. Of course, if an industrial structure transformation cannot be successfully completed, China's economic growth will stagnate or even decline in the next stage. In the transformation process, innovation is no doubt the most important driving force for industrial transformation and upgrading.

Reid Hoffman, the founder of LinkedIn, and Chris Yeh, an expert of China Thinkers Bureau, underlined the potential advantages brought about by the flexibility of China's labor market in their co-authored book *Blitzscaling*. China boasts a vast and flexible labor market, which privileges China an advantage in overcoming the growth restriction brought about by operational scaling. To illustrate this, they also specially brought up two typical examples. For example, in 2012, Apple executives needed to employ 8,700 industrial engineers to supervise and guide the 200,000 assembly-line workers that eventually participated in the iPhone manufacturing. If finding so many qualified engineers could be possible in the United States, it was estimated to take up to 9 months, whereas in China, it would take only 15 days. Another example mentioned is that even Silicon Valley enterprises could hardly match the work intensity with that of China's Blitzscaling companies. Andrew Ng, a professor at Stanford University and the co-founder of Coursera, was the head of a machine learning project of Baidu. Once he thought of a human resources problem while having supper, so he sent a text message to the human resources supervisor at 7 pm, and the supervisor immediately sent a text message to her team asking them to solve the problem. At 7:30 pm, the problem proposed by Andrew Ng was already properly resolved. Although such episode may seem to be natural to Chinese enterprises, in the eyes of Reid Hoffman and Chris Yeh, it's a very special example showcasing China's speed and flexibility.

In addition, the McKinsey Global Institute analyzed the trade transactions of 23 industries among 43 countries (accounting for 96% of the total global trade volume) and pointed out five structural changes in global trade. According to the report, though it is generally believed that global trade is driven by companies seeking lower-cost labor, it is not true, because only about 18% of global merchandise trade conforms to this labor cost arbitrage model (that is, goods flow from low-wage countries to high-wage countries). Other important factors driving international trade may also include access to highly skilled labor, closer proximity to markets and the quality of infrastructure.

The Development of Technological Dominance

In 2019, the average profit of Fortune 500 companies was USD 4.3 billion. A total of 119 Chinese companies were enlisted (not including enterprises from Taiwan Province), with an average sales income of USD 66.5 billion, an average net asset of USD 35.4 billion and an average profit of USD 3.5 billion. If ticking out banking enterprises from the list, the profit level of Chinese enterprises would be only about 1/3 of that of American enterprises.[9] For the Chinese companies listed, their average return on sales was 5.3%, which was lower than the 7.7% of American companies and the global average of 6.6%. Their average return on net

[9] mbd.baidu.com/newspage/data/landingshare?pageType=1&isBdboxFrom=1&context=%7B%22nid%22%3A%22news_8519997036444089454%22%2C%22sourceFrom%22%3A%22bjh%22%7D&from=timeline.

assets was 9.9%, which was lower than the 15% of American enterprises and the global average of 12.1%.[10] Such data show that despite the rapid development of China's top-performing companies in recent years, there is still a big gap in profitability between them and their Western counterparts from developed countries including the United States. Company profitability is closely related to their management capability, brand influence and technological dominance. Among them, for manufacturing enterprises, technological dominance has more enduring impacts, as it not only constitutes an important foundation of brand influence, but also determines enterprises' controlling ability in the whole value chain system.

In today's world, those top industrial companies that represent various countries also form intricately complicated competition relations. They are widely engaged in the industry gaming of the global technology chain. Taking the industry gaming between China and the United States as an example, we can divide this industry gaming competition into four aspects: that in product market, efficiency and sufficiency of manufacturing chain, breadth of technology chain and underlying core of technology chain. In terms of product market, Chinese manufacturing industry has obtained some advantages in market share in many product domains, where the industry gaming in this aspect is mainly seen in the fact that the United States will try to reduce its trade deficit in specific industries and to expand its exports. At the level of efficiency and sufficiency of manufacturing chain, China has also established some advantages, which could serve as an advantage foundation in China–US industry gaming.

However, there is a clear gap in terms of the breadth and the underlying core (or the depth) of the technology chain between the Chinese and American manufacturing industry. In 2019, the Chinese Academy of Engineering evaluated the industrial chain safety of 26 representative manufacturing industries, and found that among them, 6 were self-sufficient and controllable (accounting for 23%), 10 were industrial safety controllable (accounting for 38.5%), 2 were highly dependent on the outside world (accounting for 0.77%), and 8 were extremely dependent on the outside world (accounting for 30.8%).[11] Especially in terms of the underlying core of some technology chains, such as lithography machines of IC industry, high-end chips in ICT equipment industry, bearings and

[10] www.fortunechina.com/fortune500/c/2019-07/22/content_339535.htm.

[11] http://tech.ifeng.com/c/7qp0oL5yeXI.

operation control systems in rail transit equipment industry, hot parts of gas turbines in power equipment industry, along with the design and simulation software of complex product systems such as airplanes and automobiles, etc., they are highly dependent on foreign countries and constitute great potential constraints on the development of China's manufacturing industry. Through comparison with the United States, we analyze the reasons for such gap as follows. On the one hand, it is due to the advantageous breadth and depth of the technology chain owned by the United States itself. On the other hand, the overall national strength of the United States helps it to acquire dominance and influence in the breadth and depth of the global technology chain. These two advantages explain why the US can obtain clear advantages over China in the technology chain.[12]

In fact, the reason why Huawei remains the only target of oppression by the US government lies in the fact that Made-in-China still lacks enough powerful companies with global competitiveness distributed at various key nodes on the technology chain. This forced Huawei to cope with multiple points on the whole industrial technology chain alone. That is to say, Huawei is coping with multiple impacts with its individual strength. Thus, it has been fighting an unequal and unfair game.

In order to offset China's disadvantaged position in the technology chain and the consequent passive and adverse situation faced by Chinese enterprises in the China–US industry gaming, we need to well leverage some other advantages: China itself is one of the largest single markets in

[12]In this regard, the China–US trade conflict since 2018, especially the oppression of Chinese technology-oriented leading enterprises in this process, made the Chinese government and industry community realize that even in the era of globalization, the resilience of the industrial chain and the technology chain is still very important. This is why China has started to think strategically about the problem of "self-sufficiency and controllable strategy" both at the government and at the enterprise level. In fact, before the outbreak of the large-scale China–US trade conflict, China was not fully mentally prepared for this. Back then, the general trend was to dock into globalization more widely and deeply, and use the specialized division of labor in the global manufacturing chain to gain comparative advantages. The change of strategy to establish comparative advantages from simple reliance on division of labor in the global value chain to establishing comparative competition advantage based on self-sufficiency and controllable strategy has brought and will continue to bring an impact on the development trend of the global value chain. This is not only a question that China's manufacturing industry needs to think about, but is also a strategic issue that every economy around the world needs to think about in the process of their industrial development.

the world, which can not only provide the scale basis for Chinese enterprises to survive but also help Chinese enterprises to better integrate into the global industrial chain. China's complete and efficient manufacturing industry chain has the cost and value-for-money advantages to compete in the global market, except under extreme conditions. Strong government resource mobilization ability can provide initial conditions for those technical domains featured with high entry barriers and the need of substantial resource input, hence enabling them to use market mechanism to develop their technology systems. The utilization of all these advantages is based on a clear goal, that is, buffering or even eliminating the disadvantages of Chinese enterprises in the breadth of the technology chain and the depth of underlying core.

In some emerging technology fields that are highly dependent on economies of scale or network effects, Chinese enterprises may have more opportunities to build technological dominance and obtain opportunities to overtake in corners, such as the domains of Internet, big data and artificial intelligence, all of which are highly dependent on data and application scenarios. Whoever has more data and more application opportunities will be more likely to build up their own competences through the cumulative effect of data assets and the learning effect based on fast iteration. In this regard, China enjoys a huge population base, and is thus benefited with a huge data resource base and application opportunities.

It is of unprecedented importance and urgency for China to adjust its R&D input structure and improve its output efficiency so as to acquire competitiveness in the technology chain and seize the opportunity to overtake on a corner under the facilitation of technological paradigm changes. In the past two decades, China has been continuously gearing up its investment in R&D resources and achieved some accomplishments. In the "Global Competitiveness Report (2019)" released by the World Economic Forum (WEF), China's global competitiveness index ranked 28th among the 141 economies in the world. According to the 2018 Statistical Bulletin of National Science and Technology Investment jointly issued by the National Bureau of Statistics, the Ministry of Science and Technology and the Ministry of Finance of China, the total R&D investment of China was RMB 1.96779 trillion, and the R&D intensity (i.e., the ratio of R&D expenditure to GDP) was 2.19%[13] (which was quite close to 2.372%, the

[13] http://finance.sina.com.cn/roll/2019-08-30/doc-iicezzrq2338527.shtml.

average figure of OECD countries in 2018).[14] As for R&D expenditure, China has become the country with the second-largest R&D expenditure in the world, and it's second only to the United States. Although measured in sheer size, China's R&D expenditure has already reached a considerable scale, and it has become a great challenge that China's national innovation system needs to face in terms of how to support China in establishing a solid foundation in basic research, how to realize breakthroughs in key areas of the underlying technology chain, and how to improve the output efficiency of China's R&D expenditure. Simply emphasizing on quantity and scale expansion can no longer completely address China's need for quality of economic growth.

Back to the Ivory Tower

Although criticism against Chinese universities accusing them as "being far away from the market" was heard as early as in the 1990s, the efficiency of industry–university–academia cooperation and technology transfer in China's national innovation system is still considered to be sufficient today. Therefore, for a long time, we have heard the outcry of "urging universities to step out of the ivory tower". This view was generally reasonable for a certain period of time. However, with the passage of time, the situation has changed. In a sense, nowadays, Chinese universities are not too far away from the market. On the contrary, they are too obsessed with the market. A direct example is the R&D funding sources of universities, with the proportion of funds from industry much higher than that at the beginning of the reform. In 2007, for example, for Chinese universities, the average proportion of scientific research funds from enterprises was 35.09%, which was much higher than 5.41% for the United States[1]. At the same time, the proportion of government funding has also shown a declining trend since 2007. For example, in 2019, according to the statistics about budget revenue of universities directly under the China Ministry of Education, the proportion of contribution of fiscal allocation to budget revenue of Tsinghua University, Peking University and Zhejiang University was, respectively, 18.2%, 30.7% and 20.9% (Table 10.1).

[14] https://data.oecd.org/rd/gross-domestic-spending-on-r-d.htm.

Table 10.1. Sources of R&D Funds of Chinese and American Universities (2007)

Types of Universities	**Ratio of Government Funding**	**Ratio of Enterprise Funding**
China's 2+7 universities (9 universities)	66.41%	27.06%
China's "985 Project" universities (37 universities)	60.01%	35.99%
Universities directly under the Ministry of Education of China or affiliated to the Chinese Academy of Sciences and the National Defense Science, Technology and Industry Committee (83 universities)	56.26%	39.05%
Average of Chinese universities	56.47%	35.09%
Top 10 American Universities in R&D Fund	69.92%	7.66%
Top 50 American Universities in R&D Fund	68.71%	5.97%
Top 100 American Universities in R&D Fund	67.76%	5.50%
Average of American universities	67.95%	5.41%

Source: Gao Lei, G., and Z. Wenhua (2010). A comparative study on R&D funds and entrepreneurial performance of Chinese and American research universities. *China Higher Education Research* 2010(5): 39–42.

In recent years, China's central government has given more funding support to universities to facilitate their construction of world-class universities. So, top universities have received more funds from the government. Nevertheless, the proportion of enterprises' contribution in university funding still remains at a high level. Given that engineering universities might be more representative of this ratio, we chose Tsinghua University, Shanghai Jiaotong University and Zhejiang University to investigate this proportion. In 2016 and 2017, the enterprise-contributed research funding of these three universities was roughly between 20% and 25%. As indicated by Emerging Economies University Rankings 2019 released by the *Times Higher Education*, 47 of the top 100 Universities with enterprise-contributed funding were from China. And 29 Chinese universities ranked in the top 50.[15]

These data proved that, despite the fact that some universities or research institutes may still be far away from the market, as a whole, Chinese universities and research institutions have stepped out of the

[15]http://www.sohu.com/a/304631027_100169020.

"ivory tower" in the past two decades. They are increasingly driven by market forces in terms of the way of obtaining research funds and the focus of allocation of research resources. Such change has no doubt played a very important role in promoting the rise of China's manufacturing industry in the past two decades.

However, looking into the greater future, Chinese universities and research institutions face another challenge to their roles. As China's economy has grown into the second-largest one in the world, it is no longer possible to drive the further growth of China's economy without the role of basic research and disruptive innovation. Chinese enterprises can no longer benefit from global technological development through imitation and technology spillovers as much as in the past years. They need to create more technological development opportunities from basic research. On the one hand, because of the rapid growth of Chinese enterprises, the narrowing of the technological gap between Chinese enterprises and their counterparts in Western developed countries will surely reduce the opportunities of directly tapping into the current knowledge bases. On the other hand, competitive pressure will also drive the leading companies from developed economies to strengthen their control over knowledge and technologies.

As such, Chinese universities and research institutions will step more close to the market, and thereby assist Chinese enterprises in solving their engineering-oriented, manufacturing-oriented and technology-oriented problems. However, with the upward transformation of China's manufacturing industry, the need for basic research and applied basic research is stronger than ever. From the current situation of the national innovation system, the above-mentioned assistance is relatively insufficient at present. Due to economic motivation to serve industrialization, a large number of research focuses of universities and research institutions are closer to the market and farther away from science. In terms of a whole industrial innovation system, a normal system should constitute a continuous technological ladder, with enterprises evenly distributed from low to high, so as to achieve overall benefits for the industry. If the upper ladder does not move upward, and the lower ladder does not penetrate downward, the ladder will become discontinuous. Therefore, at least some of the Chinese universities and research institutions need to consider moving their positioning upward in the technological ladder within China's national innovation system.

In this sense, the biggest challenge for Chinese universities and research institutions is not how to "get out of the ivory tower", but how to "return to the ivory tower", so as to truly support the further upward migration of Chinese manufacturing industry and assume a supporting responsibility in basic research and applied basic research, which is also an important condition for Chinese manufacturing industry to move to a higher peak in the globalization system.

The Age of Discovery of China

The Age of Discovery, for the Western world, refers to the world exploration started by European navigators from the end of the 15th century.[16] It is especially represented by Vasco da Gama (about 1460–1524), Christopher Columbus (about 1451–1506) and Fernando Magellan (about 1480–1521). These navigators started their voyage from Europe to the world. To the Western world, the Age of Discovery is of extraordinary significance. Through the expansion of commercial trade, the trade and cultural exchanges between the East and the West were facilitated. Together with the Renaissance, it promoted the rise of European capitalism.

Just like when our predecessors explored the new geographical areas in history, Made-in-China, after its rise, is also embarking on a journey of exploring the world. However, to Chinese enterprises, this gradually unfolding "Age of Discovery" has its unique connotations. Because when Western navigators set sail to explore and conquer, their navigation technology and the advantageous knowledge in business rules made them invincible in the new territory. In the new age of discovery for Chinese enterprises, with the existing global business rules, China may even need a long time to learn and understand how to accept, adapt and apply these rules in this globalized system.

In the global expansion of Chinese enterprises, we can identify a "path dependence". That is to say, the strategies and paths chosen by

---

[16] It should be pointed out that, in fact, China has a prouder history in the Age of Discovery compared to the West. During 1405–1433, He Zheng, China's greatest navigator of Ming Dynasty, led a huge fleet of ships to the Western Pacific Ocean and Indian Ocean, reaching afar to the East Africa and the Red Sea.

Chinese enterprises mirror the experience and ability they have accumulated in the past.

As we know, after weathering through fierce competition in the local market, Chinese enterprises have built up very powerful experience and ability in terms of the value-for-money market. In terms of deep understanding of and survival experience in the value-for-money market, Chinese enterprises are the best in the whole world. Before they acquire cultural and brand influences across the world, especially in the initial stages of their entering overseas markets, it is an inevitable choice for Chinese enterprises to transplant and utilize the capability advantages of the value-for-money market to overseas markets.

Take Transsion Holdings, the so-called "king of mobile phones in Africa", as an example. Founded in 2006, the company was created by Zhaojiang Zhu, the former head of overseas marketing of Bird Mobile Phone, which employs over 10,000 employees worldwide. The company owns three mobile phone brands, TECNO, itel and Infinix, and its products are sold in Africa, Middle East, Southeast Asia and South Asia, which are more prone to be the price-sensitive good-enough markets. One of the important reasons for choosing to enter overseas markets was the fierce competition in the Chinese domestic mobile phone market, the rise of *Shanzhai* mobile phones, and the strong market positioning of foreign brands such as Nokia, Samsung and Sony, all of which made Transsion adopt a different way. In 2008, Transsion decided on the strategy of focusing on Africa. In 2010, its TECNO brand ranked in the top 3 in the African mobile phone market. In 2015, it decided to open up the Indian market. In 2017, the market share of all Transsion's sub-brands reached 45% in Africa and 9% in India. In order to support the cost-effective strategy and improve the quick response to the market, Transsion built its Shenzhen Yantian factory, which went into operation in 2009. In 2011, it built production facilities in Ethiopia and deployed a large number of terminal outlets in the African market to handle sales and after-sales services.

XIAOMI also chose the strategy of expanding to overseas markets because of the fierce competition in the Chinese market. In terms of its path to expand into overseas markets, XIAOMI cut in from India, extended to Southeast Asia, and then ventured into Russian and European market. It entered 82 overseas markets, and in 25 of them, it ranked top five in the industry. In its replication of its cost–performance strategy in the Chinese good-enough market, it massively incorporated localization strategies. For example, 95% of its products in the Indonesian market are made locally. It also established factories in India, and promoted suppliers to set up supporting factories. Besides, in order to replicate its ecological strategy in the home market, dozens of start-ups have been established in India and Indonesia to perfect the mobile-phone-related ecological chain system.[17]

Using local innovation to capture the market opportunities of other large emerging economies is also a common strategy of these enterprises aiming at overseas expansion. In the African market, Transsion conducted many micro-innovations for its mobile phone products to cater to the needs of local consumers. For example, in order to give better selfie experience to the local users, Transsion collected a large number of photos of African locals to analyze their face contours, exposure compensation and imaging effect.[18] The cameras of mainstream mobile phone sets mainly use facial recognition technology. However, due to the darker skin color of African people, this technology exhibited poor performance. So, Transsion developed a photo processing technology based on eyes and teeth capturing, which was combined with enhanced exposure methods to help African consumers get more satisfactory photos. Another example is Dahua, a leading video-centric smart IoT solution and service provider based in China. Dahua adopted a well-schemed strategy of product customization and differentiation according to the characteristics of different markets when entering foreign markets. For example, in light of India's market landscape with analog products as the mainstream, Dahua developed tailor-made digital-analog products that accommodate both customers' existing requirements and also the future trend of high-definition digitalization. In light of climate differences of different geographical locations, they supply Thailand and Mexico with more anti-corrosive products that are fit for use in humid marine climate, whereas they provide products that show excellent performance at ultra-low temperature for the Russian market. In fact, such customization and differentiation based on localized needs are not very substantial innovations in technology, but they meet the specific needs of the local market, which are often ignored by foreign competitors.

---

[17]Guoqing (2018). Xiaomi's global layout by Jun lei: It has entered 82 overseas markets. TechWeb, November 6, 2018. http://people.techweb.com.cn/2018-11-06/2710943.shtml.

[18]*The Paper News*: Transsion as the king of African mobile phone market: A 12 years' journey to triumph led by Zhaojiang Zhu and his team, March 3, 2018. https://www.thepaper.cn/newsDetail_forward_2015150.

Searching for a blank market with a large number of unsatisfied demands, and then penetrating into it by replicating existing business models is also one of the options sometimes. In September 2015, Ant Financial entered the Indian market by shareholding One97 Communications, the parent company of Paytm, India's largest mobile payment company. In November 2016, Ant Financial signed a strategic cooperation agreement with Ascend Money, a Thai payment company.[19] Behind these overseas market entry moves, one important consideration is that there is a big gap in terms of financial service level between these markets and developed economies. Besides, there were no long-standing strong competitors in these markets. Therefore, Ant Financial could find a huge market gap in financial services for the general public. This unsatisfied demand is very similar to the case during the early stage of e-commerce development in China. This similarity in demand makes it possible for Ant Financial to effectively replicate its previous model and accumulated experience in China's domestic market.

The great age of discovery of Chinese enterprises will demonstrate a unique feature, that is, the co-existence of local market upgrading and global expansion. Chinese enterprises will have more opportunities to benefit from the synergy of the two events. Just as Nick Leung, Chairman of McKinsey China, trenchantly summarized in McKinsey Global Institute's *China and the World: Inside the dynamics of a changing relationship*, "In the past 40 years of reform and opening up, driven by the joint efforts of industrialization, investment and trade, China's economy has achieved a miracle of sustained and rapid growth. Nowadays, the key driving force for economic development has shifted to stimulating domestic demand. At the same time, the rising dependence of the world on China's economy indicates that China is becoming an increasingly important market, supplier and capital provider". Especially when we view the global market as a bigger market ladder, we will find almost all the characteristics of the Chinese market can be identified in such a large-scale market system. For those Chinese enterprises carrying more lofty aspirations, a spectacular new age of discovery is slowly unfolding.

---

[19]How does Ant Financial nibble on the EU market? December 12, 2016. https://www.sohu.com/a/121280888_115207.

More Inclusive Integration into Globalization

After the reform and opening-up in 1978, China gradually stepped into the globalization arena. Looking back, the process of China's economic development almost coincided with China's full integration into the globalized system. Moreover, China has actually become a beneficiary of the globalization system, although at the beginning of the reform and opening-up many industries in China showed a mixed feeling of worry, doubt and confusion about globalization, fearing to be destroyed due to the huge competitiveness gap between China and developed countries in the process of opening up.

With China becoming more and more confident and willing to embrace globalization in an all-round way, the Western world's attitude toward China has undergone subtle changes. Both the China–US trade conflict started from 2018 and the US government's economic containment policy against China indicated that the United States, as the most important economy in the Western world, has been regarding China's economic growth as a potential threat to it to a certain extent. However, some far-sighted Western scholars have put forward different views on this. For example, Jeffery Sachs, an American scholar, wrote in *The War on Huawei* that "China is not our enemy. It is a country that tries to improve its living standards through education, international trade, infrastructure investment and technological improvement. In short, what China has been doing is exactly what any country should do when facing the historical reality of poverty and falling far behind. Unfortunately, the Trump administration's agenda now is all about curbing China's development. This will be proven disastrous for the United States and for the entire world".

In fact, with the increasingly closer relationship between China and the whole world economic system in the process of globalization, such a relationship not only generates important impact on China's own economic growth, it also in turn impacts on the world economic system. On the micro level, according to the estimation of Henry Yeung of National University of Singapore, more than half of the global manufacturing capacity in the field of electronic products is in China. Among the factories run by the 200 largest suppliers of Apple, 357 of them are based in China, with only 63 in the United States.[20] On the macro level, in the

[20] Electronics manufacturing the great chain of China. *The Economist*, October 13, 2018, p. 61.

report *China and the World: Inside the dynamics of a changing relationship*, McKinsey Global Institute simulated the economic value gains or loss of the economic connection between China and the world in its strengthening or weakening process. The results showed that there were plenty of opportunities for China and the world to promote mutual integration. The development direction of economic ties between China and the world will have a great impact on the global economic value. By 2040, in the following five major areas, the economic value might be as high as 22–37 trillion US dollars, which is equivalent to 15–26% of the global GDP.

From the perspective of China, in the process of China–US trade conflict, China's manufacturing industry should not face Western enterprises including American companies with a confrontational attitude. On the contrary, it should more actively embrace globalization and integrate into the global industrial chain as much as possible. This means that, in terms of the macro-level counter-measures of China–US trade conflicts, the principle of reactive reciprocity should be adopted as far as possible, aiming at corresponded industries with reciprocity, rather than picking individual American companies as targets (unless this or these American companies trespass the bottom line of China's national interests). Chinese people should also avoid emotional opposition to American products and American enterprises. In this respect, Zhengfei Ren of Huawei has set a good example. In an interview on May 21, 2019, he said, "We will not reject the United States, nor will we lock ourselves in an island. Instead, we advocate developing together ... because we cannot be isolated from the world, but we should integrate into the world. The friendship between Huawei and American companies has been forged for decades, and it will not be shattered with a piece of paper ... if they are allowed to, we will still maintain normal trade relations with American companies. And we will build an information society for mankind together, rather than doing it alone".

From the perspectives of the Chinese people, they have been upholding such a traditional spirit in culture for many generations: treat your competitors with dignity and kindness, because they are just competitors, not enemies.

From the national and industrial level, it is necessary to analyze the manufacturing chain and technology chain of some important industrial fields. It's particularly critical to identify the weak points on the technology chain to ensure industrial safety. The analysis of industrial security based on technology chain rather than value chain will become an important consideration for industrial policymaking. To address the weak points in the technology chain, it is necessary to combine industrial policies with market mechanisms to support the development of some second-best technologies, especially the underlying technological fields of the technology chain. These "spare tire" technologies, which we call second-best ones, are not meant to be technologies or products that will eventually become practical applications in the market. The greatest meaning of their existence is to let us have alternative options and game leverages in the global industrial gaming. Therefore, as for the choice of technology field, such technology is primarily aimed at the underlying technological layer of the important industrial fields, rather than the localization or import substitution over-emphasized by Chinese industrial policies in the past. In the conventional competition scenario, we still need to make full use of the division of labor and cooperation in the global industrial chain to gain efficiency advantages and win–win opportunities. In terms of supporting methods, industrial policies are mainly aimed at the early stage development of the underlying technology and some core technology fields with a feature of prisoner's dilemma. In addition, it is still necessary to give full play to the effectiveness of the market mechanism in resource allocation. What should be pointed out here is that in the early stages of developing the underlying cores of the technology chain, due to the existence of technology barrier and marked disadvantage of late-comers in user scale, it is difficult for late-comers to break through the dual barriers of technology (quality) and price (cost) in the process of competing with mature leading enterprises by solely relying on market mechanism. This is also one of the important reasons why industrial policies are needed.

For domestic enterprises, "business continuity" will become an important issue that the rising Chinese leading companies need to weigh at the strategic level. If Huawei hadn't taken precautions in developing a backup operating system and chips way before the crisis happened, it would probably have ended up with business shutdown under the recent barrage. A page has even been dedicated on its website to explain how Huawei manages its business continuity, "After years of continuous construction, Huawei has established an end-to-end business continuity management (BCM) system from suppliers to us and from us to our customers in the fields of procurement, manufacturing, logistics and global technical services. By establishing management structures, processes and IT platforms, we have formulated business continuity plans and contingency plans for emergencies, organized employees in BCM training and drills, enhanced BCM awareness and responses to respond to emergencies in various organizations, and ensured effective management of daily business risks".

Symbol of the True Rise of Made-in-China

Dickens wrote in his book *A Tale of Two Cities* that "It was the best of times, it was the worst of times, it was the age of wisdom, it was the age of foolishness, it was the epoch of belief, it was the epoch of incredulity, it was the season of Light, it was the season of Darkness, it was the spring of hope, it was the winter of despair, we had everything before us, we had nothing before us, we were all going direct to Heaven, we were all going direct the other way…"

From one aspect, it is no doubt the best innovation era for Chinese enterprises, because with China's economic growth and Chinese consumers' rising income level, the demand for product quality and service value is also growing rapidly, hence providing a tremendous market drive for innovation.

From another aspect, however, Chinese enterprises seem to be facing enormous pressure of innovation. The rapid rise of Chinese enterprises has become a direct challenge to the large foreign companies that have dominated the global industrial value chain for a long time. However, Chinese enterprises do not seem to be fully prepared for this. It must be acknowledged that there is still a big gap between Chinese enterprises and foreign multinational companies in R&D, design and branding. The true rise of Made-in-China still has a long way to go.

In such a chaotic era, how to find a suitable growth path for Chinese enterprises and switch from being long-term followers and imitators to innovators has become a pressing realistic issue that Chinese enterprises cannot bypass. Yet, how to complete such a transformation? We don't have a ready answer. All of this needs to be explored based on continuous practice.

In this process, in fact, no matter whether they are industrial practitioners, academic researchers or the general public, some of them think Chinese enterprises have unlimited possibilities, while others think their chances are slim.

It seems that we are still in confusion.

Therefore, sometimes we feel optimistic that Made-in-China has become an irreplaceable protagonist on the global competition arena. Sometimes we belittle ourselves by believing that we are falling far behind the technological level of the top companies in Europe and America. Sometimes, we eulogize the Internet and unicorn enterprises and spare no words of praise, but at others, we emotionally deny the power of business model innovations and assert that only technology has unique value and significance. In fact, innovation comes in different forms, each of which has its own value and unique strength. This is true for innovation in product, service and business model.

Moreover, a more common situation is that the combination and fusion of different forms of innovation brings us greater strength. Innovation is not limited to the play of technology, and it is not an either-or option confrontation between technology and market. Just like the real world we live in, there is no absolute black and white.

However, when thinking rationally about the future of Made-in-China, we cannot avoid one question, that is, what's the sign of the true rise of Made-in-China?

China has already become the "world factory" and gained considerable market share in global and local markets of many manufacturing products and categories. Can these be taken as a sign of the rise of the Chinese manufacturing industry?

The answer to this question not only involves a pertinent evaluation of the past and present of the Chinese manufacturing industry, it also points to the prospective direction for the Chinese manufacturing industry.

In the previous discussion, we concluded that there are two different forms of industrial value chains, namely "manufacturing chain" and "technology chain". The "manufacturing chain" takes the product form as its final output. Participants in the manufacturing chain form cooperative relations on the basis of labor division, and finally split off profits according to their premium-pricing ability in the whole manufacturing chain. The technology chain pertains to the underlying technology behind products and is closely related to product architecture, components, design and production. Based on this logic, we can understand the dominance of an economy's specific industries in global competition from the perspectives of manufacturing chain and technology chain.

The degree of dominance of the manufacturing chain depends on whether an economy is built with a relatively complete industrial chain in the matched industrial domain, whether there are strong enterprises in all links of the manufacturing chain, whether it has truly global giant companies in the core links of its manufacturing chain, and whether it has a dominant product market share in the global industrial field.

To a great extent, the dominance of the technology chain is even more critical, which is reflected in whether such a technology chain possesses and controls the core technologies of the industry, and whether it has the bargaining power on the underlying technologies of the industry (including those provided in the form of equipment and services). A technology chain has high entry barrier and is difficult to be replaced. Therefore, its dominance power can last for a longer time. With this in mind, both the China–US trade conflict that started in 2018 and the Japan–R. O. Korea trade conflict that started in 2019 can actually be partially interpreted as reflecting the competitiveness in the technology chain. In the process of China's transformation from "Made-in-China" to "Created by China", it faces a great challenge in the improvement of its dominance in the technology chain.

So, can the dominance of the manufacturing chain and technology chain fully exhibit the manufacturing competitiveness of an economy? It sounds largely right on the surface, but some key ingredients are missing.

Let us make a retrospective review on how Made-in-Japan has become a synonym for high quality in global competition. In fact, in the past 50 years, Japan was the first economy to launch a comprehensive challenge to the leading position of American manufacturing (including its advanced manufacturing) industry. At that time, the Massachusetts Institute of Technology (MIT) even set up the MIT Commission on Industrial Productivity in 1986 (which also has Robert Solow, laureate of Nobel Prize in Economics in 1987, as its member) to research into the gradual loss of US global leadership in manufacturing. After more than two years of in-depth research, the commission produced in 1989 a working paper titled "Made in America: Regaining the Productive Edge".

In fact, before the 1980s, Made-in-Japan had been striving to lift up its image in developed markets around the world — starting from the image of low price to value-for-money and finally to high quality. Through non-stop improvement on product quality and technical level, Made-in-Japan successfully became the synonym for high-quality products in the late 1980s and early 1990s. In this process, those globally renown Japanese companies such as Sony, Toshiba, Panasonic, Canon, etc. undoubtedly have been great contributors and hence were rewarded with the great developments.

In this regard, Chinese manufacturing enterprises need to learn to become creators, producing epoch-making and world-famous products, and using these products to create some new industries and bring amazing value to consumers all over the world.

More importantly, looking back to the development of the world's manufacturing industry, we can find important contributions made by Japanese manufacturing in this process. Many management concepts, tools and methods, which are critical to the management of manufacturing enterprises and are well known to us nowadays, are rooted from the practice of the Japanese manufacturing industry. For example, Toyota's production system, Kanban management, continuous improvement, 5S in factory management and so on. Although some management methods were not even first created by Japanese enterprises (such as TQM, rotation system, etc.), it is undoubtedly Japanese enterprises who worked hard to consummate them to their zenith. Moreover, another important contribution of Japanese manufacturing to global manufacturing lies in the fact that through years of continuous improvement and practice, Japanese enterprises have packaged these management methods into a management system that can be replicated by the rest of the world.

This also means that the true rise of the Chinese manufacturing industry, in my opinion, not only depends on the global competition dominance established on the industrial chain and technology chain, but also depends on whether China's manufacturing industry can, based on its previous experience of the rise of Made-in-China, develop some management theories, methods and tools transcending cultural and regional boarders, and thereby promote the global manufacturing industry to raise its productivity to a higher level.

China's manufacturing industry not only needs to contribute to China's economic growth, but also needs to contribute to management theories, methods and tools of the world.

This is not only the challenge we need to face, but also the responsibility this era bestows on us.

It is also the glory and the dream of Made-in-China.

Index

www.ingramcontent.com/pod-product-compliance
Lightning Source LLC
Chambersburg PA
CBHW071248180926
51613CB00002B/169
9789811265211